Land Reform under Structural Adjustment in Zimbabwe

Land Use Change in the Mashonaland Provinces

Sam Moyo

Nordiska Afrikainstitutet, Uppsala

This report was commissioned and produced under the auspices of the Nordic Africa Institute's programme on *The Political and Social Context of Structural Adjustment in Sub-Saharan Africa*. It is one of a series of reports published on the theme of structural adjustment and socio-economic change in contemporary Africa.

Programme Co-ordinator and Series Editor:
Adebayo Olukoshi

Indexing terms

Land policy
Land reform
Land use
Structural adjustment

Zimbabwe
Mashonaland, Zimbabwe

Language checking: Elaine Almén

ISBN 91-7106-457-5

Printed in Sweden by Elanders Gotab, Stockholm, 2002

Table of Contents

List of Tables

List of Boxes and Charts

List of Abbreviations

AAG	Affirmative Action Group
ADA	Agricultural Development Authority
ADB	African Development Bank
AFC	Agricultural Finance Corporation
Agritex	Agricultural, Technical and Extension Services
BOP	Bulawayo Ostrich Producers
CA	Communal Areas
Campfire	Communal Areas Management for Indigenous Resources
CASS	Centre for Applied Social Sciences
CBO	Community Based Organisation
CFU	Commercial Farmers Union
CIDA	Canadian International Development Association
CSO	Central Statistical Office
CZI	Confederation of Zimbabwe Industries
DAPP	Development Aid from People to People
DNPWLM	Department of National Parks and Wildlife Management
DNR	Department of Natural Resources
EC	European Community
ENDA	Environmental Development Activities
ESAP	Economic Structural Adjustment Programme

FC	Forestry Commission
FAO	Food and Agriculture Organisation
GoZ	Government of Zimbabwe
GTZ	German Technical Services
HORTICO	Horticultural Company
HPC	Horticultural Promotion Council
IBDC	Indigenous Business Development Corporation
IBWO	Indigenous Business Women Organisation
ICFU	Indigenous Commercial Farmers Union
ILO	International Labour Organisation
LSCF	Large Scale Commercial Farms
LTC	Land Tenure Commission
MPs	Members of Parliament
NGOs	Non-Governmental Organisations
NORAD	Norwegian Agency for International Development
N.R.(s)	Natural Region(s)
NRB	Natural Resources Board
OCCZIM	Organisation for collective cooperation in Zimbabwe
ODA	Overseas Development Authority
ORAP	Organisation for Rural Association for Progress
RST	Resettlement Areas
SADC	Southern Africa Development Cooperation
SHOC	Small Holder Ostrich Cooperation
SSCF	Small Scale Commercial Farms
TOPAZ	The Ostrich Producers Association of Zimbabwe
UDI	Unilateral Declaration of Independence
UNDP	United Nations Development Programme
UNICEF	United Nations Children's Emergency Fund
USAID	United States Agency for International Development
VIDCO(s)	Village Development Committees
WARDCO(s)	Ward Development Committees
WPA	Wildlife Producers Association
WWF	World Wildlife Fund
ZCT	Zimbabwe Council of Tourism
ZCTU	Zimbabwe Congress of Trade Unions
ZFU	Zimbabwe Farmers Union
ZOPA	Zimbabwe Ostrich Producers Association

Foreword

When this study was commissioned in 1995 within the framework of the
Nordic Africa Institute's research programme on *The Political and Social Context of Structural Adjustment in Sub-Saharan Africa*, little did we realise that the
issues which it was designed to cover would be at the heart of some of the
most intense political contestations in Zimbabwe's post-colonial history. At
the time Sam Moyo began his research on new land uses in the context of the
market reform programme of the Zimbabwean state, it was conceived as one
of three other studies aimed at providing a deeper, empirically-grounded
understanding of the changing political economy of land in the broader
framework of the socio-economic changes unleashed across Africa by pro-
longed economic decline and structural adjustment. That aim was clearly
accomplished by this study, together with the very rich data base on which
the analysis is built. On top of this, the report provides the reader with clear
insights into the historical and structural sources of the on-going contestations over the Land Question, contestations which have been dramatised
by the renewed "land invasions" that are, this time, tied to the struggle over
the control of the Zimbabwean political terrain.

In charting the dynamics of new land uses in Zimbabwe as exemplified
by the expansion of horticultural activities and tourism-related game ranching, Moyo's study was able to bring out very clearly, the contradictions built
into the changing political economy of access to, control, and use of land. He
underscores the point that the Zimbabwean Land Question has been ren-
dered more complicated by the structures and processes associated with the
new land uses not only in terms of the distribution of land between black
and white farmers but also among different categories of farmers. The pic-
ture of a state that attempts to satisfy the needs of the large-scale, mostly
white commercial farmer lobby whilst being buffeted by pressures from
different categories of black farmers for a greater accommodation of their
own interests, and the demands of the large army of landless people still
waiting for some form of restitution, puts into clear perspective, the swings
in state policy on land that have been witnessed over the years. Readers will
clearly find this report to be both informative and insightful and the timing
of its publication could not have been more fortuitous.

Getting the manuscript into its present state entailed a great deal of work
for which a few words of appreciation are in order. First, of course, is Sam
Moyo whom I would like to thank for all the work which he and his research
assistants put into the data collection and analysis effort. Second, Solveig
Hauser, the assistant of the Institute's programme on *The Political and Social
Context of Structural Adjustment in Sub-Saharan Africa*, who complemented
my effort in painstakingly going through the manuscript, including the

tables, for consistency of content, style and format. Thirdly, I should like to acknowledge the NAI publications department, especially Susanne Ljung Adriansson, for the additional editorial work which they did on the manuscript. I trust that the wealth of insight which the manuscript presents serves as a small consolation for the many hours of work that have gone into its production in this form.

Adebayo Olukoshi
Research Programme Co-ordinator, Programme on The Political and Social Context of Structural Adjustment in Sub-Saharan Africa

Chapter One

Zimbabwe's New Land Question

1.1 Introductory Remarks

This report examines the role of economic liberalisation in the reconstruction of the political economy of Zimbabwe's land question. Since the Economic Structural Adjustment Programme (ESAP) was introduced in 1990, the universe of policies surrounding and influencing the nature and scale of land reform has been changing in tandem with changing and varied supply responses to ESAP-related policy incentives within Zimbabwe's bi-modal agrarian structure. These responses are manifested in emerging new land use patterns and production processes oriented towards global markets. The growth of new export-oriented land uses are a key determinant of the changing land question through their salient influence on transforming the structural and technological parameters of land use, exchange values of land, and, therefore, of land ownership. This trend underlies the current development strategy of Zimbabwe's agrarian and tourism sub-sectors.

Unequal benefits from ESAP reforms, especially from new land uses, however, fuel the struggle for more land redistribution. Thus, a major result of these land use shifts is the changing organisation of the politics of land-holders and land seekers, especially in their relations to the state, reflecting renewed struggles among various constituencies for historical and norma-tive land rights against those seeking to preserve existing land rights in the context of an increasingly market-based land policy framework.

A case study approach focusing on horticulture, wildlife and ostrich land uses, their economic features and impacts, and their socio-political rami-fications was pursued between 1995 and 1997. Detailed case data and expe-riences were gathered from Zimbabwe's Mashonaland provinces. These were supplemented with information from numerous secondary sources ranging from the macro to the farmer and household levels. The study assesses the direction and scale of new rural land uses in Zimbabwe's prime lands with particular emphasis on the 1990–1996 period. It traces the new forms of land use in relation to emerging land bidding and ownership structures and/or social relations of production among large scale and small farmers, private agrarian market agents, and the state itself. The emergence of new forms of rural land and commodity markets, new trends in socio-political organisation and policy advocacy among farmers' groups and other interest groups, as well as the changing relationship of government agencies to the control and use of land and commodity production, were the main social processes and relations examined.

A complex set of economic policy and political reforms from a wide range of policy arenas, including land, agriculture, natural resources, wildlife, environment and tourism, in addition to the core ESAP macro economic policies (fiscal, monetary, trade, deregulation and privatisation), which influenced supply responses in terms of new land uses are identified. Some of the non-ESAP policy influences identified include: veterinary regulations, interest group regulatory roles, local government by-laws, indigenisation policy, tax incentives, fiscal policy, and specific monetary policies affecting exports. Evidently, Zimbabwe's economic adjustment process itself has gradually led to a shift in its land policies, land ownership structures, as well as the uses of land and natural resources towards new global markets.

Moreover, the report examines how and why there is a highly differentiated supply response among the diverse range of land users and/or landowners. Popular responses to escalating income declines and poverty as well as to the changing opportunities presented by new export-oriented markets and land uses, including technically illegal strategies of land self-provisioning, were also assessed in terms of their role in determining the new land policy. The emerging ESAP market incentives and export land uses appeared to have been shaping an essential neo-liberal land policy which was against state led land redistribution, only to culminate during 1997 in a high profile populist effort by the GoZ to redistribute land through the compulsory acquisition of about 40 per cent of the current LSCF lands.

1.2 The Research Questions

The thesis developed in this report is that SAP-oriented policies and their wider consequences over the last decade have led to a redefinition of Zimbabwe's land question through the promotion of qualitatively increased and intensifying rural economic differentiation among varied landholders and regions. Such differentiation is a result of the diversification of land use, labour management and commodity marketing, as well as of increased commercial crop and natural resources marketing, including sub-contractual systems of farm production and increased foreign financing of exports and imports induced by technological change during the 1990s. While two droughts during 1992 to 1995 influenced agricultural and land policy as well, it is the emerging wider market imperatives, rather than one-on-one ESAP policy effects, which have led to uneven capital accumulation in the rural sector.

A growing market orientation of the land question arising mainly from trade liberalisation, exchange rate devaluation, domestic agricultural market deregulation and agricultural export promotion has had far reaching institutional effects in changing the systems of land tenure and administration, and access to land and natural resources. The emergence of new and global markets for the products of rural land and natural resources, and the resultant land use conversions particularly towards wildlife management, horticultural export cropping, livestock exports and other tourism-related land uses are key consequent trends. The class, racial and regional differentiation processes of these agrarian changes are fundamental to understanding contemporary land and agricultural policy making, increasing rural poverty and the politics of economic nationalism and indigenisation.

Existing research on the land question, rural poverty and the rural impact of ESAP has focused on macro-economic and employment issues at the national level (ILO, 1994), declining incomes and access to social services among the rural poor (UNICEF, 1994) and constraints facing small and indigenous enterprises (IBDC, 1993). Little research has been undertaken on the emergence of new rural land markets, land uses and economic linkages arising from the vacuum left by a retreating state, particularly with regard to agricultural marketing parastatals, land redistribution programmes and wider rural economic deregulation. While relatively more is known about the changing positive aggregate response and export performance of large scale farmers in response to ESAP, less is known about the scale and quality of land use responses among both small and large farmers, particularly in relation to growing struggles over Zimbabwe's prime lands. Even less is known about the incipient legal and illegal land market mechanisms which drive land use and agricultural diversification, and/or intensification as well asf land tenure adjustments.

For instance, it is argued here that the growth of new export land uses has been the major political and economic force underlying the restrictive GoZ's policy tendency towards land redistribution because it argues for greater privatisation of land, including communal and state owned lands. In a related study (Moyo et al., 1998) we assess how such a market form of land reform continues to marginalise the landless people. That trend diminishes the potential for mass-based socio-economic benefits from land during ESAP, while strengthening the concentration of capital accumulation in selected rural areas and hence increasing racial and class conflicts in the agrarian sector. The state's legitimacy as an arbiter and protector of the land rights of the poor is, therefore, increasingly questioned.

The report documents the trend and impacts of land use diversification towards new export crops, focussing on wildlife, ostriches and horticulture, so as to reveal the key policy mechanisms and structural factors of export-led agrarian growth and its rural socio-economic impacts at the national and sub-regional level. The key impacts traced include the emerging property rights and struggles, employment gains, foreign currency earnings, technological feedbacks within the LSCF such as the introduction of labour displacing mechanisation, as well as income shifts among the peasantry.

The expectation that there would be increased smallholder and black farmer participation in the new high value export crop production through sub-contracting arrangements of an informal nature and through policy adjustments intended to promote smallholder export-oriented diversification is explored. The nature of agrarian politics based on farmers organisations' attempts to control land, and the racial and class issues which arise with respect to the new land uses, are integral aspects of the investigation.

Thus, the research attempts to understand the precise nature of "comparative advantages" which Zimbabwe's large, predominantly white, farmers have over small farmers in the new exports sphere. The extent to which large farmers increasingly allocate small amounts of high quality land to new exports while most of their land remains underutilised is reviewed as is the political and economic strategy to exploit economies of scale for their investments in infrastructures for handling and processing the inputs and outputs of new export commodities. The significance of local agro-ecological diversity and its nature-based land quality advantages, and unequal historical accumulation of water and electricity resources for entry into new export production are essential elements of the study.

The study argues that the emerging process of land policy formulation under economic liberalisation is a complex of power relations within Zimbabwe's highly differentiated society, based upon a legacy of racial, class, ethnic and gender disparities in the control and use of land and natural resources. Land policy involves the state, society and external forces in shaping new opportunities and resource benefits from a new, globally-focused conversion of land use in Zimbabwe.

1.3 Zimbabwe's Land Question in Perspective

Until the end of 1997 when the GoZ sought compulsorily to acquire about 1,500 of the 4,500 LSCF farms, the land reform policy, especially since 1984, had produced outcomes which were inequitable, undemocratic, inefficient and unsustainable. Land reform in the 1980s was mainly defined in the context of the dependency analytic framework which emphasized national self-sufficiency and autonomy, through import-substitution industrialisation and agricultural development strategies, that were underpinned by state intervention in "land-related-markets". This strategy reflected a critique of the inequitable results of the colonial and minority rule primary exports economic structures which had led to highly uneven allocations of agrarian resources. State interventions in the agrarian sector thus included the direct control and operation of domestic and external agricultural commodity, financial, land and service markets by state agencies, purportedly to enhance equity in favour of the black majority.

Political and academic conceptualisations of Zimbabwe's land question and land reform during the 1980s tended to focus on redressing past grievances over land alienation, promoting equity in land property rights in order to attain political stability given that there was some militant demand for land, and promoting economic efficiency through the downsizing of land holdings for more effective use of land by committed non-absentee and socially broadly-based land owners (Moyo, 1995). Land reform was promoted to enhance labour intensive small farmer production systems so as to optimise land productivity, returns to capital invested, the self provision of food and basic needs, and a less skewed income distribution (ibid).

This economic and political model promised positive macro-economic benefits in general, including "growth with equity", political reconciliation in a racially polarised society, and more broadly-based participation in the economy through the promotion of employment development (ibid). The land question embodied issues of the efficient use of scarce and abundant national resources (such as capital and forex for machinery etc.; and the self-employment of abundant labour resources), while promoting food security and household and domestic self-reliance strategies. But few of these expectations from land reform were met.

Zimbabwe's land question is continually changing in response to a shifting GoZ land policy which is inconsistently implemented, as well as hesitant donor support, despite the claim by all parties to be committed to land reform. The changing land policy interest and debates are, thus, a key process which needs understanding in order to explain recent and on-going land use shifts. Since 1990, the GoZ has made a wide range of land policy pronouncements (GoZ, 1990, 1992) some of which have been implemented in varied degrees, while others remain stated objectives. Furthermore in 1994, a GoZ Land Tenure Commission reported on a wide range of land policy issues (LTC, 1994). Some recommendations were accepted by the GoZ but are yet to be implemented while other recommendations were either rejected or have been kept in abeyance (ODA, 1996) pending further study or the development of complementary policies and legislative reforms (e.g. land inheritance etc.). It is surprising in this context that in 1997, the GoZ designated 1471 farms in the LSCF sub-sector, about 30 per cent of their number and 40 per cent of their area. Yet, this move suggests a new resolve to address the land question "once and for all".

In perspective, therefore, the study explores Zimbabwe's land question in terms of the public policy tension over balancing the issue of returning the land rights of the indigenous majority population from a minority of mainly white elite landowners against the issue of guaranteeing the dynamic productivity of land for globalised markets. This issue is reflected in the emergence of conflicting land uses underlying the interests of mainly elite whites against the rural poor. The key hypothesis posed is that the land rights of the rural majority poor continue to be eroded by elite white and black large scale land owners who legitimise this inequity through the promise of dynamic economic growth based upon new land uses claimed to be productively superior to land uses established prior to ESAP type reforms.

In theoretical perspective, it is further argued that the new, export-oriented land uses, while promising increased forex, employment and incomes growth, by definition are both a material product and ideological instrument of the ESAP programme, and that this has been crucial to private sector efforts to redefine contemporary land usufract rights in Zimbabwe. The new land uses embody complex relations among a variety of land owners, marketing agents, rural workers and families engaged in struggles to control land for their own use and private benefits rather than for a well defined social and nationally balanced project.

The growth of new commodity markets for the products of land under ESAP, including markets for tourism, wildlife products, new high value crops and the storage of biodiversity, has, thus, been critical to the changing valuation of land in Zimbabwe, and, therefore, in shaping the escalating struggles over the redistribution of land. The social validation of given land uses thus contributes to the evolution of new understandings and frameworks of land tenure and the distribution of landholdings through legitimising and conferring usufract rights to those engaged in such land uses. The importance of usufract rights in conferring land control for private consumption use values is in fact not new to "traditional" or "communal" land tenure systems.

But under a freehold tenure system whose property rights are contested in terms of their origin, equity and justiceability such as in Zimbabwe's LSCF sector, even the validation of the social benefits of land uses is severely contested. This is because private benefits from new exports to the LSCF and the state tend to reproduce a pattern of skewed rural income distribution. Moreover, the social validity of the types of benefits being emphasised in intellectual and policy arguments promoting the new land uses, such as forex and the preservation of rare species, are highly contested. The landless and some black elites judge some of these new land uses to be ideological tools used by the white LSCF sector for legitimising existing patterns of monopolistic land ownership or control.

The approach used to study these land questions was, therefore, informed both by actual social or public discourses and struggles for land in Zimbabwe, and existing academic perspectives on the land question. Specifically the study sought to answer the following questions:

- Which factors and social forces define or fuel the contemporary struggle for land?
- How does the changing use of land, including new forms of production and marketing of outputs, influence the valuation of land in terms of exchange values as well as land rights?
- Who are the major actors in the struggle to control land, and, therefore, in shaping its emerging use-values and exchange values?

• What is the social benefit or distributional outcome of the contemporary struggles for land?
• What is the role of the state in mediating changes in land rights and land use?

1.4 Study Layout

The questions outlined above define the study's broad framework and corr-espond to the organisation of the chapters in this monograph. Chapter two presents the methodological framework. The methodology is based upon a materialist assessment of how ideology and material production processes interact to shape structures and processes of struggles over economic and land policies, and the legal conditions which govern the control and use of land by a variety of actors involved as land users or as market agents. This entails understanding how land is valued socially, academically and in public policy making in terms of its relative use and exchange values among contending actors. Through this analysis, the chapter establishes the empi-rical framework within which land use and valuation changes can be gauged. The chapter then presents the study area and data collection methods.

This is followed in Chapter Three by an assessment of the evolving market-led policies that influence land use and the struggle to control or access land. This chapter assesses the interactive movement and influences of macro-level, sectoral and commodity specific policies and regulations on the evolution of new land uses. The emerging empirical patterns of new export land uses and their socio-economic impacts, as well as an analysis of how new commodity markets are evolving among the large and small landholders are discussed in Chapter Four. Chapter five entails an assessment of the politics of land and land use conversion through an analysis of how the various actors are organised and the issues they strive for, while chapter six concludes the study.

Chapter Two

Methodological Framework and Study Area

2.1 Understanding the Influences and Impact of Structural Adjustment Policy Reforms

This research is a case study of Zimbabwe's experiences with SAPs in the land and related sectors. Our study methodology builds upon on-going theoretical and methodological efforts to examine the role of SAPs in the evolving political and economic development of Africa (Gibbon and Olukoshi, 1996).

ESAP in Zimbabwe was externally imposed, although no economic crises prevailed (Stoneman, 1992; Gibbon, 1995), apart from frequent droughts, declining external terms of trade and low levels of foreign investment, which led to low levels of employment growth. While the GoZ insists that ESAP was "home grown" by the state (see Mkandawire, 1984, and GoZ, 1991), some scholars attribute its adoption to the influences of purportedly rational large industrialists and farmers, such that private domestic forces rather than external influences were primary (Skålnes, 1995). Certainly, its adoption did not involve adequate consultations with the majority of workers, small farmers and small businesses.

Indeed, this study examines, to some extent, the proposition that the ESAP macro-economic policy framework, which has largely shaped Zimbabwe's current land policy, was externally imposed and, therefore, has not been well adapted to addressing the needs of Zimbabwe's heterogenous agrarian system and dualistic economy.

It has been argued that ESAP-based macro-economic and agrarian policies were intended to curb excessive and irrational state intervention in land and related markets and to counter state corporatism which repressed the necessary pluralistic organisation and participation of civil society in policy making (Skålnes, 1995). Existing indigenous black "interest groups" in Zimbabwe's land struggle, however, were considered too atomised, "particularistic" or parochialised (ibid) to evolve an alternative coherent growth-oriented land policy. Thus, it was through that ESAP liberalisation could help to introduce more effective policies (ibid).

The fact that the land redistribution policy lobby increasingly served the narrow interests of some black elites in an orchestrated system of patronage (Moyo, 1995) has been used to argue that the GoZ as a state lacks autonomy because of its particularist interests. The Zimbabwean state is characterised as hiding behind populist rhetoric or nationalist ideology of promising land redistribution while serving the narrow and monopolistic economic interest of domestic ruling cliques (Skålnes, 1996). In this vein, the importance of external factors, such as declining terms of trade in the key products of land and aid have been underplayed in such analyses of the evolving land policy. This study argues, instead, that it is mainly the white large scale land owners who have mostly benefited from ESAP because of their disproportionate ownership or control of prime lands and natural resources at a time when an increasingly externally-oriented production structure reflected in changing land uses is being established. Such a development strategy underpins ESAP which, as we argue, was externally imposed.

In this context, a key methodological concern of this study is to trace how various organisations which represent the different and unequally endowed social constituencies competing for land have influenced the implementation of ESAP policies with regard to the liberalisation of land, natural resources and agricultural policies. This challenges the dominant SAP literature's assumptions that post-independence state corporatism inhibited the effective participation of farmer and other organisations in constructive economic policy making (Skålnes, 1996; Herbst, 1990; Bratton, 1995).

To elaborate: some argue that societal corporatism had apparently evolved during various Rhodesian regimes through their promotion of interest groups, including the mainly white industrial, mining and farmers associations which purportedly pursued nationally coherent, "redistributive" and "regulatory" policies through governmental mediation, leading to the improved overall welfare of society (Skålnes, 1995). The Zimbabwe state, instead, repressed civil society, while black economic associations should be blamed for their own organisational, political and resource weaknesses (Bratton, Skålnes, ibid). Black economic associations in Zimbabwe are, purportedly, not national and broadly-based, because of ethnicity and regionalism which reproduces localised patronage-based interest groups (ibid). This spurs conflict and incoherent policies, due to the lack of courage to confront the state, and an unwillingness to propose alternate development policies (ibid). But the tendency for some interest group policy demands of a redistributive nature to be similar to the policy pronouncements, albeit not the actual policies, of the state is not adequately explained. At best this is seen as accidental and, at worst, to reflect their fear of cooptation by the state (Skålnes, ibid; see also Bratton, 1994).

This study attempts to address some of the methodological weaknesses in the existing SAP literature on the political context of policy making and democratisation, focusing on the land question. Most notably, the study challenges the oversimplification of the politics of SAP and land policy in terms of the nature of the interest group organisations involved and underestimation of their complex political and social relations with the state, and hence their influence on policy making (see chapters three, four and five). Because many African interest groups lack a documented tradition of policy advocacy and are not visible in the media, their approaches to policy influence tend not to be familiar to analysts grounded in western-type policy advocacy processes (Moyo, 1995b).

There has, indeed, been a yawning empirical gap in our understanding of how policy making is configured by the type of relations and linkages that the African state maintains with key organs of civil society, such as economic associations, NGOs and community based organisations. The rural–urban dichotomy of this state-civil society relationship is, indeed, the focus of Mamdani's book (1996). The revised urban bias thesis underlying the latter and the SAP literature fails, however, to capture the importance of rural civil society in sustaining the dominant ruling class elites through specific political and material linkages, in spite of their externally-oriented macro-economic policies, which, proportionally, mainly benefit the national elites in urban areas and transnational capital.

A major methodological problem here is that many analyses of the policy making role of interest groups tend to rely on a superficial political-economic assessment of the domestic social classes and forces underlying the formation of interest groups, their organic character and relations with the state, and ultimately the nature of the influences they bring to bear upon particular policy reforms. In general, there is a tendency to treat the economic associations which represent farmers or land users and the state as being undifferentiated, and to exaggerate domestic policy influence relative to that of external forces, while neglecting changes in the emerging alliances between domestic and external forces. As Chapter Five will show, many high profile Zimbabwean domestic land user associations are evolving as the rural economy diversifies and becomes export-oriented. These include strong external transnational corporations which are materially dominant in such organisations and in the media they use. External factors can be both dominant in the "domestic" policy lobby process, and narrow because their interests override the smaller parties.

Moreover, there is a tendency for the SAP literature to focus upon policy processes in single sectors and to neglect macro-level and inter-sectoral processes of policy development. This sectoral chauvinism prevails in most research on land policy which has been agriculture focused, even though land use change in the broader context of tourism, forestry and the natural resources economy has been at the heart of SAP-type macro-economic policy reforms. "Getting the prices right" has indeed focused on providing incentives to expand the breadth of export land uses and market "niches". Most studies, instead, reduce the multi-dimensional cost-benefits of, for instance, emerging land use systems to the particular macro or micro economic objectives of a few farmers and the economic sub-sector rather than examining the wider goals of the variety of social forces operating at varied spatial and social levels.

The SAP literature, in particular, lacks an understanding of how the objective interests and policy demands of the majority of poor rural communities are exerted on the state and their policy making outcomes. Because such informal and even illegal interest groups and social movements lack financial and technical resources to mount national level, high profile "policy campaigns", interest group rational-choice theories which seem to require formal legal formations of "civil society" with a national profile rather than community structures which do not use documentary procedures, have been unable to capture their influences on the process of SAP policy formulation.

   This chapter sets out the broad methodological framework used in this study to examine the changing nature of Zimbabwe's land question during ESAP. We first address some of the conceptual debates, questions and issues which define academic, policy and popular understandings of Zimbabwe's shifting land problem. This discussion provides a basis for a delineation of the type of information, sources and data collection approaches which were employed to explore, analyse and explain the current struggles for land. The chapter then presents background information on Zimbabwe's land control and use patterns, and useful details on the specific sites from which the study collected its main data. Finally, the last sub-sections briefly discuss how data was collected and what the limitations of our data are.

2.2 Emerging Perspectives and Methodology on the Land Question

2.2.1 Overview of Methodological Framework

As discussed further in chapter 3, the land question is not merely a superstructural, ideological and political struggle among various farmers' organisations responding to a particular market oriented macro-economic and land policy framework postulated by ESAP. Nor does the evolution of the new land question rest solely on changing physical access and control over land among the various social forces in contest through legal and informal means. While the ideological or political struggles over land are essential to the evolution of physical land rights, the institutionalization of land ownership structures and the legitimation of land reform depend on the outcomes of land use. Legal and physical processes of land tenure only partially establish the material foundations for the actual control of land as well as the use of land and natural resources in the production and circulation process. The products from land and its effective utilisation also confer usufract rights in land, in both communal and freehold land tenure systems.

   In order to sufficiently understand the evolving character of Zimbabwe's new land question, it is necessary to evoke a dynamic perspective which sees the control of land and its utilisation as a phenomenon influenced by both changing state interventions and market processes (prices, credit, marketing channels and procedures etc.) in the agricultural and related economic sectors. This, in turn, provokes changing perceptions of the evolving values attached to land. This valuation dynamic shapes the motivations, objectives and strategies of the land struggles and policy debates waged by various players.

Thus, a critical dimension of understanding the meanings of and, therefore, struggles for control and redistribution of land, is the empirical (material) force that actual changes in land use, its products and benefits bring to bear on the public valuation of land, and, thus, the changing nature of struggles to control or access land. Thus, the feasibility of the incentives promised by SAP-type and ESAP policy changes, as represented by substantive responses in terms of land use shifts and increased financial and economic benefits, is a critical influence on the changing direction and framework of land policy and struggles.

The struggle to demonstrate the superiority of these new land uses or non-traditional export commodity production is a cardinal policy objective of ESAP given its emphasis on trade liberalization. Indeed, it has been argued that new export-oriented land uses make not only private (financial) sense at the local (individual farmer) level, but also social (economic and environmental) sense at the national as well as sub-national or provincial and district level (World Bank, 1991; GoZ ,1990).

Therefore, testing or establishing empirically, the extent to which there has been a response by farmers to the ESAP policy context through changing land uses in the proposed policy direction, especially whether it has a positive social distributional character (poverty-wise) and promotes efficiency in the utilization of land and labour resources, and thus improves national welfare in general, is a crucial objective of this research. So far, few *post facto* research and policy reviews on ESAP and the land question have done this adequately.

But establishing the nature and trend of land use changes is partially also important for us to gain an understanding of how the benefits derived from new land uses contribute towards restructuring public and private conceptions of the land question. Contemporary economic policies and political organisations seeking to establish new land uses embody new values for land property rights. The search for new patterns and procedures of redistributing land rights, establishing new social relations of production as a strategy of optimising gains from land, and the feedback of such material changes into ideological, political and policy struggles over land is, thus, an important aspect of our methodology.

In other words, a central hypothesis of this study is that the SAP-type (1985–1989) and ESAP (1990–1997) market conditions facing Zimbabwe (see also Gibbon and Olukoshi, ibid), by promoting land use diversification especially towards exports and by introducing new forms of financing and marketing of commodities derived from land, will tend to increase the effective demand for land. Through the demonstration of profitable new land uses on the one hand, and growing poverty on the other hand, the structure of demand for land thus changes under ESAP.

The major shift in demand is that more people can afford land or require land for their survival and, thus, there is demand for more land to be transferred to a wider range of actors. Since the new land uses require different kinds of land, such as extensive woodlands for wildlife and irrigated lands for horticulture, the sites of land struggles also change geographically. Furthermore, new forms of struggle to secure land emerge as the pressure for survival amongst the poor increases in scope, the accumulation needs of new elites expand and their powerful lobbies grow, and as new social movements emerge. This fuels demands for both state-led and private land reform.

This trend is contrary to claims by some analysts that market conditions introduced by ESAP would diminish the demands for land redistribution. Whereas some analysts imply that the demand for land reform during the 1980s was fuelled by a politically-motivated scheme (Skålnes, 1995) and not by real demand as argued by others (Moyo, 1995a), our expectation is that the market reforms during the 1990s increased the pressure for land reform. Increased export-oriented production and related social differentiation under ESAP are, thus, expected to broaden and intensify the demand for access to land, and the demand to participate in new higher value land uses. However, it is expected that only some of the more powerful social forces gain substantial access to land while others informally access land in a piecemeal fashion.

It is this expanded demand for land during ESAP which defines the ideological struggles for the land policy reforms which are discussed in chapters three and five. However, the main issue around which land policy reforms are being contested remains the relative values attached to different land uses and land productivity, and by implication how certain land uses imply and confer legitimate usufract rights and hence sustain existing patterns of land control. This land valuation debate is discussed next.

2.2.2 The Valuation of Land and the Rationality of Varied Land Uses

The ideological and technical debate over the relative superiority of alternative land uses is not new, although there has been a change in the parameters of the debate over time (Weiner et al., 1985; Moyo, 1986). A long standing dimension of this debate in Zimbabwe and elsewhere concerns the relative superiority or efficiency in generic terms of the large scale over the small scale farming system, and, therefore, the bundle of forms and practices of land use and returns to the resources utilized within these systems. This issue of economies of scale in land use or agriculture was also recently broached by the LTC (1995).

In Zimbabwe, this debate has been conducted in its most ahistorical and racist form, which ascribes the smallness of Communal Area "farms" (i.e. crop plots) to an immutable preference for such "household" plots rather than to the ravages of land alienation and state-led institutional controls since the early 1990s (Palmer, 1977; Moyo 1986; Drinkwater, 1991; Weiner, 1988). That line of argument was based upon the presumed preference of "African" small farmers for producing for family subsistence requirements rather than for commercial ends and large scale motives. Also, low levels of communal farm outputs, their relatively lower yields (land productivity), and their concentration on "food" crops more than "cash" crops, were assumed to imply generic internal weaknesses of the small farmer or communal farming and land use system (ibid). These weaknesses tended to be a-historically ascribed to the generic lack of knowledge, skills and technology which resulted from the distortions of "communal tenure" (Robertson, J., in *Herald*, 1992). Moreover, the lack of freehold tenure is said to exclude small farmers from access to credit and, therefore, limit their production capacity.

The presumed lack of commercial values among smallholders and the constraints on their market competitiveness and capacity to exploit local resources and opportunity in an "entrepreneurial" sense, has long been debunked (Moyo, 1995a) by perspectives which emphasized the historical effects of discriminatory state policies and, the public and private extraction from small farmers of surplus value through migrant labour, taxes, marketing price structures, etc. Most of the academic debate on Zimbabwe agriculture since the 1990s has, indeed, been focused on refuting the above stereotypes of the small farmer system, to demonstrate the structural constraints to their development and the political-economic process of the marginalisation of the poor in various markets (land, commodity, labour and inputs etc.). Many studies show how, in spite of this extra-economic colonial and racist economic management history, small farmers have achieved (and can still do so) comparable levels of agricultural crop productivity per unit of land as their LSCF counterparts, and their effective responsiveness to markets, particularly when structural conditions and specific policies were correct.

The maize and cotton output and productivity growth among some Zimbabwe peasants which began in the 1980s and levelled off around 1987 was key in legitimising land redistribution to small farmers, even in the 1997 land reform pronouncements of the Mugabe government. Their land use effectiveness (Weiner et al., 1985) and success (Cliffe, 1988; Eicher, 1995), compared to the LSCF who in gross terms have underutilized their land (Moyo, 1995a; Weiner, 1988), put paid to the racist and technical assumptions made in Zimbabwe that the small farm system was inherently deficient (Moyo, 1995a), and that economics of scale in land use favoured large farmers (LTC, 1994). Such land use valuations provided the empirical force for progressive policies towards small farmers, including the increased redistribution of land to them. But the capacity of communal farmers to efficiently use land remains contested by LSCF representatives and other analysts (e.g. Skålnes, 1995; World Bank, 1991 etc.) in general policy debates on land redistribution. Continued poverty and land degradation in Communal Areas are said to reflect the internal deficiencies of the smallholder land use system (Gore et al., 1992).

Our review of the Zimbabwean and, indeed, wider related literature suggests that from the mid-1980s, but increasingly in the early 1990s, the debates on the relative value or merits of alternative land uses have shifted methodologically. Much of the research has moved from the more micro-economic level of questions such as the scale of land (farm size), the race of land users and their static motives (subsistence etc.), towards the more macro-level criteria of assessing land use values such as the realisation of foreign currency earnings, returns to financial investments, and environmental benefits.

The latter include micro and local processes such as: the biological productivity of the system in terms of biomass, woodlands, wildlife and biodiversity; the maintenance of ecological stability in terms of well functioning soils, water and forest maintenance and watershed management systems; effective global carbon sequestration; and the maintenance and enhancement of the varied aesthetic and "spiritual" values that nature provides. This changing trend in the valuation of the use of land and its natural resources, is in keeping with global debates and efforts which promote the transnational regulation of the use of nature or the environment, as well as the growth of international eco-tourism markets.

Sitting somewhat in between the above micro-economic and general macro level poles of criteria deployed to evaluate or value land use alternatives is the more socially grounded approach which places greater relative value on land use outcomes such as the employment and incomes growth realised beyond the land owners as reflected in the national labour force in general. Although the human instrumentality criteria of land use is accepted as being important in the currently dominant neo-classical economic welfare theory framework of land valuation (Bojo, 1993) which is deployed in most existing land valuation studies, it tends therein to be measured through disputable theoretical and market criteria such as "willingness to pay" or consumer preferences.

However, this theoretical framework also accepts that political interventions to assign property rights and prices are legitimate because of existing "market failures" in the environment sector in general, and because of the unusual, historically-derived income disparities in economies such as that of Zimbabwe (Bojo, 1993). Yet, the theory also argues that direct public participation in land use (and ownership) such as is the case with state farms, forests, parks etc., distorts land use values because of the absence of market signals in many public land use decisions (ibid), and that these contribute to government or policy failures which distort the efficient or most effective uses of land.

But market failures in Zimbabwe's land use system are recognised by ideologically different analysts for varied reasons. These include historical land alienation and wider land related policy discriminations against the majority poor and, thus, income and land holding-based disparities (Moyo, 1995a), the ineffective land market transfer processes (World Bank, 1991), the racially distorted banking system (IBDC, 1994) or the land underutilisation and speculative tendencies of the LSCF (Moyo, 1995a). True, the lack of adequate land price (value) information reflects existing land market weaknesses (Bojo, 1993) which have hampered the prospects of evolving a market based land taxation system (see GoZ, 1986; Green and Khadhani, 1986; Moyo, 1993; LTC, 1995; Strasma, 1991; World Bank, 1991). This also partially underlies the current disputation by the GoZ of the validity and "fairness" of the actual land prices on sales to the GoZ for redistribution (ODA, 1996; GoZ, 1991/92, Moyo, 1995a). In part, this explains the ascribed need for the Land Acquisition Act of 1992, over and above the moral and political questions of paying for formerly expropriated land.

Thus, market valuations of current land use alternatives in Zimbabwe tend to be inadequate because of both information and market imperfections, as well as policy failures. The main land policy failures, therefore, have been: failure to intervene in the land holding structure to correct distortions such as the legacy of unequally assigned land property rights among the actors (LSCF, the state and small farmers) and because of policy failures arising from racial discrimination in allocating commodity prices, forex, import licensing and subsidies for infrastructure (roads, water, electricity, telephone system etc.) among the different land tenure regimes and land users. However, given the information weaknesses which emerge from the above distortions, residual and available information on macro policy indicators tends to be used in assessing the relative merit of alternative land uses. In effect, this focuses valuation on forex earnings and gross returns per hectare, to the exclusion of other socio-economic variables which require micro-level data.

The most visible and perhaps empirically concrete manner in which the social cost-benefits of alternative land uses have been assessed purportedly in "objective", "apolitical" or "non-ideological" terms, which it is argued remove the racial, political and class biases of the discourse, has tended so far to be focused upon the types of commodities being produced, and their aggregate values such as outputs, yields and financial returns. Most land use valuations do not emphasize the environmental, social reproduction or the employment values. In the forex-constrained Zimbabwe economy, land uses which optimise foreign currency and financial returns have, thus, been targeted for special policy attention. The success of new land uses in maximizing or realizing foreign currency earning values has thus been crucial to their further promotion by interested parties in the state, private, NGO and community sectors, and in their adoption by various landholders.

Therefore, the establishment of new export uses as valid values in and of themselves has become a primary concern of most farmer or land owner interest groups, not only because of their private interest in forex accounts but also because of the country's fixation on forex scarcity. In practice, the validation of land use diversification based upon forex earnings rather than upon the relative social and wider economic benefits has meant the validation of current export-oriented land use conversion processes in the LSCF sector. The validation of new export land uses has, therefore, also tended to mean the validation of existing unequal land ownership patterns.

Nonetheless, the limited existing technical debate over the relative superiority of alternative land uses has centred on the relative merits of a wide range of oppositional categories of land use assessed in a few local level site-specific studies, many of which have tended to focus narrowly on the specific policy objectives represented by individual outputs of given land use systems, such as fuelwood, timber, beef, wildlife, a particular crop etc.

However, the major problem in land use valuation debates has been the undervaluation of small farmer systems. Increasingly, the land use debate has begun to see Communal Area farming as a complex "high return low input" system, with a diversity of inputs (labour, technology, manure, litter, crop residues, fertilizers etc.) and outputs which include carving materials, thatching grass for roofing, various game meats, food, roots, medicines and spiritual space. Efforts to value this type of land use have been fraught with problems of placing financial values on non-marketed inputs and outputs. But there is growing recognition that the small farmer land use system has high outputs and is ecologically more benign than formerly presumed, except in areas of high population pressure where woodlands have been depleted. For instance, the World Bank (Bojo, 1992) had this to say on state forest land uses, which are akin to LSCF forest and woodland land uses:

> Even if current plans for forest development into Safari Hunting and so on are developed, there might be areas where returns to these activities are still lower than if land is redistributed (to smallholders) for livestock and crop farming (ibid, p. 235).

The general thrust of land use debates, however, has been to suggest that cropping and livestock activities in both the LSCF and Communal Areas are inferior to wildlife and tourism related uses of land in the larger parts of Zimbabwe's lower rainfall areas:

> In the same instance indigenous woodlands especially might compete well with other land uses in the drier natural regions IV and V, (Campell et al., 1991).

These conclusions follow similar efforts which have not only specifically argued that in the LSCF, wildlife ranching was superior to livestock farming in general, but that it was superior to almost all other land uses in natural regions IV and V (see Table 2.2.1), including the LSCF in these regions whose cropping regimes required heavy water and chemical investment costs (Child, 1990; Muir and Blackie, 1994, etc.).

Table 2.2.1. *Classes of Land Allocated to Wildlife Enterprises on Commercial Farms*

Land classes	Description	Area (ha)	% of total
I–II	Good arable	1,800	13
III–IV	Very limited arable, good grazing	3,700	45
V	Wetlands (grazing)	488	6
VI–VII	Limited grazing	2,920	36
Total		8,908	100

Source: Bond, 1993.

The purported superiority of wildlife land uses has been a result of detailed study and justification (see Table 2.2.2). Subsequently, however, there have been fears that wildlife land uses were being over-extended spatially into N.R. I, II and III which, it has been argued, (GoZ, 1996; Moyo, 1995) are more suitable for intensive cropping land uses.

Table 2.2.2. *Comparison of Returns/Ha of Different Types of Land Uses in Zimbabwe (Z$)*

Land use activity	Marginal land (zone 4)	Very marginal land (zone 5)
Communal farming (Crops and livestock)	12.88	5.01
Ranching	4.93	1.65
Safari hunting	2.51	2.51
Game cropping	5.06	5.06
Safari and game cropping	4.41	4.41

Source: Bond, 1993.

In this vein, the growth of horticultural land uses has tended to be viewed positively as it entails the intensive use of small-sized land areas, albeit at high financial costs for infrastructure and water. This reflects the high values placed upon land-saving and high income land use enterprises, because this trend provides scope for the downsizing of individual LSCF farms (LTC, 1994; Muir, 1994), while raising prospects for the off-loading of LSCF lands for redistribution.

Horticulture has also been favoured for its labour intensive nature and, thus, the employment expansion prospect it offers, despite its hazards for labourers due to high chemicals exposure. There is a stark difference in profitability between horticultural crops and other field crops. Horticultural crops, even when their yields are low, are more profitable by far than the other crops. Assuming little difference in fixed/overhead costs, there is a strong financial incentive for farmers to move into horticultural production. Returns to variable costs which indicate how much is earned as gross margin from every dollar invested in variable costs also indicate a strong bias in favour of horticulture. Horticultural crops have returns to variable costs greater than other crops even in cases of low yield scenarios whereas the other field crops have returns less than one even at maximum yield. Faced with high capital costs, farmers seem to be better off venturing into horticulture. Thus, assuming land or capital to be possible limiting resources, it seems to make financial sense for farmers to drift towards horticulture.

But the land question here is whether LSCF wildlife and woodland land use conversions reflect a large farmer defensive strategy against land expropriation, and an attempt to technically and economically validate the rationality of these new land uses relative to the presumed unproductive and degrading land uses of the smaller farmers. Because mainstream land use valuation mainly measures small farmer yields as "subsistence commodities" (maize and petty livestock) in the Communal Areas, other diverse incomes, self-employment and the broader use-values of the Communal Area mixed-farming-woodlands land use system have remained undervalued. The priority and importance given to the forex and narrower financial returns of wildlife and tourism related land uses, and their presumed ecological (not human) integrity, thus distorts proper analysis of small farmer land uses.

The allocation of large amounts of land to wildlife, therefore, reflects a significant socio-economic policy choice being made by the LSCF and the GoZ, and this has become a major site of contestation in the currently existing and evolving land question facing Zimbabwe. That is: the extent to which the environmental and forex earning macro-level objectives of the GoZ, and the micro-level financial returns of the few LSCF farmers involved in wildlife ranching, justify the existing levels of poverty that the above kind of land use competition condones.

The commercial production of ostriches in Zimbabwe, for instance, has direct implications for land policy because of its spatial demands for land in competition with other crop enterprise uses, the trend of reallocating financial, material, labour and expert resources towards that sector from the agricultural sector, the purported better environmental conservation implications of this land use in terms of soil erosion, and the growing interest in access and control of land that the economic benefits of the enterprise offer. Here again, however, the land question and agrarian resource efficiency issues that arise from the growth of land allocations towards ostriches have been secondary to the ecological policy concerns of the DNPWM over the security of ostriches as a wildlife species.

The land use valuation debate is not only complicated by the absence of the diverse data on outputs and inputs required to adequately derive the values achieved, but also by the market imperfections and GoZ policy intervention failures discussed above. It is also complicated by the dynamic and unstable market conditions which affect the viability of land uses. Apart from sporadic weather problems whereby good rainfall years devalue the importance of woodlands type uses relative to small farmer cropping uses, rapidly changing price signals (cost of money, commodity prices vis-à-vis inflation and devaluation), the introduction of new technologies through trade and financial (external borrowing) liberalisation, and growing competition in global markets, have all tended to shift the cost-benefit structure of alternative land uses.

Assessing the relative merits of alternative land uses is complicated by the complex input combinations which are being evolved, and the variety of commercial uses to which nature is being put without much financial input. Alternative land uses tend, in both the LSCF and Communal Areas, to be also practised as complementary activities rather than as single uses competing for the same land on a given farm. Some large farmers, for instance, combine traditional cash crops with new land uses including both horticulture and wildlife. One land use combination model we derived from findings in some of the middle-sized LSCF farms in Mashonaland (N.R. II/II), for example, boiled down to the land use structure in that farm category captured in Table 2.2.3. In such a model farm case, the immediate technical (not political) micro-land question which arises is whether 50 per cent–70 per cent (1,000–1,300 hectares per 2,000 hectare farm) of the farmland in this region should not be redistributed towards higher value, small mixed-farming-woodlands enterprises. For, that part of the farm could support perhaps over 50 landless families through the self-provision of a variety of land-based products and cash income. That gain would compare more favourably to the existing concentration of financial and forex returns to the LSCF farmer and the employment of less than 10 families on the same land for cash wages and minor benefits, which are much lower than what 10 independent small farming families would derive from their own land use arrangement. Yet, the absence of detailed empirical case data on such land allocation decisions limits the macro-level land use valuation debate.

Our combined fieldwork and macro-level data collection provides some preliminary basis for reflecting on the way in which new land uses are restructuring the debates on both the value of alternate land uses and the significance of these to the transformation of the currently existing structure of land ownership, access and use. In essence, this study gauges the relative physical response in land use terms among the LSCF and small farmers to the ESAP policy incentives for new exports in terms of their output and financial contribution, their areal coverage, the social distribution of the adoption (numbers, race and socio-economic features of adopters), their productivity and environmental benefits.

Table 2.2.3. *Middle Sized Land Use Structure in Mashonaland in 1996*

Land Use	Hectares	Percentage
Total Land Area	2,000	100.00
Traditional Cash and Export Crops (cotton, maize, small grain, tobacco, maize)	30	1.50
Horticulture (open and greenhouse)	5	0.25
Cattle (few paddocks)	50	2.5
Wildlife/Woodlands (includes chalets and cattle)	1,000	50.00
Non-Arable Area	ca. 845	42.50

Source: Field Observations and Interviews, 1996.

2.2.3 Some Further Study Assumptions and Questions

A key assumption of this study is that both land redistribution and land tenure reform are essential for broadly-based land use diversification and export growth to occur in Zimbabwe, especially if it is intended to involve the small black farmer. Increasing demand for entry into the new export land uses is, thus, expected to increase conflicts between large black and white farmers and the state over the control and access to land in Communal Areas, state lands, and private land tenure regimes. The relative disadvantages of smallholders in terms of poor access to land, their weak agricultural situation (location, infrastructure and resources), inherent policy biases (accessing forex, urban bases services and information) and various structural disadvantages (literacy, information, skills development, and capital accumulation etc.) limit their chances of capitalising on the new export land use markets. This self-reinforcing negative land use performance is, thus, key to the ideological and policy struggle over land redistribution.

In addition to the above questions, therefore, the study also generally explored the following propositions concerning the nature of Zimbabwe's new land question:

- that access to new forms of secure tenure over land and natural resources arising from ESAP may be leading to increased land use intensification, enhanced land productivity and growing fixed investments in land and natural resources among large and small farmers;
- that social differentiation contingent upon varied forms of capital accumulation from agricultural production, trade and state employment and patronage, are critical in influencing land policy and practice towards

increasingly individuated forms of land tenure in non-freehold areas, and towards increased land use diversification;

- that there is increasing black elite procurement of prime arable lands and natural resources in relation to expanding land market commercialisation, land use intensification, and the diversification of land use systems;

- that small farmers are increasingly being integrated into high value domestic and export market production through a variety of intermediaries such as large farmers, market agencies, agro-processors, and state agencies, on the basis on exploitative marketing systems;

- that central government controls over land allocations, use and management systems, as well as traditional tenure structure with broadly similar aspirations for control over land and natural resources, are rapidly diffusing into a more locally based but non-traditional or non-centralised individuated land tenure system akin to land markets in terms of the forms and means of land and natural resource transactions, security and exclusivity. Thus, informally, government and NGO agencies are promoting this trend of land individuation in spite of the absence of a formal land market policy in Communal Areas;

- that land sub-division and consolidation in LSCF areas is a growing land market process which reflects increasing government and private interest in the growth of export-oriented production a private model of land redistribution focusing on the "effective demand" of the white and black middle classes;

- that tenure systems regarding natural resources (access, use, rights and their administration) are undergoing complex changes towards their commodification and privatisation due to the wider economic impacts of ESAP reform, including the growth of tourism, a growing black orientation towards business, and the declining incomes of substantial social segments of the rural populations;

- that land self-provisioning strategies or so called "illegal" efforts at accessing land ("squatting", land and resource poaching, gold mining land "sales" etc.) are increasing due to increased economic hardships faced in Communal Areas and among working class families in urban and LSCF areas; and

- that farmer organisations and lobby processes have been reconstituted and expanded in order to manage new land related markets, protect new land owner risks, influence land policy and mediate agrarian conflict.

A wide range of specific research questions (see Annex 2.2.1) were, thus, generated to pursue the above-listed issues.

2.3 Identifying New Land Uses and New Actors

One of the assumptions guiding our study methodology, especially the choice of the land uses to examine in depth, is that emerging markets under

ESAP have shifted perceptions of the land question. Thus, the impact of new land uses in shifting the demand for land and, therefore, altering the structure of agricultural production in particular, is hypothesised to be one of the most notable contemporary economic processes which influenced change in Zimbabwe's land policies, rather than purported political demands for land.

Earlier research had shown that specific land use changes which had occurred during the 1980s (Moyo, 1989) included:

- the expansion of the area and volume of traditional exports produced, including tobacco, cotton, tea, coffee, sugar and beef;
- a division of labour reflecting smallholder focus on maize, cotton, groundnuts and other traditional foods consumed by the working class and rural poor, while the LSCF produced over 90 per cent of all other exports;
- the gradual emergence of game ranching and private tourism among LSCF farmers;
- the expansion of the cultivated land area in Communal Areas from an estimate of just below 1 million hectares to 1.5 million hectares, while the cultivated land in LSCF areas remained around less than 700,000 hectares in the last 20 years; and
- the expansion of irrigated land in LSCF areas from 165,000 hectares in the 1980–85 period to about 330,000 in 1990–1995, and from 45,000 in 1980–85 to 97,200 hectares in the 1990–95 period shows that there is continuity without change in production performance based on resource allocation.

This study, however, is focused on an examination of changing land uses and the land question through the case of three commodities that engendered peculiar but salient changes in the land use systems and underlying social relations of production, especially their dramatic influences on the nature of demand for land, and *inter alia* on shifting the supply side or general structure of agriculture. The three new land uses that were chosen for this study were expected to represent a potentially critical shift in the scale and intensity of land use in Zimbabwe and to dramatically redirect the structure and scale of the demand for land.

Horticulture provided the opportunity to examine the potential offered by more intensive land use with high returns on a relatively small area of land for potentially larger numbers of farmers and workers which could be undertaken in any agro-ecological location so long as the right inputs or technology could be mobilised. For instance, horticultural export production has meant that many land users could intensify their production on small land areas in any agro-ecological region as long as they had access to capital for water and related production infrastructure, and if there was reasonable access to refrigeration and road infrastructure towards external markets.

This meant that "large scale" commercial farmers no longer needed to own or farm large tracts of lands as they could realise superior financial returns on smaller hectarages of horticulture. Farms of between 10 and 150 hectares with access to water could earn as much and more than larger 2,000 hectare farms. This meant, implicitly, that there was potentially less of a real land shortage in natural regions I, II and even III as LSCF farmers could off load much more of their land while intensifying their production on smaller-sized farms. Economies of scale to land use in terms of farm size were diminishing for high value intensive farming, thus also reducing the importance of controlling monopoly capital to purchase large farms which was presumed to be a necessary condition to enter commercial agriculture successfully. Land intensification through horticulture meant more farmers could use less land at higher levels of return.

Wildlife provided the opportunity to examine the potential offered by extensive land use on larger sizes of marginal lands with reasonable financial returns. Ostriches offered intensive land use based on pen feeding which could be done profitably on small areas in any natural region without the need to disturb soils or use large quantities of water, if the relevant equipment and capital could be mobilised. Similarly, the increasing returns to wildlife ranching raised the margins at which productive land use could be undertaken, thus shifting the focus of demand for land from natural regions I, II and III towards the more marginal regions in N.R. IV and V where most animals thrive today. Remoteness from major infrastructure and towns, and the retention of given natural resources typical of remote areas previously not suited for cropping land uses, had become critical factors in adding value to land in mainly natural region V as discussed in section 2.2.1.

Moreover the demand for formerly marginal lands for nature-related land uses would be accompanied by increasing the variety of potential land users competing for land, adding those geared towards wildlife ranching, Campfire schemes, ostrich farming, and broader tourist uses of land, to the mixed farming land uses of Communal Area farmers and the beef ranching of LSCF farmers. This changed the sites of struggles for land geographically, in terms of the quality of land sought and the actors involved in the struggle for land.

Amongst the three land uses, therefore, the study intended to explore the potential that more people could gain access to land and farm it or manage the resources on it on a smaller scale in a variety of locations. The technological and land use system changes implied in these three new land uses also meant that agro-ecology *per se* became less important to profitable land use, and, therefore, struggles for land could be waged on a more diverse front by a wider variety of actors. These three land uses thus represented the potential to dramatically shift the structure of Zimbabwe's land use system, the agricultural sector as a whole and the nature of the land question in particular, emerging as they did during ESAP. Hence, their choice as the study focus was expected to reflect the key driving force of the broader land use changes found in Zimbabwe today.

Furthermore, the three case studies selected were found to traverse an "onion ring" model of macro-level spatial patterning of land use and emerging buffer zones as depicted in Chapter Four. In general, intensive horticultural land uses are postulated to predominate in the core of the onion which sits around the major cities and road arteries of the central parts of Zimbabwe, moving South West and South East. And the most extensive wildlife ranching land uses are postulated to predominate in the outer ring. The LSCF and Communal Area crop and mixed farming land uses are found in between these two extremes and interspersed around the various layers.

This approach to case study selection allowed us to go beyond the conventional classification categories of land use, especially the technologically static framework of agro-ecological regions used as the main reference point in Zimbabwe's land use policies. Thus, using technological and market changes, the choice of three new land uses allows us to address potential land use changes in the central, middle and outer rings of Zimbabwe.

The aim was also to transcend the use of provincial administrative boundaries that are commonly employed in the literature to locate struggles for land because of the increased trans-provincial mobility of the expanding land demand or ethnic origin of need and effective demand for land. While political constituencies of parliamentarians have been provincially structured as are the land bidding campaigns, the aim was to track a broader agency in demand for land over and above GoZ structured land offers.

A crucial aspect of the changed structure of demand for land is the expanded range of potential land users that has emerged as a result of land use diversification. The inventory in Table 2.3.1 was developed merely as an indicator of the direction and quality of such changing demand rather than the actual quantitative scale of it, and was used to guide our identification of actors to track in determining the structure of agency in the land reform debates of Zimbabwe (see also Chapter Five).

Table 2.3.1. *Changing Nature of Land Demand According to Sectors in Zimbabwe*

Sub-Sector	N.R.	Land Holders	Race	Land Use
1. Agriculture		1. Large farmers (LSCF)	White	Specialised cropping
	III–IV	2. Communal farmers	Black	Mixed farming
	III	3. Purchase area farmers	Black	Mixed farming
	III–IV	4. State farms	Black	Crops
	II–IV	5. City/District council farms	Black	Crops
	I–V	6. Peri-urban plot holders	Mixed	Residential/ intensive crops
	III–V	7. Livestock ranchers	White	Livestock
	II–III	8. Horticulture sub-divisions	White	Crops
	II–V	9. Squatter in LSCF, CA and state lands	Black	Crops, gold-mining
2. Tourism	IV–V	1. LSCF farmers	White	Tourism
	IV–V	2. Conservancy group	White	Tourism
	III–V	3. Campfire community	Black	Tourism
	III–V	4. Leaseholders	Mixed	Tourism
	V	5. State park	White	Hunting etc
	III–V	6. State forest/woodlands	Mixed	Tourism
	IV–V	7. Parastatal woodlands	Mixed	Chalets, sport, views
	V	8. Hotel group park	White	Chalets, sport, views
	I–V	9. Inland lake shoreline plots	White	Chalets, sport, views
	III–V	10. Indigenous entrepreneur plots	Black	New gold mines, tourism
	IV–V	11. NGO projects	Black	Hunting, tourism
3. Residential	I–V	1. Growth points plots	Black	Residential
	I–V	2. Communal area plots	Black	Residential
	I–V	3. Peri-urban townships	Black	Residential
	I–V	4. Squatter residences	Black	Residential
	I–V	5. Cottage plots	Mixed	Second homes
	I–V	6. Retired farm workers	Black	Residential
4. Other	I–V	1. Household energy and game provisions	Black	Forestry, tourism

2.4 Selecting the Study Area

As our earlier discussion suggested, land use patterns in Zimbabwe have been closely associated with patterns of natural agro-ecological potential due to the predominance of rainfed agriculture among all the tenure regimes. However, agro-ecological potential is, in turn, closely associated with patterns of land ownership and tenure, with the LSCF tenure regime dominating the prime lands.

Zimbabwe has five agro-ecological regions based upon soil type, rainfall and climatic factors (see Table 2.4.1 and Annex 2.4.1 and 2.4.2). The bulk of intensive high value crops are produced by farmers in Natural Regions I and II while in N.R. IV and V, beef production has been the main enterprise. Except for the few large irrigated tracts of land in the Chiredzi area, where sugar, cotton and wheat have been grown since the late 1960s, these broad macro level land use patterns have endured for about thirty years. Wheat, tobacco and horticulture production have also been extended into some parts of N.R. III, while citrus expanded into N.R. II as a result of growing irrigation capacity among LSCF farms.

Thus, in relation to land tenure and control, the white LSCF occupy 34.6 per cent of agricultural land in N.R. I, and II and 21.5 per cent in III, with average farm sizes of 2,400, while indigenous blacks occupy 42 per cent, with 7.2 per cent of this land located mainly in N.R. IV and V with poor rainfall, soils and depleted vegetation. Their land use has thus been dominated by maize, cotton and small grains. As the output data show, over 80 per cent of all commercial crops besides maize and tobacco were LSCF produced. (Therefore, in selecting where to focus our analysis of recent land use changes, careful attention was given to the issue of how existing patterns of tenure, agro-ecology and land use influenced the current export oriented trends.

In order to capture the cutting edge of such land use changes during the last decade, it was decided to primarily select as study areas, those regions with the highest potentials for converting their land uses to the three new exports of interest. On this ground, the three Mashonaland provinces were considered the most suitable given their large arable land masses, the greater rainfall they received and their Zambezi river Lowveld terrain. Secondarily, it was decided to select case studies of established new land uses outside the Mashonaland Provinces where such existed and to gain variety in our case study information on land use changes. The administrative areas and the specific sites used for case studies are briefly described in the next section.

Table 2.4.1. *Land Classification by Agro-Ecological Region and by Sector ('000ha)*

Region	CA	SSCF	LSCF	Resettlement (2)*				State farms	Forestry	National parks	Total lands	%
				A	B	C	D					
I	140	10	415	–	3	6	–	6	70	150	700	1.8
II	1,270	250	3,765	451	113	0.5	–	1	–	10	5,860	15
III	2,820	540	2,216	947	55	7	–	15	140	550	7,290	18.7
IV	7,340	520	3,293	695	9	–	–	23	640	2,250	14,770	37.8
V	4,780	100	3,284	238	–	–	94	34	70	1,840	10,440	26.7
Total	16,350	1,420	12,973	2,331	180	14	94	79	920	4,700	39,060	100
%	41.8	3.6	33.2	5.97	0.46	0.03	0.24	0.2	3.4	12.0	100	

* Including land purchased but not yet settled.

Source: Moyo and Ngobese, 1991, as adapted from MLARR, 1986.

2.5 The Study Area: Mashonaland, Shamva District and Other Sites

The Mashonaland Provinces hold 75 per cent of Zimbabwe's prime lands, and the largest number of LSCF farms, plus the bulk of the smallholder surplus producers (Table 2.5.1). The area has the highest infrastructure and urban resources in Zimbabwe, and the bulk of the country's irrigation schemes. Small-scale farmers in this area have established forward contracts with European companies to produce high-value horticultural crops such as baby corn. The underlying assumption, therefore, was that any positive effects of ESAP on agriculture would occur in this high potential region which already has significant levels of agrarian economic activity. This, in turn, would provide an active situational and contextual basis for examining Zimbabwe's new land question.

Table 2.5.1. *Major Crops in Commercial Farms in the Mashonaland Provinces 1990*

Crop	Variable	Unit	Mash. West	Mash. East	Mash. Central
Maize	Production	t	322,154	130,136	144,062
	Area	ha	74,340	28,949	30,914
	Yield	kg/ha	4,334	4,495	4,660
Sorghum	Production	t	15,715	388	2,671
	Area	ha	5,719	260	483
	Yield	kg/ha	2,748	1,492	5,530
Wheat	Production	t	96,559	45,283	80,563
	Area	ha	17,420	7,315	14,263
	Yield	kg/ha	5,543	6,190	5,648
Groundnuts	Production	t	4,839	5,021	2,452
	Area	ha	2,216	2,934	1,363
	Yield	kg/ha	2,184	1,711	1,799
Soyabeans	Production	t	53,319	18,389	30,190
	Area	ha	26,737	8,154	13,931
	Yield	kg/ha	1,994	2,255	2,167
Cotton	Production	t	25,369	359	35,815
	Area	ha	17,407	488	21,892
	Yield	kg/ha	1,457	736	1,636
Coffee	Production	t	868	57	459
	Area	ha	452	22	242
	Yield	kg/ha	1,920	2,591	1,897
Tobacco	Production	t	52,222	31,196	31,732
	Area	ha	25,346	12,629	15,132
	Yield	kg/ha	2,060	2,470	2,097
Sunflower	Production	t	1,233	678	208
	Area	ha	1,967	1,181	487
	Yield	kg/ha	627	574	427

* Productive coffee relates to large scale commercial farms only (SSCF not included).

Source: Agricultural Statistics (Ministry of Lands, Agriculture and Water Development, 1996).

Because the Mashonaland Provinces are characterised by extreme land underutilization (Annex 2.4.3), including the existence of vast tracts of virgin lands, and a few state lands allocated to natural resources management, it offers a wide potential for both land use diversification and for the redistribution of prime land to intensive smallholder farmers.

All of Zimbabwe's land tenure regimes are well represented in these provinces, both agricultural and natural resource enterprises are evidently growing here, and the most successful small and large scale farming is found in these areas. The provinces also have marginal lands and extreme land pressure and shortages, as well as a growing land occupation movement.

The broad demographic, economic and social infrastructure of Mashonaland are presented in Table 2.4.2. We see that these three, out of Zimbabwe's eight provinces, hold slightly over 30 per cent of the country's population.

Table 2.5.2. *Socio-Economic Profile of Mashonaland*

	Zimbabwe	Mash-West	Mash-East	Mash-Central	Ave. of Mash.
Demography					
1. Population	10,412,548	1,112,955	1,034,342	856,736	1,001,344
2. Population density (persons/km^2)	27	19	32	30.2	27.1
3. Sex Ratio (males: females)	95:100	101:100	93:100	95:100	96:3
4. Household numbers	2,163,389	231,340	219,516	177,011	209,302
5. Average Household Size	4.8	4.8	4.7	4.8	4.8
6. Area (Sq km)	390,757	57,441	32,230	28,347	39,339.3
7. Urban population (000')	31	24	6	8.1	12.7
8. % of rural population	69	76	94	91.9	87.3
9. % of male headed households	67	75	59.6	68.3	67.6
Economic Activity %					
1. Paid employee	44.50	49.79	36.56	39.44	41.93
2. Employer	0.39	0.47	0.43	0.33	41
3. Own account workers	24.45	22.42	36.06	30.46	29.6
4. Unpaid family worker	8.84	7.06	11.12	16.33	11.5
5. Unemployed/looking for work	21.82	20.26	15.83	13.44	21
Social Services					
1. % with electricity					
Urban	50.39	60.83	69.93	54.76	61.80
Rural	2.00	6.98	4.20	4.59	15.80
2. % main source of water (rural areas)					
Piped water inside	2.72	13.50	3.80	5.60	7.60
Piped water outside	8.34	18.81	10.29	14.40	14.50
Communal tap	11.25	23.50	11.90	17.10	17.50
Well/borehole protected	42.02	21.55	32.59	34.50	88.60
Well unprotected	21.38	14.52	33.77	15.90	64.20
River/stream	13.27	7.68	6.98	11.90	26.60
3. % source of energy (rural areas)					
Wood	95.38	93.41	94.46	94.94	94.30
Paraffin	2.02	2.57	3.20	2.39	2.70
Electricity	2.00	3.05	1.77	1.76	2.20
Gas & coal	0.16	0.43	0.36	0.57	0.45
4. % type of toilet (rural areas)					
Flush	2.21	6.33	3.96	3.27	4.50
Blair	24.65	13.34	28.38	28.86	23.50
Pit	16.76	24.74	16.13	20.85	20.60
Bucket	–	–	–	0.15	0.050
None	52.36	55.58	51.52	46.85	51.30

Source: Compiled from Census 1992: Provincial profiles for Mash-East, West & Central.

The approximately 210,000 households in the area have higher than average population densities, especially within the Communal Areas, and they occupy 30 per cent of Zimbabwe's land, most of which is prime land. About 33 per cent of the rural households are male-headed, and, thus, dependent on migrant labour wages, while over 20 per cent of the people there are unemployed. To this demographic structure must be added the 1.5 million who reside in urban areas within Mashonaland. Thus, the three provinces cater for 40 per cent of Zimbabwe's population, where also most of the county's busiest physical infrastructure is concentrated.

Shamva District in Mashonaland Central, around 100 kilometres from Harare, was selected as a district case study for more detailed questionnaire interviews and qualitative in depth investigation of new land uses. Shamva is renowned for producing regular crop surpluses among LSCF, Communal Areas and resettlement farmers. The district has notable irrigation schemes and certain small-scale farmers have established forward sub-contracting farming relations with foreign firms. Market relations are expanding in this high agro-ecological potential area which already has a significant level of economic growth.

Yet, Shamva is characterised by extreme land underutilization with vast tracts of virgin lands, a few state lands allocated to natural resources management, and a wide potential for both land use conversion and for prime land redistribution towards intensive smallholder farming. All of Zimbabwe's land tenure regimes are well represented there, and both agricultural and natural resource enterprises are evidently growing in this district, while successful small and large scale farming is found in combination with marginal lands and extreme land pressure and shortages.

Several specific case study sites were examined in Shamva to generate data for qualitative analysis. Notable projects among these were the Tsakare and Principe Irrigation Schemes, the Mwoyowamira Illegal Settlement, and the Ngome Grazing Scheme. A detailed study of dambo cultivation also was undertaken in Madziwa (see Table 2.5.3). These qualitative case studies broadly covered the three tenure categories i.e. communal, resettlement and large-scale commercial farms.

In addition to the Mashonaland Provinces, interesting data was also gathered on the new emerging land uses in other provinces. Most of the cases were on small Campfire schemes in Matabeleland North and South, Manicaland, and Masvingo. These schemes are located in Natural Regions IV and V in the marginal areas of the country which make up the dryland mixed farming zones discussed earlier. The creation of large-scale wildlife conservancies and syndicates by large-scale commercial farmers who are particularly active in the Masvingo province also provided a basis for selecting additional case studies. Furthermore, conflicts over access, control and management of resources such as forestry and wildlife were found in Matabeleland such that it was necessary for this research to briefly examine some cases there (see Annexes 4.3.3 and 4.3.6).

Table 2.5.3. *Qualitative Case Studies in Shamva District*

Site/village	Ward	Communal Area/ resettlement	Activity examined
Ngome	Mupfure	Madziwa CA	Grazing scheme
Tsakare	Mupfure	Tsakare Resettlement	Irrigation
Principe	Sanye	Bushu	Irrigation
Mupfurudzi Safari Area	–	Bushu CA	Wildlife
Mwoyowamira	Mutumba & Nyamaropa	Madziwa CA	Squatters
Gono	Gono	Bushu CA	Gold panning
		Bushu CA	Small-scale mining
	Large-scale commercial farms	Large-scale commercial farms	Ostriches
	Mutumba	Madziwa CA	Dambo cultivation

Source: Fieldwork.

2.6 The Data and Its Collection

The data for this study were collected with the assistance of three research assistants hired for that purpose between July 1995 and June 1997 (see annex for their profiles).

The study collected data mainly on the three emerging land uses and the processes influencing them in the various agro-ecological zones and land tenure regimes (Communal Areas, Large Scale Commercial Farming and Resettlement Areas) within the above-mentioned political-administrative regions. The main forms of specific data sought included the areas of land devoted to the new land uses, the production practices and inputs entailed, the nature of outputs realised and markets used, and the social distribution of the benefits of production. Data on different sociological variables such as race, ethnicity and gender, and political variables such as the nature and activities of interest groups surrounding the new land uses were collected. Annex 6.0 provides the entire range of questions and variables used to collect the data.

The study sought data which could be used to compare the changing patterns and processes of access to and use of land and natural resources among small and large farmers in relation to changing land rights and entitlements. Data on the administrative practices and market-related activities of local authorities, central government agencies, traders, agro-processing firms and farmers organisations in relation to new land uses and land markets was collected from primary and secondary sources. Attention was paid to specific information on changes in policies and regulations in the agriculture, veterinary, tourism, trade and monetary sectors as these affected land use changes in various localities and land tenure regimes. Many people were interviewed (see annexed list) to assess the emerging perceptions of changing land use and the land problem, and how struggles around this issue are organised.

Since few researchers have focused on the land uses and economic processes under study here, the definition and collection of data was exploratory and aimed to establish the basic patterns of land use change. The study, thus, used multi-disciplinary approaches to collect both quantitative and qualitative data using various methods including: rapid rural appraisal, structured questionnaires to serve as a baseline household cross-sectional data base, informal interviews, observations and secondary data sources.

Three levels of data collection were followed: national, regional and local sources. National sources of data such as central government and private records and reports as well as other studies on the wildlife, ostrich and horticulture sub-sectors were collated and assessed to gauge the aggregate and national distribution of the growth of the three land uses. National policy documents and official administrative procedures and practices related to the promotion and regulation of export land uses were reviewed and interviews held with various government officials, private agencies, NGOs involved in the sub-sectors and organisations which represent the land users. The national and Mashonaland level analysis thus informed the local level case studies data on broader policy, land use, political and economic trends. The major purpose of data collection and analyses was to inform our assessment of the efficacy of the new national level ESAP, land policy and regulatory processes, as well as responses to the policy during the 1990s.

Government agricultural statistics, district authority information sources and district level farmers organisations provided data which compares shifts in the use of arable, grazing and other marginal lands between traditional crops and new export commodities. These sources also informed us about the organisation of the export commodity input and output markets, policy lobby processes, sub-contractual and other interactive economic relations among various types of land uses and marketing agencies, as well as about the representative farming politics of these land users.

Data on the organisations which represent the farmers collected through informal interviews included information on their structures, activities and strategies and the politics of the agricultural policy lobby for land reform and land use diversification. Existing media reports and sources provided further insight into these political-economic processes.

The farmer household level formal structured and unstructured inter-views were undertaken with about 30 farmers, while the total number of open interviews involved about 100 farmers or land users operating on a small and large scale basis within the three land tenure regimes: state, free-hold and Communal Areas. The actual proportion of farmers sampled is as shown in Table 2.6.1. The aim was to balance our understanding of socio-economic and land use processes within the various tenure regimes, rather than focus on statistical representativeness *per se*.

Table 2.6.1. *Summary of Persons Interviewed at the National Level and in the Mashonaland Provinces*

Subject	No. of persons interviewed in Harare	Persons interviewed in Mashonaland			Total
		East	West	Central	
1. Horticulture	3	6	6	4	19
2. Wildlife	6	4	4	3	17
3. Ostriches	5	5	4	4	18
4. Squatting	1	2	3	5	11
5. Organisations	-	2	2	2	6
6. Other land uses	2	1	6	2	11
Total	17	20	25	20	82

Notes: Other land uses include gold panning, grazing, sub-divisions and consolida-tion, water resources. At times officials discussed more than one subject.

The investigation of new exports was conducted in a sector and area-specific manner which yielded profiles of schemes or groups of farmers engaged in these land uses (see Table 2.6.2) while data on the institutions which repre-sent the producers was guided by farmer interview information on the evolving land policy and farmer cooperation and conflict mediation. De-tailed information was collected on the specific problems and issues facing Communal Area irrigation schemes, including socio-political questions re-garding access to such schemes and other state support, in relation to the new land uses. This entailed data from 35 horticulture settlements as tabu-lated in Annex 1.1.2. Interviews and records of local private marketing groups, NGO promotional activities and the actions of various state agencies were also used at this level to marshal meso-level insights, while key infor-mants were identified to provide qualitative assessments of the impacts of the new land uses.

The gathering of various secondary sources of data has been on-going since the research was conceived. These include information on horticulture, wildlife and ostriches from written literature and records in libraries in Harare, and material obtained from interviews with officials from various institutions. The WPA, SHOC, HPC, ZCTU, TOPAZ and CFU provided some

Table 2.6.2. *Farmer Fieldwork Case Studies (i.e. CA, RST, SSCF, Stateland)*

Type of land use	Land tenure category	Area of scheme	District of study	Province of study	Site pop.	No. of questionnaires implemented	No. of respondents	% response
Squatting	CA	Mwoyowamira	Shamva	Mash Central	361	40	36	90
	LSCF	Maskum	Mt. Darwin	Mash Central	91	Qualitative interviews and observations	9	100
	LSCF	Leleza B	Chikomba	Mash East	9	Qualitative interviews and observations	5	100
Horticulture	RST	Principe	Shamva	Mash Central	60	30	30	100
	RST	Tsakare	Mt. Darwin	Mash Central	32	32	30	94
	CA	Madziwa	Shamva	Mash Central	NA	10	10	100
	CA	Mundotwe	Bindura	Mash Central	NA	10	10	100
	LSCF	Individuals	Shamva	Mash Central	35	25	10	40
Wildlife	Stateland	Shamva Campfire Fishing project	Shamva	Mash Central	92	20	20	100
	LSCF	Valley Voughan Game Park	Bindura	Mash Central	1 farmer and support staff	Qualitative interviews and observations	–	–
	LSCF	Catolina Wilderness Centre	Beatrice	Mash West	1 farmer and support staff	"_	–	–
Ostriches	SSCF	Mutoko Ostrich Syndicate	Mutoko	Mash East	–	"_	–	–
	SSCF	Musengezi Ostrich Syndicate	Zvimba	Mash West	–	"_	–	–
	SSCF	Individual	Murehwa	Mash East	–	"_	–	–
	Peri-Urban	Individual Tynwald	Harare	Mash East	–	"_	–	–
Other land uses: Gold panning	Stateland	Mufurudzi Safari Afrea	Shamva	Mash Central	More than 1,000 panners	20 and observation	12	60
	CA	Gono Area	Shamva	Mash Central	–	Observation	–	–
Grazing	CA	Ngome	Shamva	Mash Central	–	12	12	100

statistics and performance indicators on their respective areas of interest. A few interviews to understand the nature of the export producer associations, some new export producers and marketers, and the role of government officials were carried out (see list of persons interviewed Annex 1.2). Knowing the history of the associations, their constitutions, what they stand for, the nature of their programmes, their target groups and benefits derived was critical. For instance, sub-contractual arrangements in these new exports are more widespread than was initially anticipated.

Valuable information was secured from environmental and other NGOs which promote the new land uses such as ZIMTRUST, Africa Resources Trust, Campfire Association, and Africa 2000 Network, while key sources of related policy documents were the Ministry of Environment and Tourism, Ministry of Finance, Ministry of Local Government, Agritex, Department of National Parks and Wildlife Management, NRB, CASS, ADA, WWF etc.

Observations and informal meetings with farmers in the field were also a major research instrument used as a supplement to questionnaires. Three research assistants were involved in 15 field trips to the Mashonaland provinces, and they conducted numerous interviews with officials and farmers.

2.7 Limitations of Data and Sources

The greatest difficulty is that data on horticulture and wildlife is scattered, not well documented and inconsistent. Wildlife land use data is extremely complex to trace, not only because of the technical difficulties of land use valuation and the lack of transparency among wildlife ranchers who tend to combine wildlife with other land uses, but also because of the poor manner in which wildlife data is managed by the GoZ, NGOs, research agencies and private land users. A key methodological problem was that most research on wildlife land uses and, indeed, natural resources management tends to be based mainly on micro local-level studies rather than on spatially high orders of land use data aggregation such as the meso-scale (districts and provinces) and the macro or national level scale. Thus, painstaking efforts are required to aggregate land use data from multiple and, at times, contradictory sources such as interviews, records and papers written by individual land users, local area managers and authors of micro-level studies.

Another critical methodological problem found in the literature, records of land users and of GoZ policy makers, was that little importance has been placed on measuring the precise areal and locational characteristics of land uses such as wildlife, not only on the meso and macro scales but even within micro or local-level studies. There were few efforts to quantify the hectarages of wildlife "schemes", farms and parks, or to separate geographically, in agro-ecological and administrative boundaries, the precise location of these land uses.

Table 2.7.1. *Summary of Cases Observed in the Course of Study*

Type of land use	Land tenure category	Mashonaland			Other provinces	Total
		East	West	Central		
Squatting	RST	2	2	1	–	5
	CA	–	3	–	–	3
	LSCF	–	2	1	–	3
Horticulture	CA	4	8	3	–	15
	RST	12	4	4	–	20
Wildlife	CA	2	2	4	13	21
	LSCF	1	2	–	15	18
	Stateland	–	7	2	9	18
Ostriches	SSCF	2	1	2	–	5
	LSCF	1	3	–	1	5
	CA	6	–	–	1	7
	Peri-Urban	1	–	–	–	1
	ADA	–	1	–	1	2
Total		31	35	17	40	123

This data problem is not merely a technical methodological problem. It reflects wider institutional weaknesses which have emerged in the ESAP policy environment. In this context, the GoZ has "withdrawn" from various land related regulatory, marketing and production functions, which are increasingly being managed and leased privately. Furthermore, the policy emphasis of state economic management now mainly requires particular types of data critical to monetary and fiscal balances and stabilization such as the forex and financial returns, and "political" aspects such as the race and social character of the visible business people rather than data necessary for the central direction of various physical processes such as regulating specific land uses in detail. Thus, less emphasis is now placed on some forms of record keeping and monitoring which were routine before ESAP. The lack of good data on shifts in land use and related outputs markets means that merely establishing the direction and general scale of land use change is a fundamental research task.

Moreover, GoZ agrarian parastatals which are being privatised, and those which still regulate the remaining agrarian markets, have become less transparent with their data and are reportedly more fearful about releasing "trade secrets". While the GoZ has a politically charged interest in the "indigenisation" of the economy and land uses such as wildlife, its public and in-house debates on the nature and scale of land use conversions or social patterns of ownership tend to be based on general and anecdotal information when this relates to private and communal land uses at the meso and macro-scale. This suggests that there is little political support for more detailed scrutiny of land use shifts, and their true cost-benefits, in socio-economic terms. Indeed, a World Bank writer (Bojo, 1992), referring to demands for collecting data for "green accounting" land valuation approaches by some Zimbabweans, went as far as ruling out investment in such policy work thus:

> The public sector in Zimbabwe will undergo a significant reduction as part of the structural adjustment programme (GoZ, 1991). It is, therefore, difficult to get political support for increases in staff allocations for handling such a system.

While the lack of "good quality data" on land valuations is recognised, policy debate remains crippled by the paucity of efforts by government, NGOs and donors to substantively improve land use information.

The importance currently ascribed to the conversion of land use towards wildlife and related tourism activities is underpinned by the relative contributions of these sub-sectors to the formal economy. Given that there has been and remains a massive underground economy in the wildlife sector, and the fact that the available data is further limited by the "security" problems associated with data collection in contested high value "informal" markets, the information used in this monograph focuses more on formal and observable land use trends.

Although this monograph does not delve into details on the trends in land occupation and the sub-division of LSCF farmlands, acquiring such information was useful to inform us how changing land uses were closely related to the changing structure of land ownership and methods of access (Moyo, 1998). GoZ compiled records were used because fieldwork efforts to compile LSCF market data was extremely frustrated by the poor GoZ land records, the mechanical nature of these, and the over-protectiveness of officials of such data. Furthermore, the fact that most LSCF land transfers tend to entail company shareholding-based sales (ODA, 1996), the actual areal scale of sales and land prices in the land market are indeed elusive.

Data on LSCF land sub-divisions which lead to the transfer of title in land to new holders is available in various GoZ offices, including the offices of the ministry of local government, the surveyor general and Agritex. However, this information tends to be inaccessible in desegregated forms suitable for the multi-level analysis required here. We had to spend time decoding provincial records for all applications and permits provided in Mashonaland since 1980 and collating them into tables. The evidence (Moyo, 1998) on the patterns of land sub-division nationally and in Mashonaland point to a GoZ land policy of liberalising land markets from the mid-1980s. Furthermore, land use intensification based on more land owners cultivating small plots of land with high value horticulture is on the increase. Thus, the sub-division of land needs to be followed through in future land use studies.

The growth of land occupation is another signal of land use sub-division and intensification, as more land users enter the field, although this does not necessarily lead to land use diversification. The poorer landless tend to be a large proportion of the squatters, and the homeless do not invest in high value land uses (ibid). Information on land occupations tends to be scattered and elusive because squatting is constructed as either "illegal", or a deviant and private self-help aspect of Zimbabwe's land reform programme. The study collated empirical and official information on the nature and causes of the "squatting problem", its scale and patterns in terms of various land categories and its spatial configuration (provincial, intra-provincial etc.).

Given that this study examines the consequences of the ESAP policy regime on the land question, albeit in a general sense, there was need to collect detailed data on the wide range of policies which affect land use changes and land tenure *per se* (see Chapter Three). This became a time consuming research activity in its own right because few studies have attempted to assemble the comprehensive policy framework through which ESAP affects land policy. Such an exercise is methodologically complex, especially in terms of identifying the policies and the scope of their influences on a fundamental issue such as land use. The study, thus, did not emphasise precise correlations of policy impacts but rather explored the policy arenas and contexts during the ESAP reform which affected land policy change (see also Gibbon and Olukoshi, 1996).

Many of the policies identified in Chapter Three have hardly been implemented and the planning work on how to implement them is still under way. The study was informed mainly by those post-1990 land policy aspects which were implemented—even if partially—and also those which it was expected could elucidate the hypothesis that there is an evolution of increased land use diversification. This included those formal land policy shifts as well as *de facto* land policy changes resulting from GoZ inaction, omission or tacit acceptance of given policy outcomes which were not formally pronounced. Our purpose was to track policies which have a close bearing on the acceleration of the diversification of land uses, the intensification of private and informal land market processes, and organised, non-state community actions to gain access to land and natural resources.

2.8 Summary

The chapter outlined the study methodology, the Zimbabwean context and study areas, as well as the nature of the data collected, their sources and their limitations. The key methodological challenge identified was how to value land as a research tool and as an instrument for public policy formulation in a context of competing academic, political and ideological perspectives regarding the relative merit of various land uses. Thus, a multi-disciplinary and exploratory methodology to scan a range of factors and processes crucial to understanding land use change, the rationality of related policy formulation and the politics of land reform was proposed. Case studies of mainly Mashonaland traversing broad agro-ecological, provincial land tenure and land use regimes, was adopted as detailed in the chapter.

A multiplicity of data collection methods was used in order to overcome some of the data limitations encountered including: standard household questionnaires, detailed interviews of key informants to complement the case study approach, and detailed review of secondary data in the form of published essays and media articles to gauge the trends of land use change and the debates surrounding these. Indeed, obtaining data was a challenge since many commercial farmers were not willing to reveal information while small farmers do not keep records, and government bureaucracy is problematic.

Chapter Three

Policy and Institutional Context

3.1 Introduction

This chapter discusses the emerging policy and institutional context, surrounding land use change in Zimbabwe. Three policy arenas are investigated: the macro-economic and agricultural sector policy environment, specific policies and regulations affecting the three commodities or land uses under study, and the land reform policy experiences. In examining the effects of macro-economic policy factors on the emerging patterns of land use change and land control, the chapter outlines the pre-ESAP and ESAP policy framework in the context of the push to open up the economy to the outside world. The chapter then shows how specific land use policies and regulations affecting the horticulture, wildlife, and ostriches sub-sectors were changed during the structural adjustment era, especially to encourage the expansion of these land uses for export production. Finally, the chapter reviews Zimbabwe's land reform policies and experiences and shows how land issues have been changing in keeping with the above policy changes.

3.2 Macro-Economic and Agricultural Policy Influences on Land Policy

Agricultural sector policy reforms have been pivotal to the SAP-type macro-economic reforms promoted in Zimbabwe since the mid-1980s. Zimbabwe's Economic Structural Adjustment Programme (ESAP) initiated in 1990 by the Government of Zimbabwe (GoZ) promised to improve rural livelihoods through improved productivity and higher prices via market processes (GoZ, 1991). Zimbabwe's ESAP liberalisation programme promised dramatic agricultural growth beyond five per cent growth per annum and reduced poverty through employment and incomes growth and accelerated rural development. The specific policy thrust was that the concentration of agricultural production or land use on new non-traditional exports such as horticulture, wildlife and related tourism land uses would yield positive environmental and socio-economic benefits (GoZ, 1990) beyond the *status quo ante*. Liberalising domestic markets and encouraging exports were, thus, considered the main paths to the growth of Zimbabwean agriculture.

However, a fundamental problem with the ESAP framework was that it did not directly address the key constraints which confronted the small scale or Communal Area farmers prior to ESAP (Moyo, 1989) as well as after ESAP, in their efforts to respond to new market incentives. Key amongst these smallholder constraints were the narrow and discriminatory land and financial markets, distorted water rights which favour the LSCF, and the lack of access to essential infrastructure such as dams and irrigation field equipment and transportation which could make for more effective land use (ibid).

Although the Land Act of 1992 was passed well after the ESAP document had already been adopted, and although the act provided for compulsory land acquisition, it was not an integral part of the ESAP strategy. Indeed, it was considered to be a matter for markets to resolve the land question under the ESAP regime; most analysts, incuding the World Bank, favoured market transfers of land (GoZ, 1991; World Bank, 1991). Nor did the ESAP favour large scale investment in water development as had been recommended by some analysts (ILO, 1989; Moyo, 1989) in order to tackle the problems of low agricultural productivity and employment development. It was only after the 1992 and 1994 droughts that GoZ policy shifted its thrust towards mobilising more finance for dams in Communal Areas to increase the small farmers' share of water rights and to encourage private dam development.

In this policy context, the ESAP period offered no concrete resources for smallholder export-led growth in commodities such as horticulture and tourism, as had happened in Kenya, due to the restrictive land, water and infrastructural conditions of Communal Areas. The long standing skewed distribution of these resources in favour of the LSCF suggested that it was only the latter who could effectively respond to new ESAP incentives. Thus, export incentives, forex allocations and accounts as well as inherited fiscal biases in favour of the LSCF encouraged their responsiveness to land use diversification, intensification and export orientation.

ESAP was preceded from the mid-1980s by the SAP type macro-economic and agricultural sector policy incentives that were gradually introduced and which have had profound impacts on the evolution of Zimbabwe's land use and land tenure policy. Thus, the market liberalisation policies of the 1990s consolidated a particular framework of macro-economic and sectoral policies which have led to an increasingly market-oriented conception and resolution of Zimbabwe's land question. But land use and land tenure policy changes were, themselves, influenced by a wide cross-sectoral range of specific policy elements reviewed below. However, it is the changing financial and economic values and benefits which have accrued to various individual and state landholders during the 1990s through changing land and related market parameters (including commodity, financial and inputs markets) which precipitated changing demands by various interest groups for policy reforms in the macro-economic, sectoral and land- related policy arenas in order to achieve alternative export-oriented land uses.

Our analysis suggests that since the 1970s, there has been continuity with little change in the agrarian policies of Zimbabwe. By and large, the colonial and 1980s agrarian policy framework had been consolidated into an institutional bias towards oligopolistic agricultural markets. In short, following the removal of official racial discrimination in most agrarian and capital markets at independence, the macro-economic strategy during the 1980s and actually existing or real agricultural sector markets tended to favour big players or farmers with long-standing historical performances as opposed to smaller farmers. For instance, forex was allocated mainly to large farmers with a history of given scales of output to purchase imported large-scale farm machinery. Thus, pre-ESAP land use patterns were conditioned by allocations of forex to enhance import substitution and export earnings. While the new ESAP policy changed the forex factor which had driven land use changes, it did not change the policy framework with regard to the allocation of land, water and infrastructure among potential users by markets or the state. Consequently, financial markets were also distorted by this uneven structure of assets and productive capacities. Until the end of 1997, the Land Act of 1992 had remained a potential rather than a real instrument of change.

But while there was no structural break in macro-economic and agrarian policies until 1990, ESAP, and specific policy reforms in the affecting agriculture, the environment, tourism and land, as well as more broadly-based changes in the national and global markets, began gradually to generate changes in the land markets and the agriculture sector as a whole. Those changes associated with the ESAP policy framework, and the emerging market process and context which affected the diversification and intensification of land use during the late 1980s and in the 1990s, have had the most fundamental impact in shaping Zimbabwe's contemporary land question.

3.2.1 Macro and Sectoral Policy Incentives for Land Use Diversification and Intensification

The evolution of Zimbabwe's land policy, and the nature of political and economic struggles over land are a product of a broad range of policy reforms. These include the macro-economic policy framework, which shifted dramatically from the protective regime of the 1980s to the SAP regime of the 1990s, as well as agricultural, tourism and environmental sector policies, which conditioned land output markets, land commodity markets and incentives for the service and inputs sector. Together, these have influenced land uses, the changing value of land and, therefore, the demand for land. The major agricultural policy objectives after 1980 were to increase small-holder participation in markets and to diversify the range and value of agrarian markets.

Agricultural diversification towards new exports noticeably began around 1983 in Zimbabwe, through large farmer initiatives supported by piecemeal government export-oriented policy incentives. The LSCF had historically focussed production on the export of tobacco, sugar, cotton, tea, coffee and domestic urban wage-goods. Their dominance of prime lands, and discriminatory state support in the areas of credit, infrastructure (plus water and rural electrification), state marketing and extension prepared the large farmers for crop diversification. However, post-independence international market exposure and continued preferential state support to large farmers from 1980 to 1990 were critical to agricultural commodity diversification. Policy incentives for new agricultural exports encompassed foreign currency allocations, financial and transport subsidies, and wider institutional support towards the greater integration of Zimbabwe's previously isolated agrarian economy into global markets.

The most critical impact of ESAP on the land question was the liberalisation of agricultural markets and the provision of wider export incentives which changed the structure of returns to the production of various commodities. These ESAP land use policy incentives are gradually being felt through diverse rural economic changes in the form of land use diversification and shifts in the form of land control, access and organisation. As discussed in chapter fiv, meso-level actors such as local authorities, government development agencies, and organizations which represent small farmers (those in Communal Areas, small-scale commercial farms and resettlement areas) have been key elements in concretising the nature of ESAP incentives. These new administrative regulations and increasing competition, and their impact on land use change have not yet been adequately documented.

From the point of view of large farmers, economic liberalization was intended not only to improve their earnings from tradable exports, but also to expand their opportunities to realise and retain foreign currency earnings so as to improve their capacity to import inputs and to externalize their savings through export retention schemes and various export subsidies. The removal of restrictions on the remittance of dividends by foreign investors and the liberalization of foreign borrowing for export agriculture also improved the opportunity for agricultural export production through external financing mechanisms. While the LSCF have realised these gains as shown in Chapter Four, because they have been organized to capture the ESAP policy incentives, such ESAP policy benefits have yet to reach small farmers or to engender greater competitiveness and efficiency within Zimbabwe's heterogenous land economy. Since black LSCF farmers also benefit from these new exports, the incentive to promote redistributive policies in terms of land and state support to the peasantry has also been limited, as argued further in chapters four and five.

Agricultural policy impacts on the land question have varied in terms of the instruments introduced and their timing, targeting and relevance to the variety of producers, as well as in terms of the major sources of policy influences and financing. By far the most important argiculture-related SAP policy instruments, which have shaped Zimbabwe's land question, are: exchange rate management; agricultural domestic market liberalisation; agricultural export market promotion; trade liberalisation in respect of imports of inputs and equipment and labour de-regulation.

The central SAP policy experience of the 1990–1995 period has been the combined impact of the steady devaluation of the Zimbabwe dollar, the freeing of agricultural commodity markets from parastatals, and agricultural commodity price decontrol on the shift in the real and nominal prices of the entire range of agricultural commodities. By 1995, all the major commodity markets had been liberalised (Table 3.2.1), opening the marketing to private buyers and contractors, while by 1996 three of the agricultural parastatals were ready for privatisation. Massive devaluation against the US dollar occurred first in 1991 at over 90 per cent, followed by a decline of over 20 per cent in 1993 and 1994, and steady declines of around 10 per cent each year up to 1996. The nominal and real price effects of these policy instruments are shown in Annex 3.2.1 and Table 3.2.1.

But a wider range of specific agricultural policy shifts during the pre-ESAP and ESAP period directly influenced Zimbabwe's emerging land policy. The commercialisation and then privatisation of marketing boards and state credit, the liberalisation of commodity pricing, and the acceptance of private agricultural middlemen both fed into and reinforced the devaluation of the Zimbabwean dollar, and, thus, had specific effects on agricultural change and land policy. Chapter four explores the scale of the actual rather than normative and/or perceived impacts of these ESAP policy reforms on Zimbabwean agriculture in relation to other possible origins of change such as droughts and environmentalism and the responsiveness of different kinds of farmers to these policy reforms.

The role of changing agricultural producer price incentives stands out mainly because these tend to be misrepresented in terms of their value and impacts over-time. For example, the producer prices of all the agricultural commodities showed a steady rise in nominal terms, meaning that farmers could use last season's prices as guaranteed minimum prices for the current season in decision making (Annex 3.2.1).

These price shifts were accompanied by an average annual rate of inflation of about 30 per cent. However, when converted to real prices in terms of the United States dollar (using end of year exchange rates), the price trend was different. There had been a steady decline in real prices up to 1991/92 when most commodities had reached their minimum. From 1992/93, real prices started to rise again until the 1995/96 period. However, for almost all the commodities, the real prices never rose enough to reach the price levels of the early 1980s.

Table 3.2.1. *Agricultural Pricing and Marketing Policy*

Policy	Policy Features	Begun	Group affected
1. Pre-ESAP policies	Producer prices where announced before season's planting to boost producer incentives as it reduces risk and uncertainty .	1985	All
a) Pre-planting prices	Enables farmers to make decisions based on relative prices.		
b) Pre-harvest and post-harvest prices	Producer prices are set and announced around April-May. Enables government to gauge potential harvests and stocking levels beforre announcing prices.	1983	All
c) Pan-territorial pricing	Payment of uniform prices throughout the country Benefits farmers in remove surplus regions at the expense of those in deficit regions and those close to markets.	1985	
	Discouraged production of high value—low volume crops (export crops) as it infers an implicit transport subsidy to remote farmers.		All
d) Pan-seasonal pricing	Producer and consumer prices are set annually. No incentive for off season production. Encourages centralized as opposed to on farm storage.	1985	All
2. Post ESAP policies	Marketing of commodities was decontrolled as marketing boards were commercialized:	1992	CA
a) Decontrol of crops marketing			CA
	Maize (N.R. IV & V)		All
	Sunflowers		CA
	Cotton		LSCF
	Small grains		LSCF
	Beef		LSCF
	Milk		

Source: Adapted from Takavarasha, 1994 and Moyo, 1995a.

Table 3.2.2. *Agricultural Marketing Boards Reform*

Board	Established	Functions	Current State
Agricultural Marketing Authority (AMA)	1967	Coordinates and arranges financing for the other marketing board.	Dissolved in 1994.
Grain Marketing Board (GMB)	1931	Purchase, grading, handling, transport, storage and disposal of maize, sorghum, groundnuts, soyabeans, wheat, coffee, rapoko, and sunflower.	Now residual trading board.
Cold Storage Commission (CSC)	1938	Purchase and distribution of cattle. Beef exporting.	Privatised in 1996.
Dairy Marketing Board (DMB)	1952	Trading board in the purchase, processing, distribution and external trade of all dairy products.	Privatised in 1994. Now Dairy Board Limited.
Cotton Marketing Board (CMB)	1969	Trading board in purchase, processing and export of cotton products.	Privatised in 1994. Now Cotton Company of Zimbabwe.
Tobacco Marketing Board (TMB)	1936	Determines where tobacco is sold.	Opened up in 1996, new players e.g. Boka.

Source: Muir, 1994.

The phasing out of quantitative import controls was, indeed, a boost to the domestic agricultural sector. The relaxation of agricultural import and export controls had been achieved by 1995 except for the monopoly position of the GMB for maize meal, wheat and wheat flour exports. By 1991, however, special import tariffs were set for agricultural machinery, equipment and farm vehicles at 15 per cent, although local ploughs continued to be subjected to taxes of up to 40 per cent. Since the LSCF are major importers of the former items which are suitable for large-scale farms and the peasants the main users of ploughs, trade liberalization policy tended to be biased in favour of larger farms.

Differential land use responses in bimodal agrarian structures tend to mean that a growing division of labour among different kinds of farmers continues to evolve (Moyo, 1989). As noted before, Communal Area farmers have resorted to producing cheap wage foods (Shopo, 1985; Moyo, 1986) and labour intensive but low technology exports such as cotton and burley tobacco (Moyo, 1989). More recently, Communal Area farmers have been increasing their supply of low wage domestic vegetable markets for rape, cabbage, onions etc. (Weiner et al., 1988). Meanwhile, more LSCF farmers abandoned maize (Scoones, 1997), cotton, cheaper vegetables and so forth and many moved first to traditional exports, and then increasingly to new exports and land uses.

Agrarian commodity market liberalisation during the 1990s also shifted the institutional framework of extension services, market information and trading. But there are more "middlemen" (literally men) pushing new exports or land uses such as horticulture. These "middlemen" range from domestic agribusiness firms, white LSCF farmers, and indigenous businessmen to NGO officials and government officials in related agencies (see Chapter Five). This information and demand for converting or allocating land to new land uses is encouraged by a broadened business interest in such export-oriented production. Government policy towards "indigenisation" has, for example, broadened the demand among black business persons and business start-ups to engage in agricultural inputs and outputs marketing, and in small agro-processing industries. Through credit schemes for small and medium scale enterprises, a wider framework to promote land use diversification and intensification emerged.

3.2.2 Effects of Globalisation on Land Policy

In addition to national policies, the changing global economy has changed Zimbabwe's land question. Some of the key structural changes in the global economy that have had dramatic effects on policy and land use in countries like Zimbabwe revolve around the changing nature of the global demand for agricultural and natural resource commodities derived from land. In the last decade, improved air transportation technologies have made long distance tourist and business travel cheaper in a context of increased disposable incomes among elites in the northern hemisphere. The increased globalisation of business operations and travel have also certainly encouraged the growth of the markets for wildlife-related tourism in Southern Africa.

Furthermore, the restructuring of global capital itself has had profound impacts on demand for agrarian commodities and their production, leading to land use changes in countries such as Zimbabwe (Gereffi and Korneniewicz, 1994; Hirst and Thompson, etc.). In particular, buyer-driven commodity chains (BDGCC) have a profound impact in horticulture and tourist-related land uses.

The growth of the global environmental movement has also increased the allocation of development assistance and private resources towards the promotion of ecologically sustainable land uses. In Zimbabwe this has mainly taken the form of increased foreign aid allocations to wildlife land use conversions. Thus, more external private investors, NGO personnel, scientists and allied industries have been promoting wildlife conservation and related land uses than was the case before when mainly a few government ecologists did so in parks secluded from society and from entrepreneurial exigencies. These trends have increased the demand for land to be used for wildlife and related activities and broadened the range of actors involved as discussed in Chapter Five.

3.2.3 Urban Demand for Land

Beyond the global, agricultural and tourism sectoral factors, a parallel factor in shifting the demand for land has been the increased impoverishment of the urban working class, the unemployed, and various categories of the rural poor, including the 30 per cent among them who are landless (Moyo, 1995a). According to urban sociologists, during the ESAP period, wages have deteriorated to about 50 per cent of their 1982 levels in real terms (Sachikonye, 1991; Brand et al., 1995), while fewer than 20,000 jobs per annum have been created in spite of an annual addition to the workforce of 300,000 school leavers (ILO, 1994). Fewer urban dwellers can now afford township housing leading to increased urban squatting, shared lodging and living in shacks (Moyo, 1997). As a result, a greater number of the employed and unemployed in most cities are being driven into peri-urban residence in nearby Communal Areas or LSCF areas as legal and illegal squatters (Moyo et al., 1998).

The demand for land for residential purposes and to supplement the declining level of urban wages which are being shared by larger sets of dependents is on the rise. The growth in urban and peri-urban farming (Mbiba, 1995), including along streambanks and without permits, are signs of how growing poverty is increasing pressure on land. Similarly, the decline in job opportunities for migrants from Communal Areas (Maast,

1996) means that more and more people rely on land for their basic reproduction (Moyo, 1995a). Thus, poverty as a significant source of expanding
demand for land, and, therefore, as a factor in the more intensive use of land
as more people cultivate land for basic subsistence, is an important aspect of
land use change.

This source of demand in shaping the land question was also neglected
by the ESAP policy framework. Pressures for land redistribution, land occupation or squatting strategies and increased urban and peri-urban farming
suggest a trend for effective demand and aggressive land bidding strategies
on LSCF, state and communal lands around all the major cities and smaller
towns. Such demands also imply a particular structure of land use combi-
ning residential and production uses by employment-"straddling" households, leading towards diversification and intensification along the inner
ring of the Onion Ring macro-structure presented in Chapter Two. These
processes transform the valuation of land and the demands for land policy
reforms.

3.3 Specific Land Use Policies and Regulations Affecting Land Policy

3.3.1 Horticulture Sub-Sector Policy Reforms

The increase in horticultural exports in Zimbabwe is closely related to the
externally-driven marketing of inputs and outputs to the agrarian sector.
Led by Dutch agribusiness and auctioneers, and by British supermarkets
such as Sainsbury's, Zimbabwe's horticulture industry can be closely typi-
fied as a Buyer Driven Global Commodity Chain (BDGCC) (Geraffi and
Korzeniewicz, 1994). The supply of planting stocks, product design, chemicals, credit and production expertise, as well as the arrangement of external
marketing outlets from external sources have been critical in the development of Zimbabwe's horticulture (CFU, 1995).

The Government of Zimbabwe embarked on a wide range of specific
policies to promote the growth and development of the horticultural sector.
While the devaluation exercise also had some adverse effects on the horticultural industry, such as increased costs of transport, external marketing
and imported inputs, these cost increases did not negatively affect the sector
as they were more than offset by the increase in revenue resulting from a set
of incentives realised by producers.

The AFC broadened its financing to peri-urban plot holders with holdings of at least five hectares in projects which include piggeries, vegetable
growing and poultry (Box 3.3.1). Since April 1990, AFC has been financing
agro-industrial business under this scheme, and loans of up to $1 million
maximum for an irrigation project that is owned and operated by a con-
sortium and $400,000 for individuals, were instituted.

Box 3.3.1. *AFC Loan Case Studies*

Two farmers in the Trelawney area, Zvimba District, who are engaged in horticultural production applied for loans, and another two farmers from the Barwick
ICA, Murwi applied for loans for ostrich production. For wildlife, there is one famer
who applied for a loan in Karoi although most of those moving into this land use are
in Masvingo Province. Almost all of the applications have been from the white
commercial farmers but there are a few blacks who applied in Mash-West and there
is one black farmer in Chegutu who wants to have ostriches. A Mr. Matambo (Chairman of ZOPA) of Musengezi SSCF was also assisted with loans to start ostrich farming.

Source: Interviews (1996).

The AFC Development Section responsible for assisting communal, resettlement and SSCF farmers, began assisting those who were diversifying into
the new export land uses in 1988, although few were forthcoming because of
lack of information and initial capital or assets to cover risks. AFC staff suggest that most small farmers view horticulture in its narrow sense as a back-
yard subsistence activity and not as a money earner on a wider scale (Mr.
Chindove AFC Development Section—Mash-West). Thus, they have not
assisted anyone for horticulture, although funds are available.

The broad trend is a shift of AFC finances to intensive high value horticulture in LSCF and peri-urban areas, and towards wildlife and ostrich
production. The key elements of such credit included lower interest rates
denominated in foreign currency, support for irrigation systems for intensive cropping, and finance for farm-related infrastructure, as well as for
industrial processing of agricultural outputs.

For instance, under the Export Promotion Programme which operated
from 1987 to 1991, horticultural farmers had easy access to foreign currency
set aside to meet their input requirements, when they needed it, unlike other
farmers who had allocations made to them on a six-monthly basis. A special
arrangement also gave farmers planning to venture into horticultural production adequate time to secure initial capital costs and foreign currency at
times when these were scarce and costly. A special horticultural US$20
million foreign exchange facility was established in 1990 by the Reserve
Bank of Zimbabwe with a group of London-based commercial banks. The
funds were to be used in meeting the input requirements for export
horticulture and not for production for the domestic market. Such a requirement meant that it was mostly the commercial farm sector that benefited
from the fund as the smallholder farmers had very little involvement in
export horticulture. The fund was used mainly for the establishment of new
horticultural projects and the expansion of existing ones after approval by
the Zimbabwe Investment Centre. Twenty-six per cent of the fund was used
by the Ministry of Lands, Agriculture and Water Development (MLAWD) to

procure horticultural inputs. The fund was renewed by a further US$20 million in 1992.

An Export Retention Scheme (ERS) which was introduced at the start of 1991 also provided horticultural producers with foreign currency. Initially exporters of horticultural produce were entitled to retain 7.5 per cent of their net foreign currency earnings. The MLAWD retained a quarter of the forex available under this scheme for direct allocation to the agricultural sector, effectively reducing this percentage of 5.62. Towards the end of the same year, the ERS was revised to raise the percentage entitlement of individual producers to 25 per cent and to broaden the previously narrow list of goods that could be imported freely under the scheme. Half of this percentage was retained by the MLAWD. On July 1 1992, the scheme was further revised to allow up to 30 per cent retention. This scheme was a key incentive behind expanded export production among farmers.

Moreover, some specific items used by the horticulture sector were placed under the Open General Import License system. The Export Incentive Scheme (EIS) provided for a nine per cent direct payment to exporters on the basis of the net realization from exports. This was later reduced to five per cent in June 1992 as more incentives for exports were now in place. In addition, agro-industrial projects approved by the Zimbabwe Investment Centre (ZIC) were relieved from import tax, surtax and customs duties on all capital goods imported. Table 3.3.1. summarises incentives which have helped promote the horticulture sector.

Table 3.3.1. *Special Policy Incentives Promoting Horticulture*

Policy	Year of start	Year of end
Devaluation of Zimbabwean Dollar	Dec 1982	on-going
Export Promotion Programme	1987	1991
Special Horticultural Foreign Exchange Facility	1990	on-going
Export Retention Scheme	1991	on-going
Export Revolving Fund	1991	on-going

Source: Review of Government Documents.

3.3.2 Wildlife and Tourism Policy Incentives for Land Value Shifts

Among the fundamental factors influencing changes in the perceived and actual use and exchange value of land, including agricultural land, over the last 15 years are the legislative and policy incentives for the conversion and intensification of land use from older uses such as agricultural production, environmental protection and land speculation to wildlife and nature management and tourist uses. The change in policy towards the liberalisation of land use for non-agricultural purposes has increased demand among various interest groups to convert their land or intensify their activities in such uses. Various players, ranging from LSCF farmers, parastatal managers, indigenous non-farming business people and local authority income-generating managers to Communal Area communities and environmental NGO group project members, have, during the 1990s in particular, begun to place greater value on non-agricultural land use. Such uses include wildlife ranching, the creation of private or community nature and recre-ation parks, ostrich farming, forest and woodland plantations etc.

Thus, a greater part of formerly marginal lands (N.R. III, IV and V) in Communal and LSCF Areas, state-owned lands (parks, forests and reserves), as well as formerly underutilised lands in the entire country, but particularly in the LSCF and state lands, became attractive for new commercial uses. In the mid-1980s, GoZ tourism and wildlife policies began to encourage these alternative land uses on the basis of foreign currency earnings from game exports and tourism. The policy also argued on technical grounds that such land uses have higher returns to capital invested and offer better physical land productivity (see Chapter Four). These changing use values have also generated greater competition for control of and access to land, and conflicting perspectives on their values, as well as the wider cost benefits of such land uses to Zimbabwean society.

The evolution of policies which promote non-agricultural land uses has taken over 35 years. The policies were, however, consolidated into a liberal market framework over the last 10 years. Various policy, legislative and regulatory instruments characterise this policy shift. However, the key conceptual, ideological and economic basis of this changing policy direction has been the extent to which privatising nature for individual benefit was economically, nationally and ecologically sustainable. Changing global environmental perspectives and aid also played a key role in promoting this policy shift.

For instance, the Wildlife Act of 1961 legalised the issuing of wildlife cropping permits, but the first one was actually issued in 1959 to crop 350 impala. In 1960, Buffalo Ranch was issued with a cropping quota, and in that year 122 impala carcasses were exported to Holland to test the venison market. By 1964, there were 33 wildlife ranches which used 34 per cent of their total allocated quota (Roth, 1966). By 1982, game ranches with cropping permits covered 19,500 km^2 or 13.5 per cent of commercial farmland. Noncommercial hunting under landholder licences and by sportsmen under general and supplementary hunting licences on state land accounted for a greater number of animals on 14,000 km^2. Thus in 1964, game meat production and hunting were taking place on about 34,000 km^2 with a potential production of 2,350kg venison or 0.69kg of meat per ha (Roth, 1990).

Tensions arose over the existence of the two separate acts to govern wildlife exploitation: one for national parks and the other for wildlife outside national parks administered by two separate government departments. The Parks and Wildlife Act of 1975 provided a legal framework for the conservation and utilisation of wildlife resources by private owners in the LSCF areas of the country. Landholders and occupiers of alienated or freehold land were then given the responsibility for the management and utilisation of wildlife on their land (Cumming, 1990). Significantly, however, the act did not confer actual ownership of the wildlife resources on the land owners. Wildlife belonged, by default, to the state because wildlife was legally regarded as *rese nullius*, that is, belonging to no one. Yet, the 1975 Act laid the basis for private interest in the exploitation of wildlife resources, albeit within a narrow framework of commerce and land use, given that tourism during the UDI period was low and global markets for venison and wildlife products (tourism etc.) were still shallow.

Independence increasingly opened up the economy to global wildlife and tourist markets during the 1980s, especially through the promotion of export incentives and the relaxation of various environmental regulations which inhibited the commercial expansion of the wildlife sector. By the 1990s, GoZ policies on export incentives, currency devaluation, the promotion of tourism, the "sale" to private land owners of animals, and the relaxation of the licensing to convert land use from agriculture to wildlife, had, together, expanded the growing interest in the conversion towards and intensification of non-agricultural rural land uses. But some policy constraints affecting these sectors were still intact by 1990 (see Table 3.3.2).

The range of specific wildlife management incentives which facilitated the sector's growth beyond the wider ESAP policy framework is varied and detailed. For instance, more hunting licences were provided during the decade of the 1990s, hunting operations could be paid for directly in foreign currency and the proprietor could retain greater parts of those earnings. It had been argued that pre-ESAP policies led to an acute shortage of foreign exchange since its price meant that demand for it in the wildlife sector was far greater than supply, and that maintaining an over-valued exchange rate implicitly taxed the producers of the tradeables, including wildlife products, that are mostly exportable. The sector argued that the net effect of this was a taxation with a disincentive effect on wildlife producers and which also undermined the contribution of the wildlife sector to the economy. This hampered the performance and growth of nearly all the wildlife sectors, especially the tourism and hunting sub-sectors which require imported inputs, such as furnishings and vehicles.

Prior to 1990, it was argued that the wildlife sector had been more negatively affected by foreign currency shortages than the manufacturing and mining sectors, because these sectors all had access to donor-financed Commodity Import Programmes (CIPS), Export Revolving Funds (ERFs) or Export Promotion Programmes (EPPs). Thus, policy changes under ESAP were intended to improve the wildlife sector's access to forex, and to broaden their range of production inputs which could be freely imported on Open General Import License (OGIL) with private Export Retention Scheme (ERS) allocations. Henceforth, such imports were not to be regarded as luxuries for the economy as a whole, but necessities for the tourism and hunting sub-sector, and the bulk of these had been placed on OGIL by 1992 (Price Waterhouse, 1992). Thus, hunting arms and ammunition also became a major area of import liberalisation following their qualified removal from the "negative" import list.

The policy regarding the direct export of live animals has been an area of controversy as the law requires the wildlife producer to obtain permits and licences and to abide by other detailed restrictions. In 1992, the export of sable and ostrich was prohibited, while the export of other species remained at the discretion of the Parks Department which consults the Wild Life Producers Association (WPA) and the Ostrich Producers Association of Zimbabwe (TOPAZ) within the narrow framework of the wildlife sector rather than with regard to national cost–benefit effects such as the broader implications for land use change and struggles over access to land.

The investment policy debates in the wildlife and tourism sector were, however, an integral element of ESAP reform strategy. The positive environmental impact of wildlife uses have remained the main public basis of DPWLM, MET and private arguments for the above-mentioned economic policy incentives. It has even been suggested that the wildlife and/or tourism sectors are more viable than various industrial and agricultural sub-sectors and, as such, deserve greater allocations of GoZ resources, including infrastructure, finance and, indeed, subsidies, like access to cheaply priced wildlife and lands that are under the jurisdiction of the state. In fact, the Zimbabwe Investment Centre (ZIC) had placed wildlife and tourism on its priority list for state investment support by 1992. It was argued that such investments in the wildlife sector yielded greater contributions to incomes, employment and foreign currency earnings than investments in manufacturing and mining.

Table 3.3.2. *Wildlife Policy Change Demand*

Policy change	Year	Impact on sector
ESAP	1990	Improved the sector's access to foreign exchange. Inclusion of exporters' services (i.e. tourism and hunting) in the Export Retention Scheme (ERS). Under ERS, exporters can retain the rights over a certain percentage of their export earnings.
Export Restrictions	1989/90	Exports of sable and ostrich prohibited —the ban is financially motivated with the aim of restraining the price of ostriches for new domestic producers. There are a number of permits, licences and restrictions which frustrates producers.
Veterinary restrictions	Before 1980	Quarantine (lengthy) periods—increases production costs of live animals.
Tax Policy	1980	There are still ambiguities in tax policy. (When a rancher purchases wildlife, is it to be treated as a current cost, or should standard values as for cattle be used?) What types of tourism related services are subject to sales tax and which are not?
Exchange Rate Policy	1990	The policy has hampered the performance and growth of wildlife sectors, particularly the tourism and hunting subsectors which require imported inputs, such as furnishing and vehicles.
Trade Policy	1980/90	Extensive controls over international trade. A perusal of the OGIL list makes it very clear that there were few items of relevance to the wildlife sector.
Investment Policy	1990/95	Investments in wildlife sector which may make a greater contribution to incomes, foreign exchange and employment are prejudiced by being given a lower priority.
Fiscal Policy	Yearly	The sector is given a low priority in government budget. DNPWLM budgetshas provided Z$4.3 million to Treasury and received Z$21,9 million, for a net expenditure of Z$17.6 million.

Source: Muir, 1993; Bond 1993.

GoZ fiscal policy towards the wildlife sector has also been a site of heated private lobby and policy change. The evidence shows that the wildlife sector had been given a low priority in the allocation of budgetary resources. Over the last six years (Price Waterhouse, 1992), on average, DNPWLM provided a revenue of $4.3 million to Treasury, receiving $21.9 million for a net expenditure of $17.6 million. This represents 0.36%—less than half of 1%of total government expenditure. Budgetary allocations to the entire MET averaged $44.1 million, still less than 1% of total central government expenditure. Budgetary allocation to DNPWLM has not been increasing over the years compared to total government expenditure. In 1985/86, the Department received 0.46% of the total government budget. In 1990/91, this had decreased to 0.44%. MET's allocation decreased from 1.17% of total expenditure in 1985/86 to only 0.68% in 1990/91. It was, thus, argued that competing or complementary landuses such as livestock received considerably larger budgetary subsidies, which wildlife deserved more because of its larger foreign currency income and earnings and GDP contribution. For instance, the tourism sector is said to now contribute 5% of Zimbabwe's

GDP and wildlife land uses are thought to account for about half of this contribution.

Taxation policy for wildlife operators is currently under scrutiny since it is argued that safari operators are not construed as being "farming operations" for the purpose of the Income Tax Act, and, thus, do not qualify for the various allowances available under the Second, Fourth and Seventh Schedules of the Act. These allow farmers to claim the costs of erecting fences, building dams, sinking boreholes etc. There are several other "grey areas" in the treatment of tourism and safari operations under the Sales Tax Act which are under review since these are said to constrain the growth of the wildlife sector and because the Parks Department cannot give adequate support to the sector. Indeed, the wildlife and parks board and its DNWPLM were, in 1996, commercialised to enable them to run independently of the state and promote the sector better.

Various regulations affecting Tour and Safari operators in Zimbabwe, such as the requirement to be licenced by the Ministry of Environment and Tourism, and to either own or hold a lease on a suitable concession of land with accompanying animal quota, are under review. A variety of other regulations under review include: handguns for hunting which are not yet legal in Zimbabwe and recommendations to change this are being considered by the Parks Department; black powder hunting which is permitted provided the weapon complies with the requirements of the Third Schedule; and bowhunting which is permitted on private land and for non-dangerous game only, although special application can be made for dangerous game at the discretion of the Director of National Parks and professional hunters are required to have undergone a Bowhunting Proficiency Test.

But wildlife policy has been the subject of controversy because the industry has been seen to exclude "indigenous" actors, and also tends to be abused through widespread illegal forex retentions and tax evasion. Reportedly, there had been cases of private wildlife owners bringing tourists into Zimbabwe without notifying government while other producers sold animals outside the country illegally. Government policy is moving towards a:

> new system which will enable government to license wildlife farmers and control how they look after the animals and how they market them. Government intends to maintain wild animals as national property. The system will bar farmers in agricultural areas from diversifying into game production which we wish to be done in non-agricultural areas only (Minister Chen Chimutengwende, 1996).

The new Tourism Act of 1995 provides for the GoZ to regulate the sector through: controlling any service whatsoever provided for tourists; designating any premises, place or thing which in its opinion, affords an amenity to tourists, a tourist facility; requiring a designated tourist facility to be registered or graded and extracting from the operators a levy at the rate of two per cent of the gross amount, excluding sales tax or any other tax or duty, charged to any tourist making use of any amenity provided at the designated tourist amenity.

Apparently the Zimbabwe Association of Tour and Safari Operators have argued that they would be happy to pay levies as long as the money goes towards further marketing the wildlife industry, promoting better standards and "making sure that tourists are given the value of their money" (*The Farmer*, February 15 1996, Vol. 66, No. 6). However the indigenisation interests have evoked a firm GoZ stance towards controlling the sector as stated by its minister:

> Government will not allow the privatisation of wildlife resources through the back door i.e. through unplanned and uncontrolled private conservancies. We are fully aware of such Machiavellian plots to privatise wildlife resources from Kenya to South Africa. But in Zimbabwe, the state will remain in charge of this sector (Article by Ministry of Environment and Tourism, *Herald* 8/10/96).

Indeed, the GoZ and various interests support such control because it has been alleged that wildlife conservancy owners were using prime agricultural land in Natural Regions I, II and III for game ranching and lodges. And the GoZ argues that:

> If we let this pattern continue uncontrolled, then our entire agricultural production will be threatened (Minister, ibid).

The policy direction is thus that private conservancies have to be restricted to approved ecological zones of region IV and V, and that N.R. I, II and III should be exclusively reserved for agriculture except where the nature of soils does not allow conventional agriculture. According to the Minister of MET (1996):

> ... farmers who had set up conservancies in prime agricultural areas are supposed to close these down, and ... all new conservancies would be allowed to operate only after being licensed by the government, ... one condition of licensing would be that they should benefit the nearby rural communities (ibid).

Expected policy shifts are, thus, that the flow of benefits from wildlife to Communal Areas communities should be an essential ingredient of conservancies, and that the surrounding rural communities should be turned into strong stake-holders in the process (ibid).

Two GoZ policy arenas have purported to address these concerns: the Campfire programme targeting wildlife management in Communal Areas through the district authorities and the indigenisation policy (tourism subsector) wherein black elites are supported by affirmative action principles in the allocation of land leases, fishing permits and other tourism quotas and licences.

The Campfire programme has been widely documented in the environment literature and in political economy studies. The programme promotes the sustainable use of natural resources by local communities through empowering them in resource management and utilisation. The benefits from wildlife utilisation are intended to be directed to the ward, village and household levels as a source of income. Since 1989 when the programme began, it has covered 26 out of the 57 districts. The key though of related policies and legislation was to return "custodianship" or "proprietorship" over wildlife to the rural communities, the devolution of authority for wild-life management to the Rural District Councils, and the disbursement of benefits from wildlife utilisation to local communities. The Campfire concept is used beyond managing wildlife in planning the best options for the sustainable utilisation of other natural resources such as timber.

3.3.3 Ostrich Sub-Sector Policy Reforms

Policy change in the ostrich sub-sector has also been focussed on the implications of transferring or spreading the authority over ostrich management from the state in GoZ parks and forests to private ostrich operators. During the mid-1980s, GoZ policy towards commercial exploitation of ostriches was relatively *ad hoc*, given that private ostrich farming had begun mainly in the LSCF around the 1950s. However, by 1991, the DNPWM of the GoZ had produced its first comprehensive policy document on this land use. It was entitled the *Ostrich Management Plan*. Subsequently, by 1995, as the industry grew, various policy instruments intended to control the development of ostrich enterprises in the LSCF and in Communal Areas, as well as to support ostrich producer organisations and to regulate their exports were introduced by 1995 (see chart). The interesting aspect of the evolution of ostrich policy is the extent to which the GoZ tended to devolve the regulation of the industry to producers, unlike in the agricultural sector where the GoZ had always kept close control. Given that the white LSCF farmers were initially the main actors in the ostrich sector, this meant that a minority racial group tended to determine the policy environment until lately when black producers cried foul over their disadvantages, and when the viability of exports seemed to be threatened by "live bird export" (see also Chapter Five for details on the actors in this sub-sector). The GoZ had, indeed, a hands-off policy approach.

Table 3.3.3. *Ostrich Policy Developments*

Year	Policy
1991	Management Plan for Ostriches in Zimbabwe
1994	Rural Ostrich Development Programme and Rural Ostrich Finance Scheme
1995	Desertification and Poverty Alleviation through Rural Small Land Holders Participation in Ostrich Production and Complementary Projects (Draft Proposal)
1995	Constitution of the Zimbabwe Ostrich Producers Association
1995	Banning of Live Ostrich Exports

For example, under the "controversial" Ostrich Management Plan of 1991 which seeks to promote domesticated and wildlife ostrich farming, TOPAZ had been conferred with the power of self-regulation and control of the ostrich industry by the DNPWLM. Farmers who sought to utilise wild ostrich resources were required to apply for a permit in terms of the plan to the Director of Parks with a supporting letter from TOPAZ and the relevant Area Conservation Committee nominee. For all operations involving the legal sale of ostriches and ostrich trophies obtained from any source within Zimbabwe, the Director of Parks was required to issue a permit to the Chairman of TOPAZ or his/her duly authorized representative. The Chairman of TOPAZ could appoint such members of TOPAZ as he deemed fit as his duly authorized representatives.

Accordingly, applications to export ostriches within the SADC region needed to be supported by the Chairman of TOPAZ and a written guarantee was also required from the Cites Management Authority of the importing country stating that they would not be re-exported. Ostrich parts and derivatives needed to be marked in accordance with the Parks Department's instructions before a Cites export permit could be issued and all export applications needed to be accompanied by a letter of support from the TOPAZ Chairman.

Since 1993, the growth of the ostrich industry has largely benefited from deliberate policies and institutional provisions of the government, non-governmental organisations and other private ostrich producers. The Department of Natural Resources plays a leading role in promoting ostrich farming among Communal Area communities because the major cause of land degradation there is poverty, which leads to pressure on land due to the continued cultivation of marginal land. A strategy to increase incomes in Communal Areas through ostrich production and other horticultural projects can relieve land pressure. The department thus initiated the Desertification and Poverty Alleviation through Rural Small Land Holders participation in Ostrich Production and Complementary Projects Programme (DNR, 1995) to promote sustainable conservation, utilisation and careful management of the wildlife resources in the rural areas. Allied projects entail mainly irrigation projects for horticulture. Policy efforts in this area began with the pilot projects of the Chesa North Ostrich Syndicate of Mashonaland Central and Musengezi Ostrich Producers Syndicate of Mashonaland West which have had access to donor funding such as those offered under the USAID Soft and Hard Project Equipment facility and other types of assistance from CIDA, SIDA, NORAD, UNEP, Africa 2000 etc. These projects seem to have concentrated initially on Small Scale Commercial Farms (SSCF) before moving towards Communal Areas, thus reinforcing the class basis of black participation in this sub-sector.

The Department of Natural Resources' policy approach in Ostrich Development is to collaborate with private small-scale producer organisations

such as SHOC and other GoZ agencies, including the Agricultural Finance
Corporation (AFC), in providing financial aid to alternative labour intensive
and less weather-dependent crop production and animal husbandry activities. Its Ostrich Finance Scheme will operate for a period of five years from
April 1995, subject to further extensions, with funds from a grant from the
Ministry of Finance based upon donor counterpart funds (e.g. French aid), at
0.8 per cent loan rates of the amount granted, and from interest earned on
the investment of scheme funds and the repayment of loans by clients. Non-
governmental organisations, using resources derived from donors, also promote Communal Area ostrich production through grant funding to groups
of farmers. A total of $214,501.27 was, for example, given to producers in the
Chesa North ICA Project by the UNDP Africa 2000 Network.

This GoZ policy to promote land use diversification in Communal Areas
is implemented via District Development Committees, WADCOs and
VIDCOs, councillors and farmers' unions. Farmers are encouraged to group
into three or four people and to set up their own enterprises in either
horticulture or ostrich production. The DNR routinely visits projects to
monitor and evaluate progress, and approaches donors for funding for the
initial costs of projects such as the purchasing of birds, fencing materials etc.,
as well as assisting the people in obtaining permits from the Veterinary
Department for the movement of birds. The DNR also works together with
newly formed farmers organisations such as Zimbabwe Ostrich Producers
Association (ZOPA) and, at the provincial level, in a sub-committee which
brings together government (DNR, Agritex), the LSCF farmers, Communal
Area farmers and local authority structures. Secretarial services are provided
by DNR. The farmers themselves provide the chairman and the secretary.

However, some GoZ officials feel that ostrich production is an expensive
venture which needs a lot of infrastructure and have described ostrich production as not being a poor man's project as it is suitable for those who are
already "financially stable". They also insist that it should not be a poverty
alleviation strategy but seen strictly as a "business venture". Thus, land use
diversification has become an ideological site for market economic policy
debate; it is also an increasingly established site for accumulation among
competing interests in Communal Areas.

3.3.4 Ostrich Export Regulation

The export of live ostriches and eggs which had been banned temporarily in
1992 started in June 1993, "saving the lucrative industry from imminent
collapse due to the lack of a vibrant local market for ostrich meat" (interviews). The Parks Department then issued 5,000 export permits to enable
farmers to export at least two chicks per hen. Apparently, the Parks Department policy has been to provide producers a quota to export 5,000 live birds
and 12,000 eggs so as to raise money for building their own abattoir and

other facilities (*Herald*, 16/02/94), in order to meet strict European Union export product standards whenever EU veterinary officials inspect ostrich slaughter facilities at the main abattoir in Bulawayo. (In 1993, producers lost potential multi-million dollar export earnings because of the lack of slaughter facilities that met stringent export standards.) (Interviews.)

GoZ policy has also been to exert pressure on large farmer ostrich producer associations to help their Communal Area counterparts. Thus, in 1994, TOPAZ says it set aside 300 ostriches for sale to small scale farmers at a subsidized half price of $800 per six month chick in order to bring them into the lucrative industry, although, it cannot be verified if this actually happened. An interim liaison committee comprising four parliamentarians had been put in place to work out the logistics of how the small farmers could be organised and assisted by TOPAZ in the initial phases of the Communal Areas ostrich project.

The growth of ostrich production in Communal Areas is, however, restrained by the high financial and social costs associated with GoZ veterinary regulations which govern the enterprise. Thus, for instance, to enter into ostrich production, farmers must do away with chickens on their premises, special well fenced paddocks not accessible to human beings or animal traffic are necessary, while the animal stock must be from a clean stock of ostrich breeds without. Ostriches can only be moved under a Veterinary Permit affirming that the farm has not reported Newcastle disease in the last 30 days, and that there has not been an outbreak within a 20 km radius for the last 30 days. Generally, farmers are said to be adhering to most veterinary regulations, although when dealing with ostrich exports, it is reported that farmers cheat in the local translocation of animals.

Substantial effort and resources are also required of the GoZ to enforce its policy. The Animal Health Act can be used to prosecute the offenders, while the various accompanying legislation and regulations which ensure that government policy and requirements are met include: import and export regulations; animal health import and movement regulations; movement of game animal health regulations; quarantine animal health regulations; stock register animal health regulations; and carcass and game meat regulations.

The evidence suggests that the GoZ cannot necessarily cope with enforcing these regulations, hence its tendency to delegate the responsibility to producer associations. Substantial effort and resources are also required of the GoZ to enforce its policy. The increased conflicts among large white and small black ostrich producers as discussed in Chapter Five reflect their highly uneven capacities to respond to the economic incentives of ostrich land uses and to cover the costs of compliance with a multitude of regulations or even the costs of avoiding compliance.

3.4 Land Policy Changes in the 1990s

In this section, we briefly review Zimbabwe's changing land reform policy in respect of land redistribution, freehold land markets, land use conversion and sub-division, and land occupation. Three distinct phases of land reform policy have been observed in Zimbabwe (Moyo, 1995a) since independence: an early phase of radical, squatter-compelled land redistribution during 1980 and 1984 when over 70 per cent of current redistributed land was transferred from the LSCF; the dominant phase when virtually nothing occurred (1985–1989); and the current radical land policy phase (1990–1997) when the legal framework allows for easier redistribution, although little land has actually been transferred.

The section also provides the context for understanding land use changes related to land tenure policy changes.

3.4.1 Land Reform Experiences

Zimbabwe's land question is a classic case of racial and class-based inequalities in the control of and access to rural lands and natural resources of varied economic and ecological potentials, as well as of the inequitable control of related commodity and capital markets. The land reforms pursued by the state since 1980 saw the transfer of a relatively small proportion (15 per cent) of white-controlled lands to 6 per cent of the peasantry (Moyo, 1995). Communal Area land tenure was also continuously reformed as the state increased its control and regulation of the use of these lands and their natural resources (ibid). Recently, the GoZ's Land Tenure Commission (1995) proposed further tenure reforms which lean towards "radical land titling", suggesting a hesitant move to privatise Communal Areas. Zimbabwe's land-based economic structure thus retains a bi-modal character, dominated by large scale commercial farmers (LSCF), in terms of land-holding, output and productivity, technology, infrastructure resources and the concentration of rural incomes. Indeed, Zimbabwe represents a case of an attempt at agrarian and land reform policies based upon minimal agricultural restructuring, limited land redistribution and deepening market-led reforms of the so-called Communal Tenure Systems.

An important element of land property relations in the 1980s model of Zimbabwean land reform was to promote collective and public land owner-ship and its use. Cooperatives, state farming agencies, and, public natural resource and land managers were considered necessary to optimise the use of the large-scale capital-intensive machinery and equipment and marketing facilities provided by the state. The model also idealised communal forms of landholding by small individual household producers which produced "surpluses" from the detailed self-exploitation of household labour (Moyo, 1995b). These labour intensive systems especially exploited women and children, using non-monetary qualitative rewards to labour (Pankhurst, no date; Adams, 1989). Various forms of labour control and coercion were legitimised by "traditional" structures of household and community social organisation and reproduction, as well as by state policies which supported these "traditional" structures (see also Mamdani, 1996).

These "social" forms of property relations underlay an economic development strategy which encouraged the transfer of expropriated agrarian "surpluses" towards import-substitution industrialisation and the wider requirements of the state. They also benefited various parastatals and the sections of global capital dependent on primary agricultural commodity exports, a minority of white settlers and a growing indigenous capitalist group of traders and small industrial enterprises. This land reform model was sanctioned and protected by the central state and most donors.

In general, political struggles for and policy dialogue on land redistribution during the 1980s were ideologically grounded in nationalistic, moralistic, partriachal and statist philosophies (Moyo, 1996). There was, therefore, a delegation of responsibility and authority for land reform to central government bureaucracies and politicians, dominant ruling party and influential business elites (Moyo, 1995a). The pre-ESAP heterodox structure of macro-economic management and social welfare systems (social services, labour and food security), which had evolved since minority rule and had formalised rigid land discrimination by the 1950s, influenced the reproduction of this particular model of land reforms.

Since ESAP deepened the monetarist system of macro-economic management and market-based social relations of production, Zimbabwe has experienced change in land property relations, commodity trade systems involving a wide range of land products, rural labour management and, the appropriation and application of new agrarian technologies. The basic motives for and organisation of land-related primary economic production systems have changed mainly in response to new global markets and geopolitical relations.

However, there is continuity and change in the key ideological, political and economic processes which configure the land question and land reform during the 1990s. Micro-level responses to new land uses include both old conceptions and struggles for land reform infused with new forms of conception of the land question and demands for land reform. External and internal forces operate in new ways to influence land property relations and, most importantly, the use of and benefits from land in various parts of Zimbabwe. The trend in ideological terms has been an attempt to change previous (pre-1990s) understandings of the land question and policies to resolve the current problems of an emerging market economy.

Because of the importance of land-related activities such as agriculture and tourism to formal economic growth in Zimbabwe during the 1980s, and because of the dependence of a large proportion of the population on land for their livelihood, the land question poses fundamental dilemmas for public policy making. Resolving the land question in a manner that does not destabilize existing national employment and production, while increasing land-related export earnings during the 1990s, was a critical element of the ESAP reform programme. But the promises of increased production and forex from land in a diverse arena of land use and service activities (agriculture, wildlife, tourism, new exports), and competition for these by a wide spectrum of land holders and aspirants in the LSCF, among smallholders and in the state enterprise sector, has itself led to new conceptions of the land question and new specific land reform policy demands.

The 1990s have seen an increasingly market-oriented land policy with diverse implications for various constituencies, and which seems to impose far reaching political and economic restructuring processes. Furthermore, new forms of finance for agrarian change and land use such as the role of national and global credit distribution towards new exports and in relation to investment in new technologies, materials and equipment, and expertise are important aspects of the emerging land policy and the environment influencing struggles for land.

Zimbabwe's peculiar racial and class basis of land policy-making, and the co-optation strategies used by the state and markets to marginalise land reform, as well as the conservative influences of international forces on domestic economic and land policy, have reconstructed the land question mainly through the legitimisation of new export land uses as the most beneficial focus for Zimbabwe's development in a globalising world. The new political economy of land is, therefore, over the contestation of this development strategy and the continued inequitable land control that it has reinforced.

To be sure, however, the GoZ's stated land reform policy, as defined by the Land Acquisition Act of 1992 and stated land acquisition targets, is potentially radical and could be used for far-reaching redistribution. For instance, the GoZ in 1996 produced a new land policy proposal which mainly collated its immediate designs for land resettlement among various types of beneficiaries and land resettlement management, while indicating its intention to adopt some of the LTC recommendations. The massive scale of land transfer targets pronounced then as well as in 1992 in terms of hectarages and types of beneficiaries to be addressed are presented in tables 3.4.1 and 3.4.2. Indeed, various donors have been working together with the GoZ on feasibility studies, pilot projects and land management building capacities (e.g. SIDA, AusAid etc.) as part of an effort to consolidate the GoZ's land policy.

Table 3.4.1. *Land Distribution (1980 and Target)*

| Tenure Category | Area (Million Hectares) | |
	At 1980	Targets As Set in 1990 Land Policy (1996 Standing)
LSCF Sector (freehold)	15.5	5
SSCF Sector (state lease)	1.4	1.4
Resettlement (state permit)	-	8.3
Communal Areas	16.4	16.4
State Owned Farms	0.3	2.5
Nat. Parks & Urban Settlements	6	6
Total	39.6	39.6

Source: GoZ Policy Paper on Land Redistribution and Resettlement, 1996.

Most notably, the British government recently undertook a land policy and programme appraisal mission (ODA, 1996) which, among other conclusions, rallied a number of donors around supporting a gradual process of market-oriented land acquisition (of up to 2 million ha) for up to 35,000 poorer farmers in Communal Areas based upon locally-determined land requirements and agricultural land redistribution and support services designed locally.

Thus, a key land policy trend seemed to be a gradual revision of what was a radical strategy of compulsorily expropriating underutilised land with partial compensation focusing on land improvements (GoZ, Land Acquisition Act, 1992) towards an even more liberal market-based land policy, using donor funds to buy land with the owner's consent. Notable in the combined proposals of the GoZ and various donors is the continuation of a bi-furcated approach (Moyo, 1995a) of transferring land to "better off" black farmers (small and medium scale operators) and to the landless or poor but capable farmers in overcrowded Communal Areas.

Table 3.4.2. *Resettlement Beneficiaries and Programmes: 1996 Proposals*

Land Need Target Group	Packages/programmes
Group I: Landless people and people areas.	Model A (community in congested based).
.	Modified Model B. Model C. Three Tier Schemes.
Group II: Successful peasant farmers wanting to enter small scale commercial agriculture.	Self-contained Unit Model A. Small Scale Commercial Farm. Settlement Scheme (see note).
Group III0: Indigenous citizens with resources to enter large scale commercial agriculture.	Large Scale Commercial Farm Settlement Programme.

NB: Individuals might graduate through the self-contained unit programme into the small scale commercial farm settlement programme. (Source: GoZ, 1996).

Yet, a variety of official and private processes in terms of land transfers or transactions over the control and use of land have emerged in response to the wider ESAP macro-economic and land-related policies, evolving social-economic conditions, and the generally changing market place in Zimbabwe since 1990. The evolution of land bidding strategies through land sale processes and the restructuring of land ownership and management strategies, and through GoZ land redistribution programmes using official land market and administrative mechanisms, as well as through informal and somewhat "underground" mechanisms, are an integral aspect of land use change.

3.4.2 Land Markets Policy: Land Acquisition, Land Use Conversion and Sub-Division

The GoZ's land policy since 1980 has been dogged by polarised pressures for and against the full scale development of "free" land markets across the entire spectrum of the current land tenure regimes. Recent arguments for freeing land markets have, in fact, centred on preserving LSCF property rights because since 1991, they have become exposed to increased state intervention, following constitutional and legislative changes such as the Land Acquisition Act of 1992. During the 1980s, the Lancaster House Constitution compromise had required that state land purchases for redistribution be based on a "willing-buyer-willing-seller" basis, which was somewhat of a condition for donor support to the Zimbabwe political settlement and its land reform programme. The British aid establishment still maintains this as one of its conditions for supporting Zimbabwe's land reform programme.

The LSCF land markets were, thus, relatively "free" except that inherited colonial regulations which governed the sub-division and land use conversion of LSCF lands, especially for transfer or sale, were strictly guided by government regulations. The regulations had been originally grounded on technologically and socially static concepts of large scale farms which could only be viable in terms of extremely large farm enterprise areas and specified levels of incomes expected of LSCF and SSCF farmers. During the 1980s, the GoZ also adopted this policy stance in an attempt to check speculative land sales through land sub-division, and attempted to control the conversion of land uses from the technical recommendations made for given natural regions during the colonial period.

However, as discussed earlier, land use conversion to wildlife and ostrich uses in various land zones became more readily permissible as the export-led policy orientation emerged after the mid-1980s. Thus, pressure to evolve "efficient" LSCF land markets through relaxing the sub-division and land use conversion regulations was galvanised during the late 1980s. This process followed the visible individual gains from new land uses such as horticulture and tourism-oriented land uses which had begun to yield high profits on smaller land units than was the norm in the LSCF, and as the demand to enter into these enterprises grew among new black and white land entrepreneurs (see also Moyo et al., 1998).

The World Bank Agricultural Sector Study (1991) interestingly provided the most direct impetus to the GoZ's reconsideration of its land sub-division policy after the adoption of ESAP. It argued for the continuation rather than abandonment of a market framework of land redistribution, an approach which was contrary to the anticipated Land Acquisition Act of 1992. That study, while acknowledging that LSCF lands were underutilised against the claims of the LSCF lobby, an acknowledgement which validated previous local studies, suggested that land sub-division regulations could lead to the availability of more land for redistribution and more efficient LSCF land use (World Bank, 1991). However, the study also recommended that, in the longer term, LSCF lands should be subjected to effective land taxes, as is practised elsewhere in private land markets, as a further condition for enhancing land transfers and efficient land use. The LTC report (1995) merely affirmed this policy stance which proposed the sequential relaxation of sub-division regulations and the gradual institution of a land tax.

Our own work (Moyo 1993, 1995) had argued, however, for the combined use of three interventions in the LSCF land markets if Zimbabwe were to achieve efficient land use, effective markets in terms of pricing and transfers, and the deconcentration of land ownership. Compulsory land acquisition at controlled prices as enacted by the Land Acquisition Act (1992) would be the base policy instrument to drive land values and the transfer process to reflect effective and social demand for land, while land taxation and relaxed sub-division procedures within the framework of compulsory state acquisition and tax incentives would reward voluntary LSCF efforts to rationalise their land control and use (Moyo, 1995). GoZ policy seems inclined toward this stance in terms of stated intentions, but in practice it has relaxed sub-division procedures while delaying the land tax, and at the same time it spared the LSCF sector substantial compulsory land acquisition until November 1997. As predicted (ibid; also, see Palmer, 1997), the state retained its control over Communal Land transfers and effectively postponed titling there.

The GoZ's compulsory land acquisition policy position, however, also seems to be amenable to change towards the full compensation for soil approach, and even the "willing-seller-willing-buyer" approach, if donors pledge adequate, timely and less conditional funding, in terms of the organisational framework for land acquisition and resettlement (see GoZ, 1996). Contrary to the rigid market-based property rights principles highlighted by the British government land policy appraisal mission, current GoZ land policy could be defined as being in flux or under negotiation. Yet the actual GoZ land acquisition policy outcome of the 1990s so far remains slightly contradictory and hesitant in terms of the approach towards, and the pace of land acquisition. Indeed there has been an extremely low level of financial allocations made by the GoZ for the implementation of its land acquisition and resettlement programme which had targeted a further 5 million hectares and 75,000 families over 10 years since 1990 (i.e. 500,000 ha./year and 7,500 families/year).

The concrete result of the 1990s policy has been less than 50,000 hectares acquired and 2,000 families settled each year so far, which makes the British ODA proposals to acquire 250,000 hectares on a free market basis and to settle 3,500 families per year, look more progressive than the actual outcome of GoZ land policy between 1990 and 1997. The latter's remaining moral stance and pedestal at the moment is that Zimbabwe should not "pay" for land expropriated by colonialists and should not be dictated to by donors and that the GoZ can go it alone without donor funding (*Financial Gazette*, 1996).

In the above context, one of the most active GoZ land policy instruments during Zimbabwe's structural adjustment period since 1985 has been the relaxation of LSCF land sub-division procedures, as well the promotion of black farmer entry into large scale farming through GoZ loans, the provision of about 300 GoZ leaseholds to large black farmers, and the gradual sub-division of state farms for over 300 medium-sized black "tenant" commercial farmers. With regard to LSCF land sub-division and taxation, the GoZ response to the recommendations of the LTC (1994, Vol. 2, pp. 137) commission as pronounced in a draft 1996 policy instrument has been that:

> It is agreed administrative mechanisms for processing farm sub-divisions and consolidations in response to market forces should be streamlined to enable farmers with large tracts of land to sub-divide into smaller commercial farming units and sell them. Cabinet approves that an agricultural land tax based on the potential productivity and size of the farm be introduced.

In practice, GoZ land administrators in the Ministry of Local Government, particularly in the provincial offices have already been relaxing their regulation of land sub-division, as their actions and attitudes to the issue showed in our fieldwork (Moyo, forthcoming). However, a host of GoZ departments were found in Mashonaland to be still engaged in consultations to allow for LSCF land sub-divisions (Table 3.4.3), following their own policy objectives and procedures, and there is real conflict among them over the hierarchy of their powers over land administration, especially between the ministries of Agriculture, Land and Local Government (interviews).

One of the policy problems here is that not all LSCF area property falls in areas which have a development plan, where the general property sizes and land use recommendations will guide the processing of the applications in accordance with stated minimum plot sizes recommended by the plan (ibid). For example, the development plans of peri-urban areas around the City of Harare are moving the structure of land holdings towards small plots, greater than or equal to 1.6 hectares, in anticipation of expanded housing and sub-division permit demands. When there are no such plans, local land administrators have recourse to the general central government sub-division policy. In the case of agricultural applications, for instance, Agritex uses a particular approach to measuring agricultural viability as the main deciding factor in processing applications. This approach tends to require travel and expert resources which were limited in the GoZ, leading to delayed processing of applications.

Table 3.4.3. *Departments Consulted in Processing Subdivisions and Consolidation Applications*

Department	Role
Agritex	This is a critical department, comments on the agricultural viability of applications. For agricultural sub-divisions it comments on viability of both the proposed remainder and proposed sub-division. For non-agricultural applications, it comments on viability of the proposed remainder.
Administrative Court	Comments on water rights of property, if any. For a sub-division, it recommends splitting of the water rights in the event of a permit, while for a consolidation it orders the consolidation of the water rights if a permit is granted.
DNR	Comments on what natural resources are found on the property and whether the resources will be endangered if a sub-division permit is issued, i.e. it gives the implication of the application on the conservation of environment and natural resources.
National Parks	Is consulted if the property is close to the areas they administer—e.g. around parks or lakes such as Chivero, Mazvikadei etc.
Local Authorities	Often comment on the general property sizes in the area and whether resultant property sizes will be in conforming with property sizes in the areas. In turn LAs may also consult the relevant ICA.
Water Development	Gives its views when application proposes projects such as dam construction, irrigation development etc.
Deeds Registry	Checks on the title deeds on the property and conditions attached.
Surveyor General	Names the new property and checks the surveyed diagrams in the event of a permit.

Source: Field interviews and GoZ legislation.

The Agritex approach has always been based on the natural agro-ecologically determined farming system recommended using "traditional" crops such as maize and tobacco production without making reference to the requirements of new land uses such as horticulture, ostriches and wildlife. The mushrooming of specialized agriculture has resulted in more appeals to the courts for sub-division permits by farmers who argue that with five hectares, they can venture into viable horticultural or ostrich production. As a result, numerous appeals against land sub-divisions rejected have been observed in the Administrative Court (field interviews). The LSCF agricultural sector and Agritex are, thus, forced to recognise that horticulture can be a predominant land use through judicial precedence. According to one interviewee:

> People in the peri-urban areas are increasingly engaging in horticultural production and they (Agritex) have to accept the change that is going on and grant the people the sub-division permits. The major problem is that there is no general policy guiding sub-divisions, and in some cases it might be based on goodwill.

Many officials propose that a case by case approach of individual merit should be followed by the sub-division policy, arguing that the natural variability of land quality at the local level demands such an approach. When sub-division permits for specialized land uses such as ostrich or horticultural production are issued, the GoZ, however, can give conditions that certain infrastructure pertaining to the proposed activity be put in place before the permit can be registered. For example, they may require that water, pipes, paddocks and electricity and infrastructure be set up first, so that people stick to the land use that they have applied for. Some GoZ officials saw these conditions as infringements of land owners' constitutional rights. However, we found that after a period of three to five years from the granting of sub-division permits, farmers might abandon the land use for which the sub-division permit was granted and embark on a different form of land use.

What is interesting here is that the entire range of sub-division permits granted in Mashonaland was largely a private process involving land owners and new buyers with few direct national or technical inputs from the GoZ. This means that only those who can afford to pay for the sub-division process, title and land are the beneficiaries of this process. For instance, a few new black LSCF farmers in Mashonaland reportedly have pursued sub-divisions to recover from the high interest debt of the 1990s period, while it was mostly middle class people and companies which had been buying the sub-divided land, not the peasantry. This emerging *de facto* policy frame-work in essence reflects a private sector or market-led land redistribution programme for the benefit of elites.

3.4.3 Land and Natural Resource Occupation Policy

In addition to legal forms of land transfer, the self-provisioning of land rights or usufract rights and benefits therefrom for social reproduction has been gaining ground in Zimbabwe. Such land occupation or squatting as it is called by the GoZ, has been critical in spurring land transfers in the early 1980s (Moyo, 1986).

The GoZ's formal policy on "squatters" has been a critical legal and political force in the shaping of Zimbabwe's land question, and the nature of its land reform programme since 1980. The policy's legal basis is to affirm the particular land rights of land owners in the LSCF and SSCF and official occupiers in Communal and Resettlement Areas, as well as state agencies in parks, forests and state farms or leasehold lands, against the land claims and land grabbing of the landless and homeless who bid for land rights, and the long standing victims of direct land expropriation who seek restitution. In political strategic-terms, the formal GoZ squatter policy is based upon the ideology and policy approach whereby the state, particularly central government, reserves the right to direct land redistribution and to structure and allocate land rights among those who seek land (ibid).

Originally, the squatter policy was formulated against land occupations in the LSCF areas. In this context, current GoZ policy retained the colonial policy stance against squatters through land eviction measures in what are considered "undeserving cases" and the provision of resettlement land in "genuine" cases. However, since the 1980s, land occupation or squatting has tended to become a mobilidsation strategy by communities which, in some cases, are informally encouraged or defended by local politicians, and has increasingly targeted state lands and resettlement areas as well (Alexander, 1994; Moyo, 1995a). Furthermore, squatting has been occurring in Communal Areas for decades through the illegal allocation of land rights to "outsiders" in given localities, the contested provision of similar land rights in some areas, as well as through "illegal sales" of land rights in given Communal Area localities (Moyo, 1995a; LTC, 1994).

The new government squatter policy has now been directed at addressing "squatting" beyond the LSCF. This trend has introduced new policy conflicts over the very land rights of state land holders (in parks, forests, local authority lands, state farms, resettlement areas and state leasehold lands), because these were also expropriated from the people of the Communal Areas, and given that these areas are artificial territorial land holding constructs of the colonial regime which dispossessed the ancestors of the currently landless and homeless.

In many circumstances, the GoZ had turned a "blind eye" towards squatters, and indeed during the early 1980s the GoZ had formulated an Accelerated Resettlement Programme to accommodate squatters in a state-led land redistribution strategy (Moyo, 1986). However, the GoZ has been formally opposed to land "invasions" or private occupations, and has, in collaboration with LSCF farmers and local authorities, encouraged the regular eviction of squatters using the law, court action, and the police. Thus, land "self-provisioning" or popular struggles for land have always been circumscribed by the central government through its "Squatter Policy", regular promises of land redistribution, and via other forms of agricultural support schemes intended to improve the intensity of Communal Area land use *in situ* and returns therefrom.

Most notable, moreover, is the fact that individual land owners have been given greater authority to evict squatters as, since 1991/92, the GoZ has come under greater pressure from investors, large farmers and black land owners over the growing scale of land invasions to tighten its squatter policy. Accordingly, the GoZ recently instituted a range of stringent measures. Given that the scale of "squatting" and natural resource poaching has expanded over the last five years, the revised policy has led in practice to the increased identification of "squatters" in various land tenure regimes, and to the escalation of evictions (Moyo, forthcoming).

There are numerous policy problems which have arisen from the eviction strategy. State policy is now forced to define more clearly its policy on the citizenship rights of many of the squatters who are of "foreign" or "alien" origin. The GoZ also has to mediate growing problems over ethnic identity and conflicts associated with related contests over land rights in certain Communal Areas given that these have always been defined in so-called "tribal" territorial terms. Moreover, this land policy aspect has to address the social problems of homelessness and viable self-reproduction of the ex-farm workers, the landless in rural areas and the urban unemployed and employed who "squat" mainly in peri-urban areas lying within various land tenure regimes (ibid).

The new land question, thus, fuses longstanding urban and rural demands for land within the entire spectrum of land ownership (private, state and communal), pitting various classes, "ethnicities", "citizenry" and different social categories of the poor against landowners, the state and one another. Most critically, the land policy question which arises is the legitimacy of the central government's current role and legal standing in addressing popular but private strategies of land redistribution through self-provisioning, the feasibility and impacts of using state and private landholder "force" to evict land squatters and the viability of the policy alternatives proposed (meaning SAPs and current land reform policy) by the GoZ to deal with growing poverty associated with landlessness, the retrenchment of farm and urban workers, and unemployment in general.

In this context, a central policy problem which has grown is the heightened competition for political and economic power which is evident between central and local power structures in the state, ruling party, black private sector, church structures, and "traditional authority" systems over control of land allocation and of the financial benefits from explicit and informal land "taxes", transaction fees, rents and sales. Thus, local chiefs, headmen, party chiefs, members of parliament and other people not only compete with central government politicians and bureaucrats over land control, they also compete amongst themselves for the political and economic capital to be gained from the control over allocating land rights (see Moyo, 1995a).

Essentially, therefore, the squatter policy reflects an unresolved but wider political-economy problem which the market reforms have heightened as "rural monetization", land markets and social marginalisation grow in the context of the emergence of new land values derived from the new

ESAP land use incentives. Declining employment and incomes now place increased pressures on access to and the use of land for survival and "enterprise" development. The result has been an "inconsistent" policy implementation record, conflictual policy stances among GoZ officials, and increased land bidding processes through so-called squatting.

3.5 Conclusions

The land transfer processes described in this chapter are considered to have been critical in further coopting Zimbabwe's land policy towards a more conservative and elite based programme, even though this tendency is being challenged on the ground, so to speak, by the land occupation strategies of the poor, landless and homeless. The land redistribution structure which is emerging from such land transfer processes during the 1990s also reflects the structure of incentives and constraints offered so far by the ESAP policy framework, as well as a critique of the development strategy asscoiated with it.

In a related study, we found that the market responses to the GoZ land acquisition policy of the 1990s, especially in terms of LSCF land area sales and price offered to the GoZ, led to hardened land price terms, despite the GoZ policy effort to dampen prices through the "threat" of compulsory land acquisition (Moyo, 1998). Furthermore, more LSCF land was put out for ownership transfer through voluntary sales, which implies that increased land offers were made to the GoZ but that it used its right of first refusal often. In general, these trends indicate that the LSCF land markets did not panic, as predicted, because of the Land Acquisition Act of 1992 and the GoZ land policy rhetoric promising more land redistribution.

Moreover, until November 1997, other privately based land market transfer processes seemed to have overtaken the official GoZ land acquisition programme. Notable here are private LSCF land transfers through sub-division activities and popular self-provisioning strategies of land invasions and occupations. In this vein, we found (Moyo, 1998, forthcoming) that the GoZ increasingly encouraged, albeit circuitously, the sub-division of land for sale and sub-letting in LSCF areas, while turning a blind eye to the growing scale (up to 10 per cent) of squatting in all the land tenure regimes. Interestingly, the scale and spatial pattern of squatting has spread as a phenomenon from private (LSCF) lands to communal and state land tenure regimes. One third of the squatters are in communal lands, over one quarter in state lands and 10 per cent are in urban land (Ibid.). Illegal land "markets" in Communal Areas are indeed increasing and raising the costs of survival for the landless who have no free family land rights in Communal Areas.

The underlying physical and land use implication of the above trends on squatting is that there is a greater tendency towards the sub-division of lands among a larger number of people than officials planned for and that, therefore, land ownership in communal, resettlement and SSCF areas is becoming more deconcentrated. This means that land use in these areas is probably more intensively used than is formally recognised, and that production or output trends may be higher than is officially acknowledged. Furthermore, there are new trends of social differentiation and class formation processes evolving around access to and control of land, in terms of the benefits realised from new land uses and new forms of the administration and allocation of land rights.

These new trends in land occupation and use, however, reflect a critical pattern of the ineffectiveness of GoZ land policy formulation and implementation, and also the erosion of Zimbabwe's rural governance system at the local and central level. It is not surprising, therefore, that the GoZ in late 1997 identified about 4 million hectares on 1450 farms for compulsory acquisition in response to broadly based demands for land and under growing pressure from indigenous elites within the ruling party. Thus, conflicting authority over land administration, land rights, procedures of land access and over the regulation of land use are some of the key trends which must be examined further, as we do in Chapter Five.

Chapter Four

Changing Land Uses and the Reconstruction of the Land Question

4.1 Introduction

This chapter presents the results of the multilayered surveys of the nature and effects of horticulture, wildlife and ostrich land uses in the Mashonaland provinces and elsewhere. The chapter discusses each land use separately, focusing on both small and large farmers in all the land tenure categories and taking into account their diverse resource endowments as well as sharp differences in human and capital resources. The conversion of land to new export uses is both a numbers game in terms of areal expansion and an equity problem related to uneven resources distribution and social impacts. The chapter, thus, presents the number (and type) of people involved, the revenue derived from both the domestic and export market, the areal extent of the land utilised, and the quantity and quality of produce.

The distribution of benefits derived from such land uses and the role of the state in intermediating these through the implementation of given micro and macro-policies is explored. Simple cost and benefit analyses in terms of who gains and loses from the new land uses are developed and discussed. The roles of the state, NGOs and marketing agencies in promoting these new land uses are also discussed to illustrate the evolution and spread of the three land use activities among the various sub-sectors. The land and political conflicts resulting from these new land uses are also briefly discussed in this chapter, although the politics of land policy formulation is discussed more in Chapter Five.

4.2 Macro Level Spatial Distribution of New Land Uses

Based on a collection of wide primary and secondary evidence, this study identified a trend of change in the macro-spatial character of Zimbabawe's land use patterns. The emergence of improved markets for wildlife ranching and horticulture have, however, begun to reshape "traditional" values ascribed to land in terms of its agro-ecological potential. Indeed, a spatial analysis of the evolution of new land uses at the macro-level suggests that there has been a definitive change in the patterning of the use of Zimbabwe's land in relation to its control (ownership or mere use) among various categories of landholders and, particularly, in relation to the geographic variation of Zimbabwe's currently existing stocks of natural resources (especially wildlife and woodlands). While the distribution of soils and rainfall quality, and the historically evolved availability of infrastructure (roads, towns/roads, dams and energy) across Zimbabawe remain influential for intensive land use patterning, remoteness previously associated with "rejection" because of presumed low quality land has also become a defining parameter for the new land use regimes.

Some local studies capture the hangover among communal residents refusing to "live with animals" in areas previously regarded as waste lands. An "onion ring" spatial patterning of allocation of land uses is gradually emerging as shown in chart 4.2.1. Five land use regimes reflecting the emerging values underlying Zimbabwe's land markets and demand can be identified as a heuristic guide to the study approach and the selection of study sites and cases. These are: the Extensive Land Use Outer Ring; the Buffer Zone; the Communal Area Subsistence Mixed Farming Zone; the Commercial Wildlife/Cattle Ranching Zone; and the Commercial Intensive Cropping Zone. A brief summary of these land use zones provides further background and contextual information the study areas.

Chart 4.2.1. *Zimbabwe's Macro-Spatial Land Use Structure*

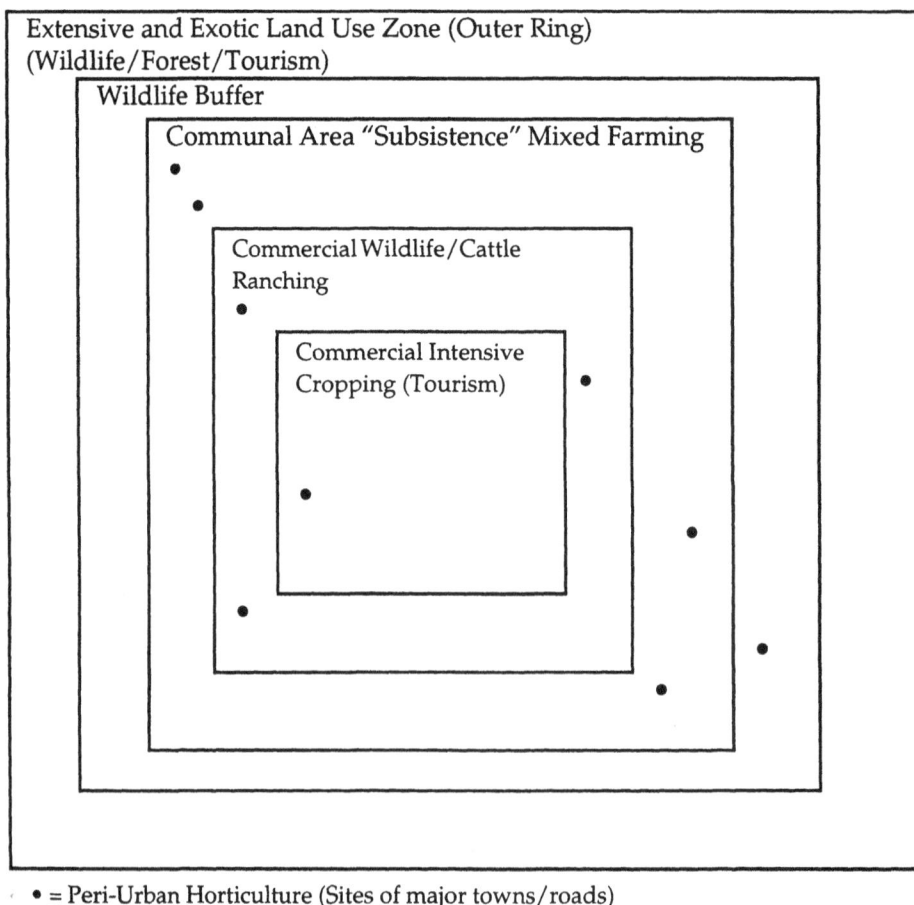

Extensive and Exotic Land Use Zone (Outer Ring)
(Wildlife/Forest/Tourism)

Wildlife Buffer

Communal Area "Subsistence" Mixed Farming

Commercial Wildlife/Cattle Ranching

Commercial Intensive Cropping (Tourism)

• = Peri-Urban Horticulture (Sites of major towns/roads)

4.2.1 The Extensive and Exotic Land Use Zone (Outer Ring)

In the outer ring can be found extremely large state controlled land estates interspersed with pockets of large LSCF estates. In this area, land ownership structures and uses have been gradually shifting towards the creation of state and private "nature conservancies". Some parts of these large state conservancies are leased out to individual tourist operators, while in some highly commercial tourist cities (Hwange, Kariba, Victoria Falls, Nyanga and Beitbridge), there has been sub-division of land for private sale to small private tourist operators and cottage owners, mainly white, with fewer black middle to upper class people.

As can be seen in Annex 4.2.1, all of Zimbabwe's provinces have national parks, although the scale and quality of these vary, as does the density of human populations and wildlife resources. Therefore, the competition for land that such parks have for the various small farmer populations is varied.

Thus, Matabeleland North with about 2.5 million hectares under GoZ state parks and forests, and numerous private parks, is one of the most extremely squeezed provinces in terms of wildlife land use. This is qualified by the fact that this province has only about 60 per cent of the average level of total human population and 30 per cent of the population densities of other provinces. However, the land quality there (sandy soils and the most erratic and lowest levels of rainfall) is only suitable for extensive farming, which requires about three times the land space for cropping and live-stocking under natural dryland conditions. The next most squeezed provinces are Masvingo with its large Gonarezhou Park (half a million hectares) followed by Mashonaland West province (about a third of a million hectares). But, as will be shown later, these latter two provinces have a growing number of private wildlife schemes which occupy significant areas.

In numerical terms, there are over 65 entities (consisting of parks and wildlife schemes) owned by the GoZ which have a wide range of facilities or provide services such as accommodation, recreation hunting, non-hunting safaris, special biodiversity protection and propagation schemes, as well as other basic social entertainment activities.

The LSCF conservancies tend to entail land tracts of between 15 and 100,000 hectares plus, and involve groups of individual farmers consolidating their former livestock ranches into huge nature conservancies. A few former state farm estates of the ADA have also been converted to nature conservancies in this zone, while the state Forest Commission (FC) has converted some of its indigenous woodlands conservation areas for touristic uses. Increasingly, companies created by groups of farmers as well as state land holders (e.g. Ngamo Safari of FC and ADA) manage these conservancies in a vertically and horizontally integrated fashion of market relations among conservancies and local tourist service firms, and in association with global tourist marketing and transportation firms.

The state Parks Authority has recently been converted into a semi-autonomous commercial entity (akin to a company), so that it can rationalise its financial base and its direct participation in the market place. Both the FC and Parks organisational and land use conversion schemes have received substantial support from donors such as the World Bank, NORAD, GTZ and USAID and from international NGOs such as the WWF and IUCN. The environmental aid lobby has focused most of its resources in this zone.

This outher ring zone, which is Zimbabwe's emerging prime tourist destination, has enhanced its land use reorientation towards wildlife and nature exploitation because of the presence there of large physical, natural and man-made attractions such as the Victoria Falls, Kariba Dam, Eastern Highlands Mountains and Great Zimbabwe. Because it had an old-established communications infrastructure, it was already a magnet for tourists. During the market liberalisation period, contiguous land holders have, thus, gradually restructured their land holdings and uses to futher capture those tourist markets and the variety of export incentives.

Some of the larger conservancies such as Gonarezhou, Beitbridge and Hwange Parks are also being converted into trans-national or "cross-border" nature conservancies involving two or more countries. The Gonarezhou and Beitbridge conservancies are evolving into an expansive territorial restructuring of land use and control across Zimbabwe, South Africa and Mozambique. The other scheme involving transnational land use under consideration is the Zambia, Namibia, Botswana and Zimbabwe wildlife conservancy around the northwest border of Zimbabwe. Already, these land use conversions are being serviced by evolving regional air-linkages, reflecting both state and private airline and bus travel investments, and the consolidation of transnational tourist companies in the hotel, tours and allied services.

4.2.2 The Wildlife Buffer Zone

The second ring of the "onion" is that strip of land which borders the large parks and LSCF areas in the outer ring which is gradually being carved out of existing Communal Areas into a community wildlife management zone. The largely donor and NGO-funded programme, Campfire (Community Management Programme for Indigenous Resources), was originally intended to benefit communities such that their interest in wildlife draws them towards protecting, together with the state, the resources within areas bordering state parks which were being "threatened" by the "poaching" activities of commercial criminal elements as well as ordinary Communal Area residents. Campfire followed the gradual policy realisation that "policing" natural resources alone had become ineffective and expensive. Moreover, growing post-1980 local demands for state and private land in the areas to be redistributed triggered the spread of Campfire.

Campfire was later employed during the late 1980s to push the case for the conversion of the Communal Area land use in that zone on the grounds that given its poor soils and water regimes, wildlife resources management yielded better and more secure incomes from tourism than extensive low yield grain cropping. Furthermore, Campfire finances from donors, project earnings and supplementary allocations, evolved into a drawing card for mobilising public investment into schools, hospitals and small infrastructures such as boreholes, as well as providing individual cash incomes for the participating community. This promoted the growth of Campfire projects from two in 1986 to about 27 in 1997, involving 60,000 families. As we have already seen earlier, over 70 per cent of the Communal Areas are within that zone which range from N.R. III and IV to V. Besides wildlife, the bulk of the farmers produce maize, cotton and various woodlands products.

4.2.3 Communal Area Subsistence Mixed Farming Zone

This zone comprises mainly the Communal Areas in natural regions III, IV and V and covers numerous food insecure households practising mixed farming with occasional surpluses in good rainy years.

4.2.4 Commercial Wildlife Ranching and Export Beef Zone

The fourth ring is largely LSCF owned land with Communal Area pockets, which had in some places been physically fenced during the mid-1980s to separate EC export beef production from the veterinary diseases of contiguous Communal Area cattle and wildlife corridors in the above-mentioned first two land use zones. It has become a predominantly mixed export beef and smaller scale wildlife ranching zone in the LSCF areas which are mainly in N.R. III land. Here, some LSCF farmers practise both wildlife and beef production as separate or integrated enterprises, as well as allocate smaller parts of their farms to commodities such as maize and cotton, and small grains or horticulture, especially among those with water resources (state and privately built dams, and private boreholes).

In this area, there have been intensely conflicting land questions raised. This is because Communal Area residents have advocated for an approach to land resettlement which is based on extending the area or territories of their Communal Areas most of which are contiguous to this and the outer zones of LSCF-owned and state-controlled lands. The "elbow room" strategy has also tended to gain credence among GoZ officials and MPs because of its potential political or electoral appeal among established communities which are more amenable to political mobilisation than those in newer resettlement areas, and because the costs of resettling people are much lower in this approach given the short distances involved. However, this approach to redistribution has tended to spare the prime lands within the onion's core from redistribution.

4.2.5 Intensive Cropping Zone (LSCF, Communal Areas and a Few State Lands

This fifth zone, which focuses on Harare and major towns in the south-west and south-east of Zimbabwe, is where we find the highest density of agrarian commodity markets, agrarian inputs, marketing and servicing enterprises and state agencies, various infrastructures (roads, dams, energy), and labour (population density), and where the rainfall is most reliable and the soils are best for crop farming. This area is mostly LSCF owned (70 per cent) with a few high density Communal Areas (Zvimba, Seke, Chiweshe, Bushu, Mhondoro and Chidhuku etc.). It is the area of most commercial grain production, the focus of Virginia tobacco output, of wheat production and of horticultural activities. This is the area in which the prime Mashonaland areas are mostly situated, and it coincides with those areas where the largest frequency of LSCF land sub-division has occurred (Moyo, 1998). Studies have also shown that horticulture in this zone has a competitive edge over other field crops (see Annex 4.2.2).

This is the area where the least land redistribution has occurred (Moyo, 1995a) albeit that as much as 50 per cent of the land or about 3 million hectares of arable land has been classified as underutilized (Weiner 1988, World Bank, 1991; GoZ, 1990). It is also the zone where a large number of black LSCF farmers and peri-urban plot holders have emerged (Moyo, 1995a). This area is the most hotly contested land zone, which has, however, been continuously intensifying its land use and from where the bulk of horticultural exports emanate. This is also an area of high levels of squatting compared to the other zones, and where the peri-urban dynamic and working class poverty have popularized "urban farming" (Moyo, 1998). In the next section, we provide the findings on the specific land uses.

4.3 Development of the Horticulture Sector

4.3.1 LSCF Horticulture Land Use Production Patterns

Commercial horticulture production in Zimbabwe has changed since the first stage of its development in the Pre-Unilateral Declaration of Independence (UDI) days. During that period, fruits and vegetables could be imported easily mainly from South Africa on OGIL at prices below those required to produce them locally (ULG, 1994). Production then was mainly for household consumption with the surplus being marketed. From 1965 to 1983, the second stage emerged. Economic sanctions had led to a foreign exchange squeeze and the implementation of stringent import controls, which forced the country towards food self-sufficiency in general and horticulture in particular. As supply decreased with demand remaining constant, the prices of produce and fruits rose astronomicially as to attract farmers, especially those located close to urban markets. A few specialist producers then started to supply the local market in a narrow range of produce consisting mainly of vegetables (rape, tomatoes, cabbage, onions, tsunga, kale and some other species) and tropical fruits such as mangoes, bananas, avocados, citrus, pineapples and guavas. After independence, the entire agricultural sector gradually increased its focus on exports, especially from the mid-1980s when deeper changes in horticultural land use were noticeable.

By 1995, Zimbabwe had over 1,600 large scale farm sector producers of horticultural produce (Annex 4.3.1) with about 60 per cent of them (1,062) being in the Mashonaland provinces (Makonde, Marondera, S.W. Mashonaland and Mashonaland Central LSCF regions). The Eastern Highlands districts had the second largest concentration of 277 producers. Thus, 36 per cent of the LSCF sector is now engaged in horticulture. About 42 per cent of the total horticulture farmers are engaged in vegetable production, while another 15 per cent are involved in cutflowers and 43 per cent are fruit growers. In contrast, by 1980, less than 10 per cent of the 6,000 farmers then were engaged in horticulture, with the bulk of the producers being fruit farmers for both domestic and export markets.

As data in Annex 4.3.2 shows, the area under flowers and horticulture grew almost three fold from less than 4,000 hectares in both the LSCF and SSCF sectors to almost 11,000 hectares of formally registered areas of production in 1993. By 1993, the area under fruits had also tripled. But by 1995, the area under fruits and vegetables had now reached about 35,000 hectares, with specialised vegetables and fruit for export reflecting the largest growth trend. In general, this suggests that over 20 per cent of the total area cropped in the LSCF was now being devoted to various horticultural products, bearing in mind that vegetables are also a second crop for many (Annex 4.3.3).

The areal growth of cutflowers was the most dramatic, increasing from less than 200 hectares in 1990 to almost 1,000 hectares by 1994 (Annex 4.3.4). Zimbabwe is ranked Africa's second largest exporter of flowers and has increasingly strengthened its competitive edge on the European market since it started flower exports in 1984. Proteas are dominant in this category, followed by summer flowers and roses. Most of the latter are grown in greenhouses.

Most of the horticulture activities take place near Harare, especially in Goromonzi, Seke and Domboshawa districts. Several notable infrastructural developments which have encouraged this trend took place in the LSCF areas around Harare during the 1990s. In the Enterprise LSCF area, electric lighting at night to facilitate photosynthesis was introduced, leading most of the horticulture crops to mature faster than they would under normal conditions, while the introduction of Nata Firm Drip Irrigation and Centre

Pivot Irrigation systems around the Harare area has given these farmers a competitive advantage over farmers in other provinces.

The distribution of horticultural production among the three Mashonaland provinces and within them is quite varied (Annex 4.3.5). This reflects the highly differentiated class structure within the LSCF itself in terms of variations in farm sizes, infrastructural resources (water etc.), available quality of soil, and access to financial resources in general. We see that Mashonaland West, followed by East, had the highest number of producers, which also reflects the presence in these areas of many smaller-sized farms (below 1,000 hectares) and plots in the vicinity of major towns. Moreover vegetables which require less capital than flowers are more common among the smaller LSCF farmers.

The value of horticultural production in Zimbabwe dollar terms has also grown astronomically since 1983 (Annex 4.3.6). From a low of Z$16,000,000 realized in 1983, by 1992 horticulture was fetching Z$121,033,000 and the value of production was expected to increase in 1996. Thus, over the 10 years from 1983, the local currency value of horticulture had grown nine-fold, against a relatively stable rate of inflation (ca 16 per cent) for most of that period until 1991 when the large devaluations led to a doubling of output value in local currency.

As we can see, the tonnage and value of horticultural exports have also grown dramatically (Annex 4.3.7). From less than US$3.5 million realized from exports in 1985/86 at a tonnage of 3,000 for all horticultural products, by 1991 the respective figures had grown to US$32 million and 14,000 tonnes, reflecting a ten-fold growth in value and a five-fold growth in volume. By 1994, however, the volume of exports had doubled while their value had grown by 50 per cent, suggesting a declining price ratio. The largest growth in volume over the years was in citrus fruit which seemed to realize a higher rate of declining prices during the period. Earnings in US dollar terms of the entire horticulture sector had doubled to about US 65 million by 1995 (Heri, 1995, *Herald*, 30/3/95).

Most of Zimbabwe's export horticultural vegetable produce goes to Europe with the United Kingdom alone absorbing as much as 73.22 per cent of it (Table 4.2.1). This is a market window for most of the produce where it is referred to as "out of season" vegetables (Heri, 1995).

Table 4.3.1. *Cutflower and Vegetable Destinations 1994/95 Season*

Country	% Produce	% of flowers
Holland	9.18	80.44
United Kingdom	73.22	8.8
Germany	8.48	3.95
France	3.86	6.33
Others	11.20	0.48

Cutflowers are exported mainly to Holland where they are sold on auction floors. Holland has the largest flower auction floors in the world and it is from here that most flowers find their way to the rest of the world. Zimbabwean flowers are mainly in demand during the winter in Europe and North America (Heri, 1995).

4.3.2 Small Farmer Horticulture Land Use and Production Patterns

Unlike in the LSCF sector, commercial horticultural production in Communal Areas has grown relatively slowly over the years. Communal farmers have always produced vegetables on vleis (dambos) and fruits around the homesteads mainly for their own consumption, with the exception of those areas close to urban markets. Peasant families have patch "gardens" of less than a quarter of a hectare each, which are hand watered. Incomes realised are used for school fees, domestic needs such as clothing, and other foods. Such gardens rely for water on: "illegal" stream bank cultivation, dambo and vlei cultivation; on legal hand-can watering from river-beds; on a few boreholes (ca 1 borehole: 10,000 households); and about 100 small-scale irrigation schemes promoted the by government and NGOs. There are about 8,490 hectares under small scale irrigation in government or community schemes, and 90 per cent of this land is under horticulture with the remainder being mainly for food crops (Agritex Interview, 1995). Besides the shortage of land and water, the main constraints to peasant land use diversification include the weak infrastructure base of Communal Areas, especially transportation, storage, markets (inputs/outputs) and other services such as credit, market and technical information. There is also evidence that LSCF farmers and small traders are beginning to fill these support service gaps for small farmer horticulture production through a variety of contractual and loose linkages.

The cost-price structure of horticulture and the intensity of land, water and labour use required by it tends to "generically" direct farmers, whether LSCF or communal, to undertake horticultural production on small areas of between less than half a hectare to currently existing maximum areas averaging 50 hectares for open irrigated field production of vegetables. In the LSCF for instance, one hectare of flowers under greenhouses tends to cost about Z$1 million (USD 100,000) per annum inclusive of capital costs, and requires large initial financial outlays. To this has to be added the costs of developing the water sources (dams, weirs and boreholes) or of accessing water in streams by hand and simple containers (water cans or bowsers). Thus, access to saving, amd credit as well as the costs of credit tend to be a limiting factor in Communal Areas. Small farmer horticulture production in communal and resettlement areas tends to be labour intensive or thin in capital investment, especially in terms of "in-field" facilities and inputs (pipes, greenhouses, chemicals etc.).

Field evidence shows that in Communal Areas, however, access to suitable quality soils, proximity to markets and water are influenced by local social and geographic differentiation. A highly differentiated distribution of access to land and water resources may arise from locational factors of a given Communal Area, such as proximity to water vleis, dambos or public boreholes and wells, or local political factors or power structures which affect the allocation of land rights in terms of land quality, quantity and its location. The capacity to use accessible land and water resources for effective commercial horticulture production is also conditioned by social differentiation in terms of available savings or remittances or access to credit for the procurement of inputs, labour and basic equipment, as well as in terms of the social composition of family labour and the nature of family expenditure on social services such as education, health and so forth. Thus, few Communal Areas farmers have accumulated both the physical resources (land and water) and the variable inputs to sustain commercial horticulture production. Those villages and family groupings in Communal Areas which have access to generally small patches of suitable land and water based upon natural conditions (vicinity to streams and dambos) or upon man-made water sources such as government and NGO-funded dams, boreholes and full-scale irrigation schemes are, therefore, the most likely to participate in horticulture.

Given that these resources are limited and more importantly underdeveloped due to a historical neglect of infrastructure development in Communal Areas, the scope for small farmers to participate in horticulture is limited. Currently, therefore, the growth of horticulture in Communal Areas is mostly dependent on the rate of public allocations to water development, which are low, and land redistribution towards more suitable land sites.

As box 4.3.1 field case study of an irrigation scheme in Shamva District (Mashonaland Central) shows, the GoZ and NGOs have been promoting such schemes using their own and donor resources. The schemes are usually targeted at between 10 to 50 families on areas of less than half a hectare each. Indeed, the irrigation capacity is low in Communal Areas which hold less than five per cent of available irrigation resources in Zimbabwe compared to over 80 per cent in the LSCF, with the rest being held by ADA of the GoZ (Madondo, 1996). In general, local labour and cash are used to supplement the GoZ's expenditure on irrigation schemes which tend to be regarded as social subsidies for food security (drought relief and recovery) by the government and donors (such as UNDP, FAO, ORAP, NGOs) rather than as critical economic investments.

Box 4.3.1. *Case Study of Tsakare Irrigation and Dryland Resettlement Scheme*

Government structures involved in the scheme include an Agritex Officer, two Re-settlement Officers, a Veterinary Services Official and a Councillor. Agritex and re-settlement officer and people in the resettlement area provide advice on who should be part of the management committee. Women are increasingly having a say in management issues. The irrigation scheme started in 1991.

The irrigation scheme was planned by ten people in 1991 who wanted to make a garden during the peak of the drought. The resettlement officer suggested that the initiators consult an irrigation company called Dore and Pit. People got interested and the numbers swelled to 31 members. The land was borrowed permanently from dry land plot holders and a total of 16 ha was acquired. Agritex pegged the land and the construction of drains began. About $9,600 was raised when maize was donated by members of the scheme to the committee and sold. The money was used to dig the trench from the plots to the engine. Electricity was not available then. They used three diesel engines donated by FAO, but had to buy diesel. During the drought, the market was flooded and this led to a loss as irrigators did not get much.

In 1993, a bean crop was planted and farmers (irrigators) got good profits. Income realised ranged from $3,000 to $8,000 the whole season for this crop. By the end of 1993, electricity was drawn from the village to the dam by Government. Farmers also had to help ZESA dig the holes for the poles. With electricity, green maize was planted. But a new problem cropped up i.e cholera. Vendors could not sell the crop well, but a profit was made, incomes which ranged from $2,000 to $7,000 were realised for the whole season. In 1994 similar profits were realised from beans, tomatoes, rape and cabbages.

The net effect of this has been a high demand for plots on the irrigation scheme. However, expansion cannot be done unless a new engine with a higher capacity is acquired. Irrigators and farmers feel that with the huge water resources from "Kariba" dam, irrigation has a potential of checking the effects of drought and ESAP. During the drought, a loan was sourced from AFC for both dry land and irrigation. The dry land loan was repaid, but the loan for irrigation it is still outstanding. AFC is now refusing to give more loans to the irrigators because they have outstanding bills. Irrigators believe that rival credit institutions must be created so that they can compete with AFC.

Our interviews found that the establishment of irrigation schemes also tends to introduce varied local conflicts over such issues as the land and com-pensation rights of those displaced by dams, and local competition for the few irrigation plots available as well as over selection criteria. Conflicts also arise over GoZ credit provision, especially over interest rates and repayment schedules; over local vegetable trading arrangements; and over GoZ dictation of the cropping regimes to be followed. Furthermore, social con-flicts are growing in relation to the sharp socio-economic differentiation which emerges around schemes, particularly in terms of income, food consumption and assets accumulated where the schemes are successful. Nevertheless, there is a tendency for irrigation to increase local incomes and food security such that popular demand for such schemes is found among peasants, local authorities, MPs and various GoZ provincial officials. The development of irrigation among small farmers is, thus, a critical aspect of building political capital in communal and resettlement areas. Irrigation resources are also easily traded off by some communities against demands for land redistribution (interviews).

Irrigation schemes in Communal Areas are clearly one of the key instruments in the restructuring of local power relations, which have been diversifying from the older "traditional" authority, including the ruling party and GoZ-led development committees (VIDCOs), towards a variety of specialised management structures (see Annex 4.3.8).

The Tsakare irrigation scheme was found, for instance, to be comprised of a relatively young leadership (below 40 years) inclusive of females, an ethnically homogenous group which is not the norm in most resettlement areas and of people with relatively higher levels of schooling. This contrasts with the socio-economic features of those who hold power and have greater access to local natural irrigation resources (dambos and stream banks) who tended to be older male members of the Communal Area communities with a high status or traditional authority. Thus, the evolution of irrigation schemes for horticultural development is critical in the process of local social differentiation, political restructuring and in the changing patterns of access to and use of land in communal and resettlement areas.

As can be seen in Table 4.3.2, Mashonaland has a number of small irrigation schemes which have evolved particularly over the last decade. Whereas the data is not well recorded in terms of operationality, area irrigated, and number of families participating, we were able to scour provincial and district records and aggregate the findings. We found that there are a total of 144 schemes in the three Mashonaland provinces with an area of almost 33,000 hectares, intended for about 60,000 families, which would each cultivate an average of 0.5 hectares (Table 4.3.2).

Table 4.3.2. *Overview of GoZ Small Farmer Irrigation Schemes: Mashonaland, 1996 (planned/operational)*

Province	District	No. of Schemes	Area/Farmer (est/ha)	Hectares (est/ha)
Mash-Central	Bindura	14	1	930
	Shamva	9	1	780
52 schemes	Centenary	4	1	1,200
	Guruve	11	1	9,000
12,880 ha.	Mazoe	6	2	600
	Mt. Darwin	5	1	150
	Muzarabani	1	1	120
	Rushinga	2	0.5	100
Mash-East	Chikomba	3	1.5	80
	Harare	4	0.5/1.5	750
	Macheke	2	0.5	55
50 schemes	Marondera	6	0.5	205
	Mudzi	8	0.2	160
1,567 ha.	Murehwa	1	0.3	12
	Mutoko	9	0.5/0.7	100
	Rudhaka	1	1.0	20
	UMP	4	0.5	40
	Wedza	12	0.2/0.5	145
Mash-West	Chegtu	14	0.5	535
	Hurungwe	7	0.5–3.0	1,910
	Kariba*	–	1	12,627
42 schemes	Kadoma	8	1.0	195
	Karoi	3	1.0	620
18,480 ha.	Makonde	4	0.5	66
	Musengezi	2	0.5	82
	Zvimba	4	1.5	2,445
Totals		144	ave. 0.5 ha.	32,927

* No data on the number of schemes for Kariba district could be established during field work.

Source: GoZ records (provincial interviews).

This suggests that less than ten per cent of the over 60,000 Communal Area families in the Mashonaland provinces have any real chance of entering into horticulture, and that a maximum of five per cent of their arable land (most of which is already cropped) is actually or planned for intensive high value horticultural crop production. Thus, those 30 per cent of Zimbabwe's communal and resettlement areas which are favourably located within the prime land area (N.R. I, II and II), have a limited possibility of intensifying or diversifying their land use and, therefore, of participating in the export-oriented agenda of the 1990s. But this rate of areal and farmer involvement in horticulture suggests a significant loss of potential incomes and productivity among the 2.7 million people of Mashonaland.

   Nevertheless, it is instructive to examine the land use and socio-economic outcomes of those few small farmers who are engaged in horticultural production in order to gauge the qualitative implications of this new land use for the participants, the impacts of this on local land and economic issues and on the evolution of rural markets targeting horticultural growth in Communal Areas. In addition to the above-cited Tsakare irrigation scheme case, we analyse in more detail, based on field observations, interviews and a survey, the performance of the Principe Irrigation Scheme case, and the performance of a local community-initiated horticultural scheme based upon dambo and streambank cultivation. These are presented as detailed narratives of each case. Our major findings on these cases suggest that there is a diverse range of socio-economic, political and marketing practices which are evolving from small farmer horticultural growth.

Principe Irrigation Scheme: Shamva District (Mashonaland Central)

The Principe irrigation scheme, which is also part of a resettlement project, is a typical GoZ-led type of avenue for smallholder entry into horticultural and land use diversification in general. The scheme which began in 1993 is approximately 30 km from Shamva town. It sources water from the Eben (Umfarudzi) dam, 20 km upstream on Mazowe river. This water is shared with LSCF farmers in the district. The scheme of 144 hectares is divided into two blocs (Blocks A and B) with 30 irrigators using each block. The scheme's population currently stands at around 200 people. Each plot holder is allocated 2.4 hectares (6 acres) of land for both farming and residential purposes. The cropping patterns so far reflect an inclination towards those crops with high returns (Annex 4.4.9). The farmers decide on the cropping regimes with the major focus being on horticultural crops. However, dryland planting is also done on a small scale to cater for some of the dietary needs of the irrigators. The government, which was fully involved in the land use planning of the scheme and which separated grazing areas from residential sites and the fields, supplied the scheme with irrigation equipment, such as two 25 electrical horsepower engines, pipes and other small materials, while the irrigators constructed their own accommodation and secured their own draught power. The irrigators were "allowed" to bring a maximum of six cattle for draught power purposes while small animals such as goats were prohibited. But the number of cattle have out-grown the permitted limit by two-fold, and the resettlement officer has not been able to control that trend. A grazing scheme was also initiated in order to limit the time farmers use in herding their livestock.

The settlers were mainly drawn from the Mashonaland areas. Their average age is 30 years, although there is a mixture of both the old and the young. The farmers selected are said to have "proved themselves" in the communal sector through "surplus production". Thus, Communal Area farm success is a critical qualification for "promotion" into horticulture. A selection score sheet examines the farmers in terms of their age, labour resources and farming experience as designed by the Department of

Resettlement of the District Development Fund (DDF) which operates directly under the local authority, the Chaminuka Rural District Council.

An Agricultural Extension Officer and a Scheme Resettlement Officer (who is the resident manager of the scheme), both of whom live near the scheme, oversee the project and mobilise other government departments for the provision of various services to the irrigators. The irrigation scheme is located near the Communal Areas proper and this area provided the initial market for its horticultural produce. The irrigators have maintained a cordial relationship with the people in Sanye Communal Area (Ward 16) who provide labour in exchange for both cash and part of the harvest. This linkage is said to have improved the nutritional status of communal people (interviews).

Dambo Horticulture Case Study: (Madziwa Communal Lands, 1996)

Dambos are another common avenue for small farmer diversification into horticulture because of their natural features. The land quality of the Madziwa community dambo was ideal for horticulture. Kaingidza and Chiwisayi II villages between the Mt. Darwin to Bindura road and the Pfura mountain range, lie within a large sandy dambo (vlei) with homesteads situated 2 km off the roadside. The vlei holds much water and the grazing areas are wet during the dry season. Cultivated lands were littered with wells and small ponds within the fields due to good rains last year.

Table 4.3.3. *Differentiation of Garden Plots and Field Plots (Ha), Sales, Income and Retentions*

Household	Garden (acre)	Field (ha/acre)	Sale	Retention	Potential income Z$
1	1 acre	1 ha	x		2,700
2	10x10 m	2 ha		x	
3	2 acres	4 acres	x		5,000
4	1 ha	1 acre	x		2,800
5	4x3m	5 ha		x	
6	1 acre	4 ha	x		725
7	10x8m	1 acre		x	
8	2 acres	2 ha	x		4,180
9	20x7m	2 ha		x	
10	1 ha	4 ha	x		7,450
Schools 1	2 acres	–		x	
2	2 ha	–	x		2,000
3	1 acre	–	x		800

The natural vegetation left is mainly tall grass, a few mutukutu trees, and occasional musau and mkuyu trees, and vast patches of thorn scrub in the grazing areas. Much of the land has been planted with eucalyptus (gum) trees. Soils range from clay/loam to loam and sandy/loam west of the road and mainly sandy soils to the east of the road. Key land features and outputs information show that there is extreme unevenness in access to land and water and, thus, outputs (Table 4.3.3).

There was a wide range of crops grown in the Madziwa case dambo area, which was less than twenty hectares large. The most common crops were those with a high local market and home consumption potential such as tomatoes, rape and tsunga (Table 4.3.4). The few commercial vegetables grown were dispersed in small patches among the farmers. 20 per cent of the ten families held over two or more dambo acres of an average of less than a quarter of an acre. The schools held two hectares on average reportedly for public benefit. About 60 per cent of the dambo area dwellers grew horticultural crops on a commercial basis with the remainder doing so only for home consumption. Incomes were reasonable on only two of the sites (house 10 and school 2) which realised close to the potential amounts.

Table 4.3.4. *Madziwa Dambo Horticultural Cropping (1996)*

Crops	H1	H2	H3	H4	H5	H6	H7	H8	H9	H10	S1	S2	S3
Tomatoes	x		x		x	x	x	x		x	x	x	x
Rape	x	x	x	x	x			x	x	x	x	x	x
Tsunga		x			x		x		x		x		
Rugare		x		x			x				x		
Onions		x	x	x		x				x	x	x	x
Cabbage		x					x	x		x	x		
Peas			x	x								x	
Carrots				x		x			x	x			x
Okra				x									
Rice						x							
Sugar cane													
Beans							x	x	x	x			
Potatoes						x		x					
Covo									x	x			
Spinach													x

These two cases entailed land users who owned an engine (pump) for irrigating their gardens and a truck to transport goods to Mbare market in Harare. The school had access to large free labour resources (1,100 pupils), and the headmaster (Mr. Mangwanya) had access to a friend's truck which transported crops to Bindura market. The remaining commercial horticulture farmers relied on the local community coming to them to buy, leading to much crop rotting.

Thus, water pumps, transport and labour were key constraints to small horticulture growth on a commercial basis. Also, many crops were affected by pests (Red Spider Mite) and farmers said the costs of herbicides and fertilizers were prohibitive. Experience and skills also mattered, as in the case of House no. 7 which had used the wrong chemical on a crop of tomatoes which was infested with Red Spider Mite, resulting in the destruction of the crop. The lack of tools and gardening implements was also raised by some farmers as a problem although in some cases, even the relatively wealthy farmers (large crop producers of cotton and maize) cited this. Lack of good quality reliable fencing was cited often as a problem, because of theft.

All of the plots used fertilizers and pesticides rather than traditional methods of soil enhancement and pest control such as green manuring and inter-cropping. Widespread gullying was observed throughout the area, as were overworking of soils, overcrowding and overgrazing. All livestock owners grazed their cattle in the vlei leading to erosion around water pools and streambanks. After a few seasons of cultivation, the dambo is reported to dry out, leading to soil crumbling.

NGO Promoted Small Farmer Horticultural Land Use

Another growing way in which small farmers are getting involved in new land use is through training schemes organised by various NGOs, LSCF and trusts such as the Farmers Development Trust. Our case study, however, involved an international NGO. In 1995, DAPP an NGO working in Shamva district of Mashonaland Central, began training communal farmers to become commercial farmers, reportedly in fulfilment of the strategy to indigenise the commercial farming sector. DAPP bought three farms in the Shamva land market (Table 4.3.5) to train farmers in commercial horticulture, cattle ranching, and woodlands development. DAPP has developed land use models which combine horticulture, forestry and livestock reflecting a small scale of intensive horticultural practice complimenting the more extensive land uses (Table 4.3.6). The farmers are trained for five years and then promised resettlement land. The training land is sub-divided into 3 hectare units per family.

Table 4.3.5. *Smallholder Training Farmlands*

Name of farm	Land Area (ha)	Activity at Farm
River Estate	1,082	Training communal farmers to be commercial farmers
Park Estate	1,280	Cattle production as well as eucalyptus, citrus, mango and litches
Forest Estate	1,200	Mangoes, litchis, eucalyptus for commercial purposes
Total	3,562	

Source: Field interviews (1996).

The communal farmers are identified by DAPP fieldworkers in consultation with Agritex, chiefs, headmen and headmasters in their local areas, and those selected include the unemployed and married. Over 650 communal people applied for training while only 82 were selected in the first intake.

Table 4.3.6. *Land Use Structure of Training Farms*

Type of Activity	Name of Farm	
	Park Estate	Forest Estate
Cattle Production	150 ha	24 ha
Eucalyptus	240 ha	230 ha
Citrus	24 ha	25 ha
Mangoes	5 ha	
Litches		2.5 ha
Total	419 ha	281.5 ha

These benefited from $500,000 worth of seed packs sourced through AFC credit, while the farmers prepared the land. Each farmer has access to 3 ha allocated for the residential stand (0.25 ha) composed of a homestead, a small vegetable garden, orchard and a plot for planting traditional crops while the 2.75 hectares are devoted to cash crops. During the first season, the farmers incomes ranged from $10,000 to $32,000. But some farmers focused on traditional cash crops with one producing 32 bags of maize on the 2.75 hectares, which was far ahead of most communal and LSCF sector yields. Crop rotation is a key practice in the training, and most of the farmers produce paprika, beans, maize, cotton and vegetables. Since DAPP is an anti-smoking agency, tobacco is not produced. Vegetables produced are sold to the DAPP's Frontline Institute and in Shamva town, which is, thus, a captive market.

The programme also promotes conservation practices such as tree protection, the use of fuel efficient stoves and solar water heating systems. Joint decisions by husbands and wives in setting production targets and sourcing of finance is promoted, since both are treated as trainees. This NGO approach to small farmer diversification has far reaching socio-cultural as well as economic implications. In contrast to the above cases of small farmers endowed with water resources and who engage in horticulture, the rest of the small communal farmers pursue dryland farming. Dryland uses yield one seasonal crop on an extensive land use basis, but rely on mixed farming activities including livestock production. Thus, even small farmers who practise dryland farming on resettlement schemes which provide more land per capita to individual farmers, realised incomes which are well below those of their counterparts engaged in horticulture (Table 4.3.7 and Annex 4.3.10). For instance, average annual incomes per family in the four cases here varied as shown in Table 4.3.7.

As the next section shows, the land questions confronting these different farmers also vary extremely. Indeed our detailed survey of communal farmers in Shamva demonstrated a variety of land grievances related to tenure.

Table 4.3.7 Small Farmer Land Use and Estimated Benefits Profile: Mashonaland Central–Shama District (1995–96)

Land User	No. of farmers	Land Resources Arable	Grazing	Water Resources	Crops Produced/products	Average yield/ha	Labour Resources Own	Hired	Machinery Annual Income	Marketing	Average (Z$)
Communal farmers	Several villages (13 wards)	–	–	Dambo well, rivers and boreholes	Maize, cotton, tobacco sorghum/millet, garden vegetables	–	X		DDF tractors, plough, cultivators, harrows, planters	Cargill, COTTICO, GMB. Retain for own consumption	–
Tsakare dryland resettlement	160	700 ha	–	Rainfed & boreholes	Cotton, maize	–	X		DDF tractors, plough, cultivators, harrows	Cargill (Tafuna) COTTICO/GM B Mt. Darwin	10,000–15,000
Tsakare irrigation resettlement	30	16 ha	–	"Kariba" a local farm dam	Paprika, okra, vegetables green mealies	–	X		Irrigation equipment (pipes and engine)	Mt. Darwin and local schools	3,000–8,000
Principe irrigation resettlement	60	144 ha	–	Eben dam upstream of Mazowe river	Baby corn, vegetables, cabbages	–	X	X	Irrigation equipment (pipes and engine)	Mbare, Shamva, Bindura	10 000–15,000
Madziwa Dambo cultivation	Several villages	80 ha	–	Wells, rivers	Vegetables, sugarcane	–	X		Hoes, picks, buckets	Local market	4,000
DAPP—communal to commercial famer	82	300 ha	900 ha	DAPP sunk boreholes	Cotton, maize, eucalyptus, citrus	–	X		Tillage unit from LSCF sector	COTTICO, GMB	10,000–30,000
Ngome grazing	2 villages	–	–	–	–	–	X		Fencing material from Africa 2000 network	–	–
Mufurudzi Campfire fisheries project	–	–	–	Eben dam	Fish	–	X		Nets	Local market (Bindura/Shamva)	–

Source: Interviews (1995/96)

4.3.3 Changing Marketing System and Small Farmer Land Use Diversification

Apart from the GoZ, NGO and community initiatives to promote water development for the diversification of small farmer land uses into high value commodities such as horticulture, the emergence of new marketing systems in communal and resettlement areas has become a "driving force" in this process. As a result of trade liberalisation, the deregulation of the rural transportation system, and of agricultural markets, we observed a variety of new marketing procedures which increasingly condition small farmer land uses and the social relations of production. The range of marketing channels observed since 1991 include:

a) The old GoZ parastatals buying mainly grains and cotton;
b) LSCF farmers now supplying horticultural inputs to small farmers and buying their crop (e.g. paprika) for further processing and onward sale;
c) Large multinational corporations now engaged in horticultural, cotton and wildlife production sub-contracting or making leasing arrangements;
d) Traditional shopkeepers and hammer millers (mainly older patriachs) and new younger shopkeepers, many of whom were GoZ approved buyers of grain for onward sale to parastatals, now buying for themselves to grind and sell retail and wholesale, and no longer merely grinding for individuals. These have also diversified into buying and selling a wider range of crops;
e) New "indigenous" traders located in major cities and larger towns, who organise mobile buying and temporary storage facilities which truck products to larger markets (see Box 4.3.2, Walk Project);
f) The continuation of small farmers clubs or cooperatives pooling marketing resources;
g) Individual mobile agents operating on behalf of various end-user industrial firms (e.g. Hortico) or for international export agencies who spot buy or contract small farmers.

In our survey of new marketing channels and horticulture growth, we examined the evolving marketing systems at Principe Irrigation in more detail. Most of the crops produced there, including green mealies, cabbages, green beans, okra, onions, tomatoes, water melons, and groundnuts were, in the past, mostly sold in Shamva town, surrounding Communal Areas and at Mbare Musika (market) in Harare. The latter market now seems to be their major marketing centre. The irrigators had to market their crop in direct competition with local LSCF farmers and Communal Area horticulture producers in Mashonaland East whose marketing scheme is donor-funded. Given the problem of remote competitive markets, in 1992 about 20 Principe irrigators entered a verbal agreement with an LSCF farmer to supply him water melons. Initial communication difficulties led the small farmers to harvest their entire water melon crop at once, instead of delivering the crop in batches. As a result the LSCF farmer failed to market most of the produce and it was written off.

Box 4.3.2. *Marketing Case Study: Walk Project (Pvt) Ltd.*

- Walk Project (Pvt) Ltd. started in 1995. The company is based in Masasa (Harare) and buys sunflower and maize from resettlement farmers in Tsakare Resettlement Scheme and other surrounding areas which include Chihuri and Mupfure Communal Lands. The company holds a private licence for buying crops.
- The company buys over 100 bags per day from the farmers and by September 1995 had bought more than 10,000 bags of maize at a price of $1.00 per kg. The produce bought from the farmers was later transported to Harare using company vehicles and the maize was re-sold to the people in town. The company also buys beans and groundnuts, but the farmers in Tsakare do not plant these for cash sales.
- The company has five employees who receive cash, write receipts, procure and measure produce. It has apparently been agreed by Walk that local youth be employed as part of local development input.
- The local farmers benefit from Walk because it pays ready cash and they do not incur transport costs any more. Walk buys the produce on the "spot". Business was booming for the company, such that they often ran short of cash to pay the farmers, until more cash was delivered from Harare.
- The company does not sell maize to the local farmers even though such demand was high.
- Walk employees argued that conditions under ESAP were now better, because they could now buy directly from the farmers as well as sell directly to millers and consumers in town!
- The owner of Walk is a black professional worker who works for a government parastatal.

However, since 1992, the small farmers began contract crop marketing based upon individual plot holders engaging in informal or verbal agreements with various private companies. But in 1996, a large private firm, HORTICO, entered into a written agreement with the irrigators to produce baby corn for export. Another large firm, Olivine Industries (Pvt) Ltd., then followed suit in August 1996, and it "engaged" the farmers to produce Red Canadian beans. By the end of the year, all the Principe farmers were signed up in two major contracts producing entirely new horticultural produce (Table 4.3.8).

Table 4.3.8. *Principe Contract Farming Arrangements*

Name of Company	Type of Contract	No. of Beneficiaries Block A	Block B	Crop Produced
HORTICO	Verbal, then written when crop planted	30	12	Baby corn
Olivine Industries (Mrs Mhende)	Verbal, and written later	30	15	Red Canadian beans

Source: Field interviews (1996).

In both contracts, the companies provide inputs such as fertilizers and chemicals, although HORTICO also provides extension services through a field officer who visits the scheme at each stage of the crop's growth. HORTICO provided the irrigators with seed, fertilizer (Compound Z, ammonium and dymathiote cyranuous) and transport right to the field. In contrast, Olivine Industries, through its agent, expects the farmers to transport the crop to Chegutu town (approximately 220 km) at their own cost. There is also uncertainty among irrigators as to whether they are contracted by Olivine Industries or its agent and, thus, how to negotiate better marketing conditions. Some of the irrigators believe that the agent either sourced money from embassies and bought inputs from Olivine or that the agent is an outside employee of Olivine who is paid a 10 per cent commission by Olivine. The Olivine contract was only signed when the crop was already planted and inadequate inputs were supplied. Furthermore, the irrigators suspected that they were supplied with untreated Red Canadian bean seed, which led to poor yields.

In general, the horticulture crops planted by 42 irrigators on 0.4 acres to 6 acres of land was a success compared to other horticultural crops produced. The crops matured in about 6 months time and farmers obtained high incomes, with some in excess of $10,000. At least five farmers are said to have obtained over $8,000 on 1 to 1.5 acres of land, after selling around 60,000 cobs of baby corn at 16 cents a cob. One farmer sold 80,000 cobs of baby corn from a plot of 0.10 of a hectare and obtained $13,000, a comparatively high return against most other crops (Table 4.3.9).

Table 4.3.9. *Principe Contract Sales Incomes*

Income-Ranges	Frequency	%
0–1000	1	5
1001–2000	1	5
2001–3000	3	15
3001–4000	3	15
4001–5000	1	5
5001>	11	55
Total	20	100

Source: Field interviews (1996).

The irrigators were charged Z$0.02 per cob for transport and deductions were made to meet their loan obligations. Thus, 55 per cent of the irrigators obtained more than $5,000 from selling baby corn (Table 4.3.9). The irrigators believe that their crop has been exported and that HORTICO benefited more from the foreign currency transactions than they did. Few farmers feel cheated because they did not quite work out how sales and input costs were balanced out.

Table 4.3.10. *Principe Farmer Grievance with Sub-Contracts*

Problems	Hortico		Olivine		Total	%
	No.	%	No.	%		
1. Restricted Market	6	21	8	20	14	23
2. Low Profits	2	7	4	10	6	7
3. Delayed Cash Payment	1	3	0*	0	1	2
4. Poor Harvest	5	17	5	13	10	5
5. Contracts Cheating	3	10	9	22	12	17
6. Unfair Prices	2	7	8	20	10	15
7. None	6	21	0	0	6	7
8. Diseases	4	14	6	15	10	15
Total	29	100	40	100	69	100

* Cash for Red Canadian beans not yet paid.

For example, HORTICO had promised to buy baby corn at 25 cents/ kilogram and when the contract had been signed, they stated that they were buying at 10 c/kg, less 2 c/kg for transport charges. Farmers did not have the option to refuse because the crop was already in the soil. In general, the farmers cite a range of difficulties with the contract farming system (Table 4.3.10), although they acknowledge that their current incomes are now higher and more certain. Thus, by and large, the Principe farmers saw contract farming as beneficial to them in the meantime (Table 4.3.11).

Table 4.3.11. *Farmer Perceptions of Contract Farming Benefits*

Benefits	Frequency	%
1. Input Supply	20	25
2. Guaranteed Produce Price	15	19
3. Processing of Product	2	3
4. Transportation of Produce	18	22
5. Extension	15	19
6. Easy Marketing	4	5
7. Payment of Cash on Time	3	4
8. Others	2	3
Total	79	100

Note: The frequencies of 79 are more than the sample of 30 because some respondents provided more than one answer.

Source: Field interviews, 1996.

The key problems which small farmers felt were being resolved by contract farming were transportation, guaranteed prices, cash payments and extension advice (Table 4.3.11). However, the two companies do not seem to want to take the risk of crop failure in the contracts undertaken, and at any rate the contracts are written in legal jargon which the small farmers do not understand. Farmers feel they have no option but to sign the contracts because inputs are expensive and inaccessible. Our analysis of sales shows that Olivine buys the beans at $7,50/kg which was the price as at 1993. However, local institutions such as Frontline College are prepared to buy the same at $9.00 to $10.00/kg, although the farmers are not yet organised enough to exploit such options or to press for better contractual terms.

4.4 Wildlife Land Use Patterns

4.4.1 The Role and Development of Wildlife Land Uses

By 1994, the wildlife sector was found to employ over 38,000 formal sector workers, which is about four per cent of the national total (Table 4.4.1). If we add on to this the unrecorded numbers of communal people and LSCF staff who are involved in the sector, and the "underground" workers, as well as all those who indirectly service the wildlife sector, it seems plausible that the sector may be engaging up to about eight per cent of the country's total formal sector employees. Indeed, most of these employees were full-time, not casual. Even so, using a lower estimate of five per cent, the sector has grown into a significant private and public wage provider, although the earnings are highly concentrated because the ownership of most wildlife resources is in government and LSCF hands.

Table 4.4.1. *National Employees in Tourist Industries*

Period	Full-time	Part-Time	Casuals	Total
1986	13,213	130	471	13,814
1987	13,385	127	392	13,904
1988	13,512	170	445	14,127
1989	13,732	193	708	146,633
1990	14,464	263	991	15,718
1991	15,530	292	1,075	16,897
1992	15,329	445	1,075	16,849
1992 March	16,020	348	943	17,311
June	14,761	771	905	16,437
Sept	15,137	337	730	14,100
Dec	15,396	325	1,008	16,729
1993 Jan	13,094	276	730	16,204
June	13,031	271	676	13,978
Sept	13,317	301	621	14,239
Dec	19,528	261	744	20,533
1994 March	20,055	263	243	20,561

Source: CSO, 1994.

Apparently, the sector earned Z$0.5 billion in 1994 (Table 4.3.2), mainly from tourism in general, which as we have argued is wildlife-dominated or associated. Hunting and ostrich production are key contributors to the "wildlife" sector boom.

Sub-Sectoral Land Allocations to Wildlife

The pattern of land allocations to wildlife among different land tenure regimes or sub-sectors has been changing. Out of the total land in Zimbabwe which had been allocated to wildlife, the biggest shifts since the 1960s occurred within the LSCF where, by 1970, such land had grown ten-fold, albeit remaining relatively static from then on until 1980 (Annex 4.4.1).

By 1994, however, the LSCF land under wildlife had reached 31 per cent of such land use compared to three per cent in the 1960s. The slight decline in LSCF land allocated to wildlife during the 1980s mostly reflects the marginal N.R. lands which were redistributed from that sector to smallholders under the resettlement programme. These land use changes at the national level were relatively gradual since the 1970 level, when the national proportion of land allocated to wildlife moved from 16 per cent, towards 22 per cent in 1990 (Annex 4.4.2). By 1996 however, the national level land allocation to wildlife had jumped up to 27 per cent (Cumming, 1990).

Table 4.4.2. *The Role of Wildlife in the Formal Economy (1994)*

Sector	Total Earnings (Z$ million)	Forex Earnings (Z$ million)	Number Employed
Tourism	500.0	300.0	35,000
Hunting	46.2	41.8	2,000
Wildlife management services	6.2	–	375
Live animal sales	1.0	–	25
Game product (hides, skins)	15.0	negligible	100
Crocodile production	30.0	15.0	500
Ostrich production	–	20.0	100
Total	588.4	376.8	38,100

– Indicates that no data was available at the time of the research.

Source: Adapted from Muir, 1993.

During the 1980s, the biggest jump in land allocated to wildlife was in the Communal Areas, or smallholder sector, which had gained three million hectares under the resettlement programme. These new lands mainly in N.R. IV and V brought with them the wildlife resources in the indigenous woodlands which were added on to existing small farmer woodlands within the Communal Areas where such lands have functioned as mixed livestock grazing and natural wildlife and woodland resources preserves. The introduction and spread of the Campfire programme from the late 1980s served to formalise the exclusive and commercial use of some of these Communal Area woodlands for wildlife management rather than for livestock or cattle grazing. This conversion process also reduced the significant trend in Communal Areas of allocating more grazing lands to new families for crop husbandry (see Cousins, 1991).

As stated before, state lands with wildlife resources remained static, although even here state agencies such as the Forestry Commission, ADA and the Parks increased their formal and commercial use of some of these lands as wildlife enterprises. There, the growth of tourism during the 1990s has also been an incentive for the conversion towards formalised commercial wildlife management as opposed to their mere "ecological conservation" approaches of the past. This shift heralded the era of so-called "eco-tourism" and sustainable exploitation of natural resources in Zimbabwe.

Comparatively speaking, therefore, the small farmer areas have remained with the lowest areal space of land allocated to wildlife resources as opposed to the combined state and LSCF owned lands. This reflects the unequal land distribution and high population structures which have led to the large scale conversion of communal woodlands into extensive cropping and livestock grazing regimes, combined with the foraging of nature for various domestic or household requirements such as shelter and energy. But this pattern also reflects how the agriculturally underutilised lands in the LSCF areas (ca 40 per cent) in terms of cropping and livestock ranching, have gradually been converted into commercially-exploited wildlife land uses.

In one sense, this trend reflects a growing choice by the LSCF to retain woodlands for wildlife enterprises over agricultural uses proper given the financial returns to this land use in relation to their capital investment requirements. Moreover, the maintenance of this trend has been justified on environmental grounds, defending thus the unequal land distribution patterns or delaying the land redistribution process while building up the market value of such land.

The uneven or unequal areal distribution of land allocated to wildlife land use is also matched by the less pronounced but uneven endowments or control over wildlife resources themselves in the three major land tenure regimes or socio-economic sub-sectors (Table 4.4.3). The state and LSCF control slightly more of such resources in value terms of "trophies" actually realised from harvesting wildlife, while control over most of the large and prized animal categories is dominated by the state followed by the LSCF which controls larger numbers of middle-sized and rarer species.

Table 4.4.3. *Distribution of Wildlife Resources by Tenure (1992)*

Species	National Parks	Forestry Lands	Communal Lands	Commercial Farms	Total
Elephant	60,270	1,040	7,070	420	68,800
Buffalo	57,300	1,800	9,800	210	69,110
Lion	3,080	180	460	240	3,960
Black Rhino	1,870	60	150	110	2,960
Giraffe	2,510	740	460	6,470	10,180
Sable	7,100	1,320	1,340	10,700	20,530
Eland	4,390	2,400	1,330	22,990	31,110
Kudu	24,100	3,920	5,350	58,370	91,470
Impala	145,950	7,120	29,780	204,940	387,790
Leopard	4,030	740	1,770	3,050	9,590
Cheetah	620	180	200	1,280	2,280
Crocodile	5,350	350	1,680	410	7,790
Zebra	14,860	1,520	2,020	15,550	33,950

Source: Jansen et al., 1992, p. 23.

Sub-Sectoral Land Allocations to Wildlife

The pattern of land allocations to wildlife among different land tenure regimes or sub-sectors has been changing. Out of the total land in Zimbabwe which had been allocated to wildlife, the biggest shifts from the 1960s occurred within the LSCF where, by 1970, such land had grown ten-fold, albeit remaining relatively static from then on until 1980 (Annex 4.4.1).

Table 4.4.4. *Analysis of Origin of Trophy by Land Tenure (1990)*

Species	Total No.	% DNPWLM	% C. Areas	% LSCF
Elephant	134	48	52	0
Buffalo	503	54	39	7
Sable	317	27	8	65
Kudu	737	27	12	61
Leopard	182	44	45	11
Zebra	465	32	10	58
Waterbuck	244	46	17	37
Eland	237	4	9	87
Impala	1,517	48	40	12
Wildebeest	279	0	2	98
Warthog	728	29	16	55
Tsessebe	147	0	27	73
Reedbuck	1,860	14	8	78

Source: Jansen et al., 1992.

These patterns reflect a realisation of GoZ policy towards the allocation of land to wildlife and its commitment to defend that land use. Today, the government spends US$100 per km^2 in protecting these areas which has tended to be used to justify the official GoZ's international lobby for Cites to allow increased elephant culling and the export of ivory to compensate for the wildlife management costs. The destruction that elephants have increasingly brought onto Communal Area crops as wildlife numbers and land uses expand is also used to lobby for the global liberalisation of the ivory trade. There is, thus, a definite trend of growth in wildlife land use which is aimed at attracting high value wildlife tourists to Zimbabwe, and whose forex earnings have been used to justify the efforts to increase the returns to land from wildlife management.

Sport Hunting in Zimbabwe

Sport hunting in Zimbabwe is the chief form of consumptive wildlife utilisation in the state lands administered either by DNPWLM or the Forestry Commission, Communal Areas and Commercial Farmland. Sport hunters are divided into three categories: international clients using Zimbabwean outfitters; international sport hunters who have purchased the Zambezi Valley Auction Hunts; and Zimbabwean citizens. These three different types of hunters do not have equal access to the land available for hunting. Out of the land under DPNWLM, only about one third of the total is allocated to Zimbabwean citizens who purchase "cheap hunts" in the Zambezi Valley, while the remainder in the Parks estates, the state land under the Forestry Commission, the Communal Areas and commercial farmland is almost exclusively hunted by international clients in the company of locally-based outfitters.

But game viewing has also grown tremendously within the lands allocated to wildlife. Prior to independence, there were 13 registered safari operators (Child, 1989), while by 1986 there were 55 registered safari operators, and the latest estimate of active safari operators is in excess of 150 (Price Waterhouse, 1992). Game viewing also involves boat trips and bird watching, in addition to viewing large animals. This reinforces the market driven shift towards wildlife which has led to increased LSCF farmer involvement. The number of LSCF wildlife farmers was 183 in 1974, while the number of farmers registered under the Wildlife Producers Association in 1990 was 436, of which only 187 were reported to be involved in active wildlife production (White, 1990).

4.4.2 The Distribution of Wildlife Resources in the LSCF

Since gaining proprietorship over wildlife in 1975, LSCF land owners have increased the amount of private land under wildlife in Zimbabwe from (1,700,000 ha) 17,000 km^2 to (3,000,000 ha) 30,000 km^2. By 1994, more that 500 of Zimbabwe's nearly 4,000 commercial farms derived all or part of their income from wildlife and more than 75 per cent of the private ranches earned some revenue from wildlife. Martin (1994) reported that the LSCF area allocated to wildlife was increasing at the time at an annual rate of six per cent: a significant trend given that approximately 35 per cent of Zimbabwe's land is in private hands.

One interesting feature of the growth of wildlife land use in the LSCF is the agro-ecological distribution of wildlife resources to this land use, given that policy debates focus on the moral and socio-economic value of allo- cating prime land uses and control in relation to the utility of such land uses to the majority of Zimbabwean human beings (small farmers) vis-à-vis the few individual large farmers and the animals themselves. The general trends in this respect are that the LSCF areas in natural region V have by far the largest number of animals (ca 58 per cent) which is in keeping with the argument that those lands are too marginal for proper farming and should be left to natural uses such as wildlife. Equally, wildlife resources in the prime LSCF lands of N.R. I and II are the least (three per cent) given that these regions are relatively smaller in area and more densely divided into LSCF farms contiguous to major urban areas and numerous high density Communal Areas which, together, have "crowded out" wildlife.

However, these relatively few but substantial wildlife resources in the prime lands occupy some of that land which is widely contested as being underutilized. Moreover, their conversion into exclusive cropping, grazing or mixed farming would essentially imply the spatial dislocation, not neces- sarily the loss, of only about three per cent of the LSCF sector's wildlife resources, and of course less than one per cent of the national wildlife re- sources. It is little wonder that GoZ officials have mooted a general public policy statement which, while not yet effectively implemented, is intended to disallow wildlife ranching in natural regions I and II. The argument here is that even small amounts of prime land would substantially improve the livelihoods of a significant number of families.

However, beyond these ideological and technical debates, the most pro- nounced and grounded contestation of land allocations towards wildlife we rather than farming proper is the allocation of LSCF lands to wildlife in N.R. III and IV. Given the existence of technical doubts over the relative financial returns of these areas to crop production, and the fact that most of Zimbabwe's communal population borders the LSCFs in these regions, there are heated debates over the land use allocations there. The evidence is that up to 40 per cent of the LSCF wildlife resources are contained in these two agro-ecological regions (Table 4.4.5). These wildlife resources occupy about 11,000 km^2 of land. Were such land to be allocated instead of resettling peo- ple under existing individual settler models, many farmers could benefit from such an alternative approach to land use.

Table 4.4.5. *Numbers of Carnivores on Commercial Game Ranches by Natural Region*

Species	N.R. I&II	N.R. III	N.R. IV	N.R. V	Total	Total[*]
Lion	26	–	28	187	241	243
Leopard	150	120	430	1,890	2,590	3,050
Cheetah	5	235	149	707	1,096	1,280
Wild-dog	43	–	58	157	258	290
Hyena	36	2	194	898	1,130	1,170
Jackal	–	680	1,140	770	2,590	4,140
Caracal	–	60	40	50	150	700
Serval	–	–	120	70	190	360
Civet	–	–	160	210	370	690
Crocodile	–	110	10	210	330	410

*Includes cattle ranches.
– Indicates that no data was available at the time of the research.

Source: Jansen et al., 1992, p. 29)

Therefore, in the Mashonaland provinces, which encompass mainly agro-ecological N.R. II and III, the allocation of inequitably held prime arable lands therein to wildlife, when these areas could potentially offer greater crop production security for small farmers compared to their predominantly poorer and densely settled lands in N.R. IV and V, has become a hotly contested spatial and political domain with regard to Zimbabwe's land question.

Scouring the scattered information sources on wildlife in Mashonaland, for instance, we identified about 13 privately run safari establishments mostly on LSCF lands (see Annex 4.4.3). Over 90 per cent of these were in Mashonaland West, which also has much more N.R. III land within the LSCFs of Mashonaland. But the most dynamic and controversial trend in the conversion of LSCF to exclusively wildlife and nature-based land uses is that of the consolidation of farms into large scale "conservancies". In general these are billed as market approaches to the environmentally, socially and economically sustainable management of land and natural resources within N.R. III, IV and V. Our review of this trend exposed interesting case studies on the state of the art in the creation of such conservancies (see Box 4.4.1). This "art" has become a significant prism through which Zimbabwe's land question has been mystified under ESAP through processes of creating a "market economy", based upon the restructuring of forms of ownership and distribution, decades after non-market land alienation processes.

Box 4.4.1. *Save Conservancy*

- The Save Conservancy, formed in 1991, is located in the South-East Lowveld of Zimbabwe and stretches from Birchenough Bridge in the North to the Mkwasine River in the South. The Save River forms the eastern boundary of all but 20 kilometres of the conservancy's 100km length. The conservancy is bordered to the west by the Devure Resettlement Area and Matsai Communal Land and to the South by the Mkwasine Sugar Estate and the Sengwe Communal Land. The conservancy covers 3,200 square kilometres (326,000 ha) and is the largest privately owned nature reserve anywhere in the world today.
- From the early 1920s onwards, cattle ranches were established in the area. By the late 1980s, overgrazing and a series of droughts are said to have begun to threaten the environment. Then cattle ranching was considered no longer viable from both the financial and ecological points of view and individual land owners took to wildlife management because of its higher profitability. According to the conservancy owners, the initial aim was to facilitate black rhino breeding in the area.
- Before 1991, restocking of wildlife involved a few giraffe, waterbuck, nyala and tsessebes, elephants and rhino on individual farms. Wildlife was introduced after cattle de-stocking began. The 1991/92 drought led to large scale wildlife feeding and faster de-stocking of cattle to prevent loss of wildlife. Further species were introduced in and after 1993 and a double 7.5 metre electrified fence built around the perimeter to regulate foot and mouth disease from infected buffalo that were under free-range conditions.
- About 84 per cent of the conservancy is bordered by communal and resettlement areas, with little irrigation facilities and cattle overstocking. Apart from self-provisioning farming, the communal farmers also provide short-term labour in the sugar industry or government schemes. The areas are poverty-stricken and environmentally degraded. The conservancy promises to provide employment and "entrepreneurial opportunities" to the surrounding populations and enhance the area's economic development.

Growth of Wildlife Conservancies

Conservancies which have become popular in the LSCF during the 1990s entail the creation of private companies which hold and manage groups of farms in one block. These are being used mainly to attract financial investment in the form of equity so as to capitalise large expanses of land with more wildlife, tourist infrastructure, and basic machinery and equipment. They are a focus for attracting national, regional and international capital in the tourist sector. In essence, conservancies remove the visibility of the human face of individual land ownership from the struggles over land and shift these to abstract legal entities of ubiquitous domicile.

Data on the structure of land ownership and amalgamation in the three conservancies examined (Annex 4.4.4 a, b, c) shows the enormity, by Zimbabwe land distribution standards, of the scale and form along which landholdings and uses are being restructured. In our largest conservancy case from N.R. V, 17 farms whose land sizes ranged from 10,000 to 44,000 hectares were amalgamated into the Save Valley Conservancy of over

326,331 hectares. The other two conservancies involved 7 and 12 farms amalgamated into units of 127,546 and 89,482 hectares each. In the Chiredzi River Conservancy, nine smaller farms, varying in size from about 1,800 to 5,000 hectares, were amalgamated with three larger farms ranging in size from 9,000 to 32,000 hectares, to form a conservancy.

Thus, the socio-economic differentiation of LSCF farms based upon land ownership is now being transformed into shareholding structures (Table 4.4.6). Essentially, these structures are a form of "communal" land use, although the more regularly used terms for this land use include: "common property management regime", "corporate management of natural resources" and "conservancy". These land structures reflect a more encoded regulation of land rights, obligations and management rules than their counterpart land use system in the Communal Areas.

Of immense interest also is the type of admixture of bedfellows found in these conservancies. In the Save case we find a major corporate hotelier, Zim Sun Ltd., which owned a farm of 12,976 hectares. Also involved the Zimbabwe Hunters Association (15,792 hectares), ADA, a state farm parastatal (12,146 hectares), a syndicate farm (Savule), and five other private corporate (company) land owners as well as individual family farm members.

This reflects a somewhat growing cohesion in the economic strategy of LSCF land users regardless of their socio-economic differentiation, and the political value that the transformation of land use and ownership structures brings them in terms of resource pooling for policy lobbying and investment portfolios (Table 4.4.7).

The "unique opportunity" thus identified by the conservancies is the bringing in of external investors into these land use structures in order to facilitate tourism, heralding a new wave of foreign land ownership in Zimbabwe.

Public controversy has, however, been stirred by some local politicians, including the provincial Governor, Dr. Hungwe, and the Vice-President, Muzenda, who, together with some local traditional leaders, focus on the more "parochial" issues of seeking ways in which people from neighbouring Communal Areas (and it seems some indigenous elites from the area) can also be "given" shares by the Save Conservancy. But statements from what are considered a "rival faction" of politicians in the Masvingo Province (such as Dr. Eddison Zvogbo etc.) suggest that the conservancy notion is welcomed and that they do not want the issue to become "over politicised". Local communities are, therefore, expected to cooperate because of the employment and development benefits that tourism in the conservancy will bring.

Table 4.4.6. *Allocation of Save Valley Ordinary "A" Shares*

Ranch	Hectarage	Share Entitlement
Angus	15,792	1,548,563
ARDA-Potential	12,146	1,191,036
Bedford Block	12,215	1,197,802
Chanurwe	44,348	4,348,762
Chapungu	12,976	1,272,426
Chishakwe	9,977	978,344
Gunundwe	11,374	1,115,334
Humani	41,158	4,035,991
Impala	8,097	793,991
Levanga	13,040	1,278,702
Makore	7,451	730,645
Mapari	23,153	2,270,382
Masapas	15,437	1,513,751
Matenere	13,123	1,286,841
Mkwasine	12,547	1,230,358
Mkwasine Estate	3,502	343,406
Msaize	16,340	1,602,300
Mukazi	11,457	1,123,473
Mkwasi	12,549	1,230,554
Savuli	5,529	542,173
Senuko	24,120	2,365,206
Total	326,331	32,000,000

Source: Save Valley Wildlife Services Limited, Eighth Draft, August 1995.

In the Mashonaland area, we also found some information on LSCF land use conversion towards wildlife in the form of conservancies. But these schemes occur on a much smaller scale, ranging in size from 1,000 to 2,700 hectares (see Annex 4.4.4). A key factor behind some of these private wildlife and nature parks is their vicinity to Harare (ca 40 kilometres), which is strategically intended to draw in domestic Harare-based and international tourists. Besides regular holiday-makers, the former include the market for business "retreats" (seminars, planning etc.), children's tours and educational conferences which, it is reported, have been growing considerably (field interviews).

These Mashonaland wildlife ranches offer chalets for overnight stays and guided tours, but they attract those tourists with less time and who seek an intensive sighting of a wide range of animals. The costs of running these small types of wildlife ranches are much greater than the "naturally" managed parks because of the higher feeding costs and more intensive care required by the animals.

Table 4.4.7. *Estimated Numbers of Wildlife to Be Acquired for the Conservancy*

Species	Already present, to be purchased from land owners	To be purchased externally	Total to be purchased	Unit cost Z$	Total cost Z$
Buffalo	120	3,750	3,870	3,000	11,610,000
Eland	370	500	870	3,500	3,045,000
Elephant	84	250	334	7,000	2,338,000
Giraffe	100	1,000	1,100	6,500	7,150,000
Hartebeest	–	100	100	50,000	5,000,000
Hippo	–	10	10	9,000	90,000
Nyala	125	500	625	7,000	4,375,000
Ostrich	–	500	500	4,000	2,000,000
Roan	–	100	100	40,000	4,000,000
Sable	–	500	500	9,500	4,750,000
Waterbuck	230	400	630	9,000	5,670,000
White Rhino	–	75	75	100,000	7,500,000
Wildbeest	1,200	1,500	2,700	3,200	8,640,000
Zebra	230	1,200	1,430	3,800	5,434,000
Total	2,459	10,385	12,844	255,500	71,602,000

Source: Save Valley Wildlife Services Limited, Eigth Draft, August 1995.

4.4.3 The State in Wildlife Management

Large scale wildlife ranching is also undertaken by the state on its own. In the ADA case, four of its farms, ranging in size from about 5,000 to 28,000 hectares, have been converted towards wildlife conservancies (Table 4.4.8). Two such farms are in Mashonaland (Battle Fields Range in Kadoma and Sesombi Ranges in KweKwe) while the rest are in N.R. IV/V. The lands had been procured by the GoZ for redistribution to smallholders but were handed over to the ADA for interim management.

Apparently, ADA is evolving a wildlife ranching policy for its farms (interviews, 1996) which proposes that 40 per cent of the land on most of its 20 large estates, located mostly in N.R. IV and V and amounting to about 0.5 million hectares, would be devoted to wildlife land uses because these can be more profitable and the land already holds wildlife resources. The ADA approach is to sub-contract hunters and safari operators for fixed periods or to form joint ventures with them (Box 4.4.2).

Thus, through the involvement of numerous state land managers and others who oversee or gain from these programmes, the state has consolidated its interest and policy design towards a favourable stance on the use of LSCF and state lands for wildlife, as opposed to its redistribution.

Table 4.4.8. *State (ADA) Wildlife Ranches*

Farm name	Acreage (ha)	Assumed area under wildlife (40% of total/ha)
Vungu ranges	71,190.00	28,476
Mkwasine	12,146.00 (potential)	4,858.4
Battle fields (some parts were taken for resettlement)	45,171.08	18,068.4
Sesombi	Approx. 49,000.00	19,600
Total	Approx. 177,507.08	71,002.8

Source: ADA Files.

As mentioned before, the involvement of other state agencies such as the Forestry Commission and District Councils in wildlife land uses reinforces the land policy orientation towards export land uses. But the state in collaboration with other actors has gone further to promote the conversion of Communal Area land into wildlife uses.

Box 4.4.2. *Contractual Arrangements between ADA and a Private Safari Operator*

- A year long joint venture between the Agricultural Development Authority and a local safari operator to carry out hunting safari operations has been so successful that an application has been made to the state farming agency to extend the agreement. Under the current hunting lease (up to December, 1994), ADA offered hunting, shooting and safari rights over Vungu and Sesombi Ranches to Connel Safaris.
- The deal guaranteed that the state farming agency would get trophy fees for all safari operations while the operator would receive all the daily rates. At the end of each month, the safari operator posted to ADA a return of all animals shot or wounded during the month and made full payment for the value of wounded animals.
- The concessions covered about 300,000 acres and are owned by ADA but managed by Connel Safaris. In line with economic reforms, ADA was now offering exclusive private hunting safaris on its wildlife estates in the region since it diversified its operations to include wildlife conservation.

Source: *Herald*, 24/11/95

4.4.4 Small Land Holders' Communal Wildlife Land Use: The Campfire

The involvement of smallholders in wildlife land use has been growing in terms of areas allocated, incomes being realised and the organisational strategies of the actors. For instance, in 1992, Campfire realised an income of about $2 million, 40 per cent of which was derived from trophy elephants. However, the Campfire communities had $1.6 million worth of unrealised incomes in the form of stockpiled unsold ivory (6.5 tons of the 27.5 tons are currently in the national ivory store) due to the trade ban on ivory. It is estimated that about 60,000 to 120,000 Communal Area people were directly involved in Campfire (see also Box 4.4.3 for details on the Nyaminyami Case).

Box 4.4.3. *Nyaminyami Campfire Case Details*

Nyaminyami is one of the earlier Campfire projects begun in 1989, with over 6,000 families managing 3,000 km² of wildlife. Twelve wards divide revenues, which in 1994 amounted to about Z$200 per household, while Z$1,097,000 was realised by the project. Actual net allocations of cash to individual households amount to below Z$50 (US$5.00) each year; school classrooms, a teacher's house, clinics, feeder roads, an electric fence and some small income-generating projects (boreholes) were constructed for the community. Up to 40 persons were also directly employed by the project.

The growth of Campfire projects is part of the growing signficance, over the last decade, that sport hunting has achieved. In 1990, the gross value of sport hunting in Zimbabwe was US$9.4 million based on a total of 11,338 hunting days sold (Table 4.4.9). In 1991, 11 Campfire districts generated Z$3,073 million, and Z$2,668 million of this was derived from sport hunting. In 1990, 52 per cent of the national elephant trophies were from communal land and the remainder were shot in protected state land areas. Gross income rose from over US$2 million in 1984 to US$9.4 million in 1990 (Table 4.4.9). Five species have consistently contributed to over 50 per cent of the total sport hunting trophy fees. But the income from these trophy animals is now less secure since the Cites ban on elephants and because of the fact that buffaloes have been a major threat to cattle in Zimbabwe through foot and mouth disease transmission.

Table 4.4.9. *Growth of Sport Hunting in Zimbabwe*

Year	Hunting days	% Increase	Income (US$)	% Increase
1985	7,966	–	4,313,343	–
1990	11,338	42	9,368,171	117

Source: Adapted from various media articles.

In the Campfire Project, professional hunters will pay as much as $12,000 per trophy to the district, which divides the money amongst individual families, the project management and the community as a whole through investment in services (Table 4.4.11).

Table 4.4.10. *Contribution of Five Species to Total Trophy Fees*

| Year | Species | | | | |
	Elephant	Buffalo	Sable	Kudu	Leopard
1987	19	14	13	11	7
1988	24	12	9	9	10
1989	21	13	11	10	8
1990	23	13	10	9	7

Source: Price Waterhouse, 1992.

Table 4.4.11. *Household Dividends Paid under the Campfire Programme in Mashonaland (1992)*

District	Ward or Village	No. of households	Dividend per household ($)	Date
Guruve	Kanyurira (1)	86	200	1990
	Kanyurira (2)	140	400	1992
	Chisunga	449	150	1992
Hurungwe	Ward Vidco I	198	190	1992
	Vidco III	243	90	1992
	Vidco IV	200	290	1992
	Vidco VI	208	325	1992
	Nyamakate	554	50	1992

Source: Bond, 1993.

For example, Clive Stockhill (a Chiredzi farmer and Safari Operator) and other safari operators charge hunters who come in search of bull elephants around US$1,000 a day and an additional US$7,500 trophy fee for the elephant itself. The Campfire concept thus promotes the idea that the elephant is worth Z$65,000 to the community, and that allocating land and other resources towards the maintenance of such animals is worth their while (Interview with Stockhill, 1996). The overall income and expenditures of Campfire (Table 4.4.12) show that the communities get about 47 per cent of these incomes. Campfire district earnings increased from Z$648,620 in 1989 to Z$11,508,538 in 1993, with 90 per cent of the earnings being derived from sport hunting, and almost 70 per cent from elephants alone.

In 1989, 35 per cent of all revenue derived went to the district councils for "management", 15 per cent was retained by these local government agencies as levy, while a minimum of 50 per cent was to go back to the wards. In 1992, only 40 per cent of the revenue from wildlife on communal lands reached the people who bear the costs of living with wildlife, though in 1994, 65 per cent was then being expected to go back to the producer communities. The new goal is to return at least 80 per cent of resource revenues to the producer communities.

Table 4.4.12, *Sources and Allocation of Wildlife Revenues under Zimbabwe's Campfire Programme (1989–1992)*

Category	Absolute Revenue (in 000' Z$)	% of Total Income
Total income	11,509	100
Sport Hunting	10,307	90
Tourism	164	1
Problem Animals	244	2
Hides and Ivory	–	–
Other Revenues	740	7
Allocation		
District Councils	1,339	12
Wildlife Management	2,533	22
Local Population	5,460	47
Other	298	3
Unallocated	1,772	15

Source: Arntzen 1994, from Bond, 1993.

The latest data suggests that up to 60 per cent of the revenue is today reaching the community directly. Although low, these types of incomes have, indeed, provided the incentive for small farmers to engage in formal commercial wildlife management. In all of Zimbabwe's provinces, there is at least one Campfire project, while the outlying provinces in N.R. IV and V tend to have about four or more Campfire projects each. There are at least 25 Campfire projects in various districts throughout Zimbabwe's Communal Areas (Annex 4.4.6), while new projects continue to be initiated. The outlying districts of the Mashonaland provinces in N.R. III and IV have among them at least nine Campfire projects each in one district.

In essence, therefore, while less than 10 per cent of the Communal Areas land has been allocated to commercial wildlife management, and is, thus, not available for mixed farming or livestock rearing, there is an increasing trend of land use conversion in Communal Areas (Annex 4.3.6). However, the economic returns to and specific land use productivity of Campfire are, however, a contested policy terrain. Data on a range of Campfire projects indicate that in some districts, large areas are now devoted to Campfire while less than 5,000 families are direct beneficiaries even in the largest schemes. Thus, for instance, in Nyaminyami,on average each family has foregone some hectares of land for wildlife land use as opposed to cattle or mixed farming and realised about Z$533 in 1991 (Table 4.4.13). In 1996, Mola A and B wards got an average of $1,000.00 per family, whilst Negande, Musambakaruma etc. got an average of $100.00 from wildlife proceeds.

Table 4.4.13. *The Economics of Campfire: 1991 District Performance*

District/no. of Campfire wards	Size of district (ha)	Campfire pop. (0,000)	H/holds no.	Value of 1992 quota (Z$)	1991 net surplus (Z$)
Nyaminyami (12)	363,000	40,0	5,000	1,645,688	266,212
Guruve	415,700	24,6	3,100	1,257,940	380,117
Binga (11)	225,734	37,0	4,900	935,625	367,219
Gokwe (9)	–	66,48	8,300	399,988	305,573
Hwange (7)	–	28,5	3,800	232,000	63,187
Tsholotsho (7)	–	30,0	3,700	790,663	339,940
Bulalima Mangwe	–	30,0	4,000	260,000	218,150
Beitbridge	–	40,0	5,000	–	102,000
Gaza Khomanani	–	–	–	771,125	292,000
Gazaland (1)	21,000	2,4	391	214,675	65,528
Muzarabani (10)	277,400	24,0	3,000	110,080	22,375
Hurungwe (5)	40,000	–	–	539,375	217,000

Source: Child, 1991.

These data suggest that although more cash is immediately being realised, the combined incomes of the Campfire project and other agricultural activities are still below Zimbabwe's rural poverty datum line of Z$ 1,058.00 for seven people in a household and below the average earnings of (Z$1,500) of "capable" Communal Area families with access to good arable land in other Mashonaland areas not far from Nyaminyami. This pattern begs the question whether resettling some of these families onto underutilized prime LSCF lands within Mashonaland would not yield better net results for them and Mashonaland West.

Some of the key problems also associated with Communal Area wildlife projects through Campfire are that external NGO advisers dominate the programme while locals are not trained in management, marketing and "professional" hunting. Most important the among local criticism that have been made is that donor funds for the projects are being diverted to Rural District Councils whose expenditures do not directly benefit communities (various interviews).

Another critical land use policy arena which is contested in Campfire projects is the manner in which the GoZ (DNPWM) regulates the quotas of animals permissible in such projects and allocates the trophies which can be hunted. These are normally determined in terms of the land carrying capacity and sustainable rates of off-take through hunting combined in an overall sense with the culling programmes and the rates of animal losses from crises such as droughts. Given that there are limits to the demand for sport hunting vis-à-vis the supply of trophies, there is growing competition over the allocation of hunting quotas among various wildlife land use sub-sectors and individual operators. The value of elephant trophies is relatively evenly spread among the sub-sectors, but it is not clear whether this represents an equitable and "efficient" pattern of allocation of the "rights" to exploit such trophies.

4.4.5 Wildlife Markets and Export Trends

A critical trend associated with the shift in land use towards wildlife, and indeed one of the driving forces of this, is the evolving nature of the wildlife markets beyond the basic tourist markets discussed above. This evolution became noticeable from the mid-1980s. A key finding is that the range of wildlife products or by-products being traded, the kind of domestic and external markets that are served, and the forms or procedures of marketing products have increased quantitatively, changed qualitatively and become more complex.

In this context, one of the fastest growing and most controversial aspects of wildlife markets is the sale of "live" animals domestically and abroad. The essential problem here is that there is contestation of the "ownership" of wildlife between the state (treated as public ownership), the local indigenous communities (especially in Communal Areas or the community as such), and private land owners who have a natural stock of wildlife on their properties. The latter have procured these through various mechanisms such as purchase and legal public transference of animals onto their property for safe-keeping or sustainable management, as well as through the "illegal" or "informal" activity of "enclosing" wildlife onto their properties.

In Zimbabwe, it is only since the mid-1980s that the notion of and problem over "owning" wildlife has emerged because wildlife export and tourist markets have grown. For, legally speaking, rights over wildlife have tended to be limited to their controlled ("sustainable") exploitation, such that even the so-called "sale" of animals by the state to private landowners or sales among the latter are intended to transfer a limited right over the animal to the land user. The privatisation of "common property" has been occurring without policy consensus over the rights of the majority over wildlife resources (see Chapter Five).

The domestic meat economy has been thriving in urban areas since the 1980s in higher class restaurants. While this cannot be said of the rural formal meat market, there is widespread "unrecorded" consumption of large populations of impala, kudu and eland which provide important sources of protein to the rural people. Formal urban meat sales among the poor tend to be lower than the potential because of the constraints set by the veterinary and health department regulations and local cultural considerations. Meat sold for human consumption must be inspected by the Meat Hygiene Department and by-laws in various urban areas may require an additional inspection before the meat enters into urban butcheries. While this constraint is common in township butcheries, the higher class restaurants can afford these "transaction" costs. This unrealised potential market, thus, essentially affects low income working families who can barely afford game meat prices in distant supermarkets, let alone in restaurants. Cultural factors such as the respect of totems also inhibits the widespread consumption of game meat (consumption of a "totem" species is "forbidden") among the working class indigenous population. These totems are mainly nature-based and are a product of indigenous systems of sustainable management of natural resources (Matowanyika, 1991).

The sale of live animals in Zimbabwe really took off from September 1990 through wildlife auctions which grew from a handful to 11 auctions throughout the country (Price Waterhouse, 1992). There are two methods of live animals sales: by video or by the auction of penned animals. Buyers appear to favour the sale of penned animals because they can inspect the animals personally (FAO, 1991) whilst the video sales require later capture and can entail losses of animals before delivery or exchange of animals at delivery. The number of animal sales increased from almost zero sales in the early 1980s to over 2,469 animals sold at a value of Z$6 millions (US$2 millions) in the 1990s.

Table 4.4.14. *Live Animal Sale Prices in 1991 Compared With Those Achieved in 1990 for Triangle/WMS Auctions (Z$)*

Species	1991 Prices	1990 Prices	1990 Prices as % of 1991
Bushbuck	2,090	1,179	56
Eland	4,110	1,736	42
Giraffe	10,500	6,798	65
Impala	558	288	52
Sable	5,125	6,870	134
Waterbuck	6,679	3,406	51
Wildebeest	965	525	54
Zebra	3,136	1,631	52

Source: Price Waterhouse, 1992.

By 1991, only a small number of large animals (elephants and hippos) were being sold compared to the medium (giraffes, zebra, tsessebe, impala and eland) and smaller-sized animals. Individual prices realised showed a dramatic jump between 1990 and 1991 (Table 4.4.14) following the devaluation of the Zimbabwe dollar, although this rate of prices growth for animals was not sustained in the following years mainly because the high prices were a function of the novelty of the sales and the desire of some farmers to purchase game irrespective of cost (FAO, 1991). Prices of live animals are affected by the cost of production or capture. Most of the current capture techniques require the use of a helicopter to drive the animals into a net or boma. The current cost of hiring a helicopter is R660 per hour and the cost of capture will mainly determine the reserve price of the animals on sale. The viability of the market for live animal sales seems to be based on the development of new technologies which reduce capture costs.

However, the data also shows that "underground" forms of ivory production and, thus, sales which the state managed to monitor, have always been substantial, ranging in various years from 2 per cent to 14 per cent of the total output. The large volume of sales in 1986, however, reflects ivory accumulated over the preceding years since 1981/82. Furthermore, the "nuisance value" of elephants, especially in destroying the crops, property and ecology of peoples within Communal Areas, is reflected in how the Problem Animal Control (PAC) source has each year contributed between 10 per cent to 45 per cent of the ivory put up for sale.

The marketing of sport hunting rights by the state (Parks) and small farmers (Communal Areas) is varied and complex and has also undergone qualitative change during the 1990s as competition for such rights and for licenced hunting operators has grown. The diverse marketing practices range from systems of tender, lottery, auction, fixed price contracts and fixed allocation of hunting rights. The Communal Areas have mainly used the tender system in recent years to improve their prices following the earlier emphasis placed on contracts based on the allocation of fixed hunting rights to particular operators. But most such tenders have had to be renegotiated with external (GoZ, NGO etc.) "technical" support, as there has been a tendency for the prices and terms of trophies sold to operators to be under-valued. In Mashonaland, Campfire also negotiated some forms of "joint ventures" with private operators who play a broad resource management role. Most contracts are fixed over three years such that land use and income determination tends to be fixed and ceded to hunting operators.

The sale of ivory is based on a variety of sources including the culling of elephants, the elimination of problem elephants which maraud people's habitats, natural deaths and "poached" elephants. Thus, various GoZ offices collect and transmit ivory for sale. Other indirect sources of ivory are district councils and the Department of Tsetse Fly Control. Communal Area ivory is recorded separately from National Parks ivory so that the district councils which have "Appropriate Authority" status can collect such revenue and spend it. This status entitles them to directly receive revenues arising from ivory produced in the communal lands.

The patterns of ivory "production" from 1985 to 1991 are shown in Table 4.4.15. We can see that ivory production and sales in general declined from 1985 to 1991 because of the international ban on its trade and the reduction of culling and poaching, while the growth in natural production is identified with the effects of droughts on increased animal loss. Thus, ivory as an additional source of revenue to the state, LSCF and smallholders, and which complements other tourist sources of wildlife revenue has diminished, with at least Z$3 million being lost because of this each year.

Table 4.4.15. *Ivory Production 1985 to 1991 (Kgs)*

Year			Source of Ivory		
	Culled	PAC	Natural	Poached	Total
1985	17,962.20	2,225.0	672.60	683.5	22,668.8
1986	11,660.25	2,873.25	1,010.75	346.0	16,738.75
1987	6,822.25	3,235.55	2,467.30	681.0	13,739.15
1988	5,586.50	3,143.25	2,043.00	365.25	11,859.00
1989	672.75	1,993.8	2,474.51	408.25	5,969.16
1990	223.50	2,701.1	1,677.15	820.35	5,957.55
1991	312.75	2,324.0	4,502.45	665.75	7,690.00

Source: Murphree, 1992.

These patterns of trophy sales, especially the fixed contracts, raise questions about the actual form of land use control that Campfire and state parks wildlife hunting is propagating. To what extent are the private operators, through their marketing of hunts or tours and their supervision of these activities, actually the key decision-makers on the structure of wildlife resources kept in the different land tenure regimes, and on the distribution of financial benefits among various players: the state, communal people, international tour firms and local tourist operators?

Live Animal Exports

Live animal exports, especially of large and prized ones, have been limited in the last three years because of a growing consensus both within the government and the private sector that exports be restricted so as to maintain Zimbabwe's competitive edge over neighbouring countries in the quality of hunting offered. Thus, export sales have been constrained through the small number of licences provided to game capture firms in the country. However, when exports have been undertaken, the prices were higher than domestic prices. The Republic of South Africa appears to be the largest potential market for live animals and game meat, although the latter market is limited to preserved and processed biltong. In 1993, Zimbabwe exported 940 wild animals worth over $5.5 million to South Africa, Namibia, Botswana and Zambia. The exports included 232 sables and 20 tsessebes and elands. The highest price fetched for a sable, for instance, was $22,000 while the average price was $17,000. Prices for elands averaged $2,750 and for tsessebe $2,400. In 1994, export quotas had been set for middle sized animals (Table 4.4.16) through the Wildlife Producers Association (WPA), although the 1992 drought had restricted the country's capacity to meet that quota.

Table 4.4.16. *The WPA Quota for 1994*

Specie	Number	% Stock
Sables	300	15.0
Tsessebes	240	12.0
Elands	400	20.0
Giraffes	100	5.0
Zebras	300	15.0
Reedbucks	170	9.0
Kudu	500	25.0
Total	2, 010	100.0

Source: DNPWLM, 1994.

Some wildlife farmers sell their excess animals at wildlife auctions that have attracted European and America buyers. For instance, at an auction on the Gronvlei Farm in Doma in 1994, sables were sold at Z$8,870.00, waterbucks (a highly protected species) at Z$8,800, and elands at Z$3,920 (*Sunday Mail*, 16/10/94). These auctions have also served to popularise wildlife ranching. Over 500 international buyers participated in the Department of National Parks and Wildlife Management's Zambezi Valley Hunting Camps auction in February 1996. One buyer at the auction paid $170,000 (Table 4.3.17) for an elephant bull with a reserve price of $50,000. Buyers were drawn from all over the world with the majority coming from South Africa, England, United States, Germany, Australia, Switzerland and India.

Table 4.4.17. *Department of National Parks' 1996 Zambezi Valley Hunting Camps Auction*

Specie Sold	Highest Price (Z$)	Lowest Price (Z$)
Elephant	170,000	160,000
Hippo	16,000	10,000
Leopard	37,000	25,000
Zebra	8,000	5,000
Crocodile	17,000	11,000
Bushpig	900	500
Warthog	2,900	1,400
Kudu	4,800	3,000
Waterbuck	1,600	1,200
Impala	400	300
Bushbuck	4,600	4,400

Source: Compiled from *The Farmer Magazine*, 22/2/96, Vol. 66, No. 6.

In terms of hunting exports, a few countries, including the USA and some European ones, account for 80 per cent of the elephant trophies shot annually in Zimbabwe. Even the small farmers have become a major export arena for trophies. In the Nyaminyami District, for instance, 38 per cent of the trophies went to Spain while the US accounted for 29 per cent in 1991 (Table 4.4.18). Another significant policy and international market problem which has emerged from this growth in wildlife markets is the manner in which multilateral conventions (e.g. Cites) and the laws of major export market countries emphasize the importance of external forces in conditioning national land use change processes.

Table 4.4.18. *Number and Value of Trophies by Nationality of Sport Hunters in Nyaminyami District*

Country	No. of Trophies	Percentage	Value of Trophies (Z$)
Austria	25	5	21,710
France	31	7	23,120
Germany	46	10	53,973
Namibia/RSA	30	7	53,610
Spain	179	38	210,128
USA	136	29	189,358
Others	18	4	28,225
Total	465	100	574,146

NB: The data is for three safari operators.
Source: Anonymous (undated).

For example, more than 80 per cent of the species listed by the US Endangered Species Act are foreign: they are found in Africa, Asia and other continents.

> Most of the elephants, which include Southern Africa's over-populated elephants ... found their way on to that list without proper consultation with host countries or adequate research to show that such species were endangered in the first place (Campfire Deputy Director, Interview; *Sunday Mail*, 15/10/95).

Thus, internal and foreign lobbying for the further liberalisation of wildlife markets has become a growing industry in itself, especially among NGOs. As some of their representatives see it:

> The Endangered Species Act, as currently written and enforced, discourages and sometimes prevents foreign countries from implementing the most appropriate measures for their human and wildlife populations to thrive in tandem (ibid).

> For developing countries to lift their citizens out of poverty while maintaining native wildlife species, well regulated and profitable tourist hunting programs are of utmost importance (Congress and Sportsmen Foundation of US, one of the organisations supporting developing countries), (*Sunday Mail*, 15/10/95).

In these debates, the evidence shows that conflicting wildlife data sources and interpretations have become an important site of contestation. For example, the Minister of Environment recently dismissed as misleading, a report by the Wildlife Society of Zimbabwe (an NGO) that there are 17,000 elephants in Hwange National Park since the government's count was over 30,000 and the official level of recommended population is 15,000.

> The society's report is a typical case of misleading information. Actually there is conflict among conservationists. Some want us to say there are many elephants so that we agree to their demands to sell some, while others are saying elephants are few so that we will not sell (Minister Chen Chimutengwende, *Herald*, 4/11/95).

Moreover, there are different opinions on how effective GoZ wildlife management is, as acrimony over recent reports of the death of 17 elephants in Hwange National Park due to lack of water has shown. The underground nature of some of the markets and allegations of increasing corruption in the wildlife industry, indicate that wildlife product markets are extremely volatile.

For instance, it is reported that the government lost more than $3.7 million through the illegal export and translocation of more than 900 elephants and other animals in the Gonarezhou National Park during and after the great drought of 1992. A report by the Comptroller and Auditor General detailed cases in which officers in Parks and private organisations exported the recently locally translocated or culled elephants without authority from Government and in flagrant violation of Treasury rules (GoZ, 1996). The report strongly criticised the suspended Director of Parks (Dr. Nduku) and called on the Department to recover the full export value for 200 elephants exported by Wildlife Management Services, a private firm controlled by Dr. Nduku, as the illegal action cost the government Z$2 millions in export earnings.

The report also recommended Parks to recover park fees in respect of 255 elephants and other animals captured and translocated to neighbouring LSCF conservancies in 1992. Each recipient had signed an agreement which required that recipients pay park fees in addition to capture and translocation costs payable to Wildlife Management Services (WMS). National Parks was supposed to recover Z$78,000, being the total value of 6 elephants captured and auctioned by WMS and a further Z$811,800, being the market value of 451 elephants captured and translocated to neighbouring LSCF conservancies and farms in 1993. Thus, the state is alleged to be subsidising wildlife markets for the private gain of a few. This queries the overall efficiency of this land use at the national and social level. As the politics of this sector shows, wildlife markets are indeed hotly contested.

4.5 Intensive Wildlife Land Use: Ostrich Husbandry

4.5.1 Expansion of Ostrich Land Use Pattern

The development of the Zimbabwean ostrich industry predates direct settler rule. Indeed, it goes back to the mercantile era when the export of ostrich feathers began in the late 1800s and domesticated flocks were being reared both in Northern and Southern Africa only for the harvesting of feathers. The indigenous birds of both Southern and Northern Africa were cross-bred to achieve the ultimate feather producing bird. Fashion businesses world-wide supported the ostrich industry for over 50 years primarily based on the feather trade alone, while prior to the first world war, ostrich feathers were recorded as the fourth most valued traded commodity in Southern Africa after gold, diamonds and wool. Thus, ostrich and related wildlife land use (ivory from elephants) are not actually new, as they were a key element among the factors which attracted settlers to the region in the first place. This type of land use was to lead not so long after to land alienation, as well as to the wanton decimation of much of the country's wildlife which was considered at the time to be vermin (Machingaidze, 1980).

The export of ostrich leather represents the second stage in the development of the industry. This leather is currently one of the most exclusive leathers in the world. The third stage in the development of the ostrich industry, which represents its most widespread growth, is the present one that is dominated by the ostrich meat trade. Although it is true that the meat has been utilised for many years in Africa, its unique low cholesterol qualities toghether with its leather and feather potential, has recently formed the basis of the phenomenal international demand for breeding stock, thus setting in motion the boom in the ostrich industry.

During the early 1900s, the ostrich population in Zimbabwe declined due to its over-exploitation through hunting and other land use conversions such as the fencing of veld for cattle. Currently, the largest concentration of ostriches in the country is in Hwange National Park. Ostrich populations also occur naturally in small numbers in places such as Tuli Safari Area, Matetsi Safari Area and Gonarezhou National Park. Some small natural populations have been introduced into the Lake Kyle, Mushandike, Nyamaneche and Macilwaine National Parks areas. Ostriches also occur naturally outside the Parks and Wildlife estates in places such as the Matibi II and Diti communal lands, and on some resettlement areas in the Matabeleland and Midlands provinces.

Ostrich land use is a less land consuming endeavour than wildlife in general, as well as in comparison to the allocation of prime arable areas to cattle production. On one hectare, for instance, it is recommended by experts that three hen and two cock ostriches can be intensively (high feeding) produced, and this requires a financial investment of at least Z$75,000 leading to a gross income of at least 5 times the investment per hectare in 1995 prices.

Thus, all the land users in Zimbabwe, including those in the LSCF sector, individual land holders, groups of smallholders, state agencies, local councils and central GoZ parastatals such as ADA, and the Forestry Commission which has large estates, have been rapidly involved in allocating land to ostrich production during the last decade. In actual practice, it is rare to find ostrich enterprises on individual farms, estates or community projects which occupy more than 100 hectares, although a few large LSCF firms are reported to exceed this. The minimum size allocated tends to be about one hectare for those who only sell the eggs or have intensive feeders, given the management requirements of the various stages of ostrich production.

We found that because of the areal "scale neutrality" of ostrich production and higher financial returns per unit of land and money in all the dryland farming zones of Zimbabwe, and the ecological advantages of its production when appropriately stocked (1 large bird-grower to one hectare) (see Annex 4.5.1), the promotion of this land use to achieve sustainable development has become a common clarion call among varied types of development agencies, producer interest groups, experts and politicians. But given the low level of savings and access to credit, the financial investment required for even one hectare is beyond the majority in Communal Areas in the absence of subsidies.

When ostriches are slaughtered for meat, their sizes range around 100 to 110 kgs of meat after 8 months, and they yield about 12–15 square feet of leather per bird, which costs about US$39 per square foot of finished skin and about US$125 per square foot of manufactured hide. However, an ostrich has a lifespan of 20 years and the meat which can be produced per breeding hen amounts to 1.8 tonnes per annum, at a high rate of bird survivability of approximately 95 per cent.

4.4.2 LSCF Ostrich Land Use

In Zimbabwe, it is estimated that there are about 300 LSCF producers of ostrich birds who are predominantly in the white farming community, although their production is slowly penetrating the black commercial farming community in the LSCF, the small scale commercial farming sectors (SSCF) and, in exceptional circumstances, the Communal Areas. The national ostrich flock is estimated to be between 12,000–15,000 which experts say is decreasing owing to slaughter, high mortality rates and live bird exports. Of these, over 90 per cent are held between state and LSCF large-scale land owners.

The land intensive management of the ostrich industry in Zimbabwe, which started around 1985 with 30 LSCF producers and with 100 birds, has been expanding rapidly in the 1990s. The major ostrich LSCF producers are located in Mashonaland East, West, and Central provinces in the areas of Mvurwi, Concession and Karoi, and in the Midlands and Matabeleland provinces. Other important producers are also located in Masvingo province around Chiredzi.

The government which recognises the potential of the ostrich industry to earn foreign exchange through meat, skins and feathers, promotes the development of ostrich farming in Zimbabwe and seeks to use this development to increase wild ostrich populations. It has focused its attention on the conservation of wild ostrich populations with the long-term plan of preserving genetic diversity and benefiting the industry. The Department of National Parks, through the recommendation of TOPAZ, has re-instituted the ban on the export of live birds which it had previously lifted, in order to increase the availability of breeding stock for farmers intending to diversify into ostrich production.

Innovators of ostrich production include the Lonrho-owned Savanna Estates, a transnational corporation which, in 1985, supplied the early farmers: (*Herald*, 14/02/93). Zimbabwe's industry is minute compared with the industry world-wide: the world ostrich population is between 700,000 and 1,000,000 birds (*Herald*, June 1996) and Zimbabwe has only three per cent of these. As observed by on farmer:

> The world market is much bigger than what Zimbabwe is ever going to supply. We just have to expand from here (Cunningham, BOP Chairman, as quoted in *The Farmer*, 13/06/96).

The LSCF interest in ostrich production has become so over-zealous that, for example, the Bulawayo Ostriches Producers (BOP) agency which represents dry land LSCF farmers has, in times of capital shortages, tended to strongly support live bird exports so as to inject much needed capital into the industry. "The ostrich industry worldwide is expanding tremendously fast and here we are actually going much slower—in terms of our growth—than the rest of the world. The main constraint we are facing is a lack of capital. The industry is very capital oriented and intensive. We see exports as a way of introducing that capital and allowing our production to grow. As a result we support it..." (ibid).

Because neighbouring South Africa exports between 3–14 tonnes of meat a day while Zimbabwe exports 78 live birds (equivalent of 1.2 tonnes of meat), ostrich producers feel they are underachievers:

> Our industry is exporting one plane load every three weeks at the moment and the detraction of 1.4 tonnes from our exports, compared to other exports of 14 tonnes per day is not going to take away our market share .... What we need are time and money to develop the infrastructure so that the industry becomes viable. Exports will provide that money needed for the long term survival of the industry and its producers, (ibid).

The urgency to expand ostrich production has, thus, been expressed in terms of fears of global competition since it is also believed that soon, when the Far East begins to slaughter its birds, the Zimbabwe ostrich industry and BOP as a company will have to depend on the increased numbers of birds to compensate for the drop in profit margins because of more meat on the market:

> With an industry siting at between 30–40,000 birds, we are not going to be a player. We need to build the Zimbabwe industry to 100–150,000 birds slaughtered per year at least, to be something of a player on the world market. (*The Farmer*, 13/06/96.)

As a result of an organised effort to expand LSCF ostrich production, the number of ostrich producers increased by 25 per cent and in 1993 (Table 4.5.1), it was expected that more than 40,000 ostriches would be provided in a period of five years. In December 1993, there were over 200 commercial ostrich producers with over 10,500 birds and the population was expected to earn $160 million a year within five years of which 75 per cent would be in foreign currency (*Herald* 28/12/93) (Table 4.4.2).

Ostrich meat which was only introduced in late 1992, has quickly found its way into the country's hotels and restaurants:

> Ostrich meat is the latest food here, tourists try it because they think its African while Zimbabweans want to try something new (Monomotapa Hotel's Assistant Food and Beverage Manager, Elizabeth Wells).

Monomotapa Hotel started serving ostrich menus at three of its restaurants and bought 45 kg of ostrich meat a week. COPRO has sold 3.5 tonnes of ostrich meat a week in Zimbabwe and was planning to export. The country, however, faces stiff competition from South Africa which produces 90 per cent of ostrich products and controls the already established markets.

Table 4.5.1. *Ostrich Stock for a Selected Number of Years*

Year	No. of Birds	No. of LSCF Producers
1980	47	1
1985	100	30
1989	1,500	85
1993	10,500	200
1994	20,000	230

Source: Compiled from *Herald*, 28/12/93, *Herald*, 23/07/94, *Herald*, 14/02/93, *Herald* 04/08/94.

A co-operative in Insiza in Matabeleland South has successfully launched an ostrich rearing project which started by collecting ostrich eggs in a nearby veld and selling them to commercial farmers. Each egg fetched $25 and they raised $40,000 which they used to launch the co-operative. They later collected 42 eggs which they took to the farmer for incubation and when hatched these formed their breeding stock (*Herald*, 05/06/94).

Marketing Ostriches

As a result of these growth trends, the export of ostriches has become increasingly more organised, grown in scale and become more diverse in market determinations (Tables 4.5.2 and 4.5.3). But in 1994, changes had occurred in the marketing of the birds in Europe where exported ostriches were being auctioned because the ostrich trade had attracted many dealers who added their mark-up, making birds extremely expensive for genuine farmers (*Herald*, 16/02/94).

Table 4.5.2. *Actual Export Earnings*

Time/Year	Income realised (Z$)	No. of farmers exporting	Destination	Source
1993	$15.4 million	–	United Kingdom, Netherlands	Sale of 896 birds and 350 eggs
By Feb. 1994 (total exports so far)	$29 million	–	United States	Export of 1,854 birds and 614 eggs
May 1994	$500,000	2*	Austria	18 large adult ostriches and 28 young ones
May 1994	$4 million	30	United Kingdom	176 birds
July 1994	$200,000	7	China	91 two-year old ostriches
July 1994 (were in quarantine)	–	–	Thailand, United States	100 young birds, 350 eggs
October 1994 (total export so far)	$58 million	–	United States, China	Export of 6,375 eggs, 3,587 birds
March 1994	$6 million	15	Italy	Export of 232 birds
January 1995–April 1995	$55 million	–	China, United States	Over 2,000 birds, 400 skins & 900 eggs
January 1996	–	–	China	Export of 78 live ostriches

*1 in Kadoma, 1 in Chinhoyi.

– Indicates that no data was available at the time of the research

NB: Most of the exports in 1994 were single deals at the pick of the ostrich industry in Zimbabwe.

Source: *Herald*, 28/12/93; 26/05/94; 07/07/94; 01/10/94; 17/05/95; 03/08/95; 05/01/96; 09/05/94.

COPRO believes that the Far East has potentially lucrative markets for live birds and meat because of its requirement for high intensive production of meat per unit area. Countries like Thailand and Malaysia, have in fact, shown interest in ostriches and in July 1994, about 100 young birds were under quarantine prior to be exported to Thailand (*Herald*, 07/07/94). Copro, as the marketing company of TOPAZ, had in a period of about 15 months, supervised and facilitated the slaughter of 800 birds and developed a local market to cater for a weekly supply of 3.5 tonnes of meat, compared to 1992 when Copro was slaughtering more than 30 ostriches a week for the domestic market. The co-operative has since embarked upon a huge campaign to inform consumers of the merits of ostrich meat. As a result, ostrich meat has expanded its market into the country's hotels.

However, Zimbabwe's ostrich market is also threatened by pressure groups in Europe which are trying to press for the inclusion of the ostrich in the Convention of Trade in Endangered Species (Cites, Appendix II) which restricts the sale of all animals considered endangered and their products (Source: *Herald*, 13/03/93).

Table 4.5.3. *Expected Income by TOPAZ Breeders*

Year/Time	Expected income (Z$)	Destination	Source
1992	$9 million	UK, China	Slaughter of 3,000 ostriches
1993	$24.7 million	USA, UK	Export of live birds and eggs
Dec. 1993 (1 month)	$9.3 million	Netherlands, UK	Sale of 532 eggs and 670 birds
1994	$100 million	USA, China, Malaysia	Export of ostrich products
1995	$155 million	USA, UK, Thailand	Export of ostrich products

Source: *Herald*, 06/08/92; 28/12/93; 16/02/94; 03/08/95.

4.5.3 Small Farmer Ostrich Land Use

The small farmer production of ostriches has grown quite gradually. In Mashonaland province, we identified less than 20 ostrich producers in the form of NGO-led community groups, individuals and local council projects (Table 4.5.4). By and large, the LSCF breeder supplies small farmers with the stock for start-up as well as the markets, while some assistance is sought from NGOs and newly formed small ostrich producer associations. Some of the interesting smallholder ostrich projects studied were at their early stages. At the individual farmer level, it is mostly SSCF medium scale farmers who are involved in production on extremely small areas of around 1 hectare (see Table 4.5.6). The individual ostrich land users tend to be in clusters of contiguous farms in given localities where particular agencies have promoted the activity.

NGOs such as Africa 2000, funded by international environmental programmes (UNDP) assist projects such as the Musengezi Ostrich Producers Syndicate by meeting the costs of purchasing the birds for the farmers in the project and buying equipment such as hatchers and incubators. Two farmers, namely John Waterfield and Phillip Rowe, who are fully fledged commercial ostrich producers, are providing subsidized birds at $3,000.00 per ostrich hen and $4,000.00 per ostrich cock.

SHOC, which was basically a one man institution, is also working towards promoting ostrich farming in the small-scale and communal farmers sector through the Rural Ostrich Development Programme financed by the Rural Ostrich Finance Scheme which is administered by the Agricultural Finance Corporation (AFC). The funds available for the scheme are in the form of a grant sourced from the French Embassy as counterpart funds through the Ministry of Finance. The loan amount is used for lending to the farmer, for the procurement of ostriches, equipment and accessories at a 15 per cent interest rate.

Table 4.5.4. *Project by Sponsor and Supporting Agencies*

Project	Source of Birds	Source of project funding	Other Agencies Involved
Chesa Nyajinje	Philip & Wakefield of Cowbird and Big Bird Zimbabwe	Africa 2000, UNDP	Dept. of Natural Resources
Musengezi Syndicate	Philip & Wakefield of Cowird and Big Bird Zimbabwe	Africa 2000, UNDP	Dept. of Natural Resources
Domboshava Training Centre	Philip & Wakefield of Cowbird and Big Bird Zimbabwe	Africa 2000, UNDP	Dept. of Natural Resources
Mhondoro (Proposed)	Philip & Wakefield of Cowbird and Big Bird Zimbabwe	Africa 2000, UNDP	Dept. of Natural Resources
Mudzi	Crundall and Inyati Estate	DNR	–

Ostrich production in Mashonaland provinces is largely intensive ostrich production where the birds are all kept in paddocks. This has meant that there is no significant loss of land from other agricultural uses to ostrich production. In specific ostrich projects like Mutoko Ostrich Producers Syndicate, Chesa Nyajenje Ostrich Producers Syndicate and Musengezi Ostrich Producers Syndicate, ostrich production is under intensive management and ostrich paddocks are more or less of standard size: 1.0 ha per five birds. The areas under ostrich production per individual farmer are all below 1 per cent of the individual farm area (Annex 4.5.2).

Ostrich production is seen as beneficial in terms not only of export realisations but also of more efficient land use productivity, improved environment management, increased employment opportunities and income generated, and improved nutritional standards in the country. For instance, ostrich land use efficiencies are said to be superior in terms of financial returns compared to beef (Chiromo, 1995).

The development of the smallholder ostrich industry has largely taken the form of project specific syndicates. This has beneftted farmers in that there is communal sharing of plant and equipment such as hatchers and incubators which would have been donated by various institutions. A good example is the Musengezi Ostrich Syndicate which sourced donor funds for a hatcher. All farmers who belong to the syndicate collect eggs on a weekly basis and ferry them to the nearby fellow-member's farm where there is electricity and where the hatcher is situated. For the Chesa Project, the farmers are utilizing the hatcher and incubator facilities of Mr. John Waterfield and Phillip Rowe in the Concession ICA (Annex 4.5.3.). However, the farmers can only utilise the facilities if they are not competing with the owners' requirements. Nevertheless, such kinds of contractual agreements are benefiting the industry, especially in the early stages of production when the farmers do not have enough capital to buy their own equipment. (See also the Mudzi Ostrich Case, Annex 4.5.4.)

Table 4.5.5. *Distribution of Ostrich Projects*

Project	Location	No. of farmers	Birds per farmer	Total birds in projcet	Year	Sponsor/ Agency
Chesa Nyajenje Ostrich Project	Mt. Darwin District, Mash-Central, Chesa SSCF	11	5	55	1993	DNR
Musengezi Ostrich Syndicate	Zvimba Rural District Mash-West, Musengezi SSCF	15	5	55	1995	ZOPA
Makumbirofa Project	Chirau Communal Lands	–	–	–	–	Individual
Chiwanzamarara Project	Chihota Communal Lands	–	12	–	–	Individual
Mhondoro (proposed)	Mhondoro-Ngezi Communal Lands, Kadoma Rural District, Mash-West	–	–	–	–	DNR
Mudzi Ostrich Project	Mudzi Rural District, Mash-East	–	–	33	1990	DNR
Domboshawa Training Centre	Goromonzi Mash-East	–	–	–	–	Ministry of local gov.
Mutoko Ostrich Syndicate (proposed)	Mutoko Rural District Mash-East	11	(5)	(55)	1995	Africa 2000

– Indicates that no data was available at the time of the research.

4.5.4 Overall Conclusions on Ostrich Land Use

Ostrich land use is considered by the GoZ and others to promise growing employment benefits as many of its activities are more labour intensive than wildlife and cattle ranching, and may compete well with the extensive cropping patterns of Communal Areas (Table 4.5.6). But the available evidence on this is as yet inadequate for us to conclude that this is really the case when compared with the back-breaking labour requirements of mixed farming and the wider social reproduction activities of Communal Area families.

Table 4.5.6. *Expected Employment from Ostrich Work*

Activity	No. of workers per activity	Total no. of jobs Per 800 units
Feeding and caring of mature ostriches	1 per 2 units	400
Incubation process	4 per 2 units	1,600
Chick-rearing and care	2 per 2 units	400
Paddock fence erection	8 per 2 units	3,200
Feed delivery	3 per lorry (10 tons)	240
Abattoirs	6 per 2 units	2,400
Ostrich health care	4 per 20 units	+160

Source: DNR, 1995.

Ostriches, however, tend to have the negative impact of market instability arising from the introduction of a common poultry disease (Newcastle disease) when not well attended to. For instance, Newcastle broke out in Masvingo in January and June 1994 (Sengwa and Matibi areas) and South Africa was thought to be the source of infection by local veterinary experts. This led Canada, one of the leading importers, to suspend imports of ostrich and poultry products from Zimbabwe. The major previous outbreak lasted for a year from 1985 to 1986, and the disease spread rapidly to all Mashonaland provinces and Manicaland, owing to the lack of awareness about the danger it posed and the alleged spread of the disease from Mozambique. At that time again, all countries importing poultry from Zimbabwe were notified and the European Union suspended planned imports of ostrich products until the disease was brought under control:

> Newcastle disease is a very contagious disease and if it were to spread to mainland Europe, the multi-million dollar EU industry there would be in danger (Leahy, EU Agricultural Advisor, *Herald*, 23/08/94).

Another growing political and economic problem which faces farmers engaged in ostrich production is the monopsonistic structure of its related markets. Ostrich producers complain of too many middlemen and as a result producers are not realising maximum profits on exports (interviews, 1995). It appears that too many middlemen are involved in ostrich exports (Chief Executive of TOPAZ). Indeed, even in the LSCF, the low profit margins realised by some TOPAZ members, reportedly because of middlemen's off-take, were part of the reason for the ungraceful resignation of the organisation's National Chairman, Mr. Hamay Hamilton. As a result, producers seek to improve their profits from exports by marketing their own products, by-passing export companies, and taking advantage of improved communication among producers and with marketing bodies. As noted by a senior TOPAZ official:

> The difficulty we have experienced is that small scale producers haven't been well co-ordinated. They are an unrepresented body and we have dealt with

them in an uninformed and unstructured way" (TOPAZ Chief Executive, Phil Hasen).

There are also allegations that LSCF producers are selling sub-standard or "sick" birds to the small scale producers. A case in point is the Musengezi ostrich producers syndicate which has allegedly been provided with new-castle infected birds (*Herald*, 09/01/96). TOPAZ argues that the allegations of newcastle infested birds being sold to small scale producers passed un-noticed by the association. TOPAZ further argues that if the allegations were to be proved true "on good evidence", that would be contrary to veterinary regulations and the association would support the prosecution of the offender. Indeed, the GoZ Veterinary Department did confirm in its report of July 3 1993, that birds sold to Musengezi small producers by commercial breeders had "traces of antibodies similar to those associated with New-castle, and that the birds were sold to the smallholder producers at a "give away" price of $3,000 instead of $10,000, and that subsequently the birds failed the export test although the smallholders were not told of this prospect in advance" (*Herald*, 19/01/96).

As in the case of the export of other live animal exports in the overall wildlife sector, there is growing conflict over the GoZ live sale of ostriches in society. The contentious issue is whether exporting live birds and eggs for breeding in Europe and North America will not be suicidal in that up-coming ostrich producers in the northern markets may soon pose stiff com-petition to ostrich meat imported from Africa. Since the bird is uniquely African, it is felt that the long term economic interest of African countries is not to help establish overseas ostrich farms by exporting live ostriches and eggs. But the relative returns of live ostriches to slaughtered ones are so un-equal that it has forced a short term view among producer organisations in support of live exports.

COPRO argued, for instance, that in 1993 up to Z$20,000 had been realised on each live bird exported unlike the $2,000 per bird that was fetched locally:

> The export of live birds is so lucrative that as a business-oriented organisation, we cannot overlook it. There has been a policy discrepancy in that during the time the Department of National Parks and Wild Life Management had prohibited the export of live birds, a Canadian with business interests in Zimbabwe had secured a permit to export 400 live birds to Canada and began buying the birds from local producers for export. (*Herald*, 23/11/93).

Other conflicts are also brewing between ostrich producers and market agents over the liability of farmers for birds in quarantine pending export, amid suspicion that birds could be selling at higher prices on the export market than producers were being told. The struggles are now focused on efforts to ensure greater transparency, including the setting and publication of benchmark prices expected by Zimbabwean producers. Income losses and bird quality downgrading which have been experienced during quarantine periods have forced the question of liability into the open, as many producers believe that agents are failing to pass on to the producer the "full benefits" of export markets (*Herald*, 16/02/96).

4.6 Summary of New Land Use Developments

This chapter has examined the evolution of new land uses during the period of Zimbabwe's structural adjustment programme in the 1990s. Several case studies were reviewed to show concrete evidence of the growing trend towards the new land uses. More large than small farmers engage in these new land uses on much larger areas than small farmers, leading to differential benefits among the farmers. Even among blacks, the elite have taken up the new land uses more rapidly. Patterns of land allocations to the new land uses revealed that the estimated number of farmers engaged in the three new land uses in Zimbabwe still remains low relative to those involved in producing other land-based traditional commodities. In general, our best estimate is that about 50 per cent of the LSCF farmers are involved in the new land uses, although this is combined with other land use enterprises. Among Communal Area farmers, the maximum number of households involved in the new land uses would be 100,000 families, which amount to a maximum of about 10 per cent of the Communal Areas (Table 4.5.1). For Communal Areas, the estimates on horticulture exclude the small gardens averaging less than 0.01 hectares in size meant mainly for home consumption, as at least 30 per cent of the 1,000,000 families there have such gardens.

Table 4.6.1. *New Land Uses in 1995/96 (Estimates)*

Land Tenure Regime	Horticulture No. farmers	% Sector	Wildlife No. farmers	%	Ostriches No. farmers	%	Total No. farmers	%
LSCF	1,700	30%	500	15%	300	>%	1,500	50
C. Areas	5,500	>1%	100,000	6%	30	>1%	100,000	10
State Estates (parks)	5	>5%	30	<70%	3	>5%	40	60
Total	6,000		100,000		500		100,000	100

Note: Because of estimates used, the totals are best estimates not necessarily meant as sums. Although Communal Areas have large numbers of participants in horticulture the areas used are small (average below 0.5 ha. each), and the LSCF wildlife areas owned by their 500 players are much larger than the Campfire areas of the 60,000 Communal Area farmers.

Source: Compiled from the various sources used in Chapter Five.

However, the rate of growth in the number of farmers involved and area devoted to these land uses has been rapid and may yet grow even faster if current economic conditions remain or improve. Horticulture has generated

much interest among large numbers of the smallholder and large scale producers in the Mashonaland provinces. However, the ostrich sector still remains depressed in spite of its positive benefits so far. The involvement of
numerous state land managers and others who oversee or gain from the new
land uses, has consolidated the interest and design of policy towards a favourable stance on the use of LSCF and state lands for wildlife, as opposed to its
redistribution. State agencies such as the Forestry Commission and District
Councils involved in wildlife reinforce the land policy orientation towards
export land uses. Thus, the state in collaboration with other actors has
promoted the rapid conversion of Communal Area land into wildlife uses.

NGOs have also been engaged in promoting the new land uses, particularly horticulture production which mainly relies on the local markets,
and smallholder participation in wildlife land uses as witnessed through
their participation in the Campfire programme mainly in the marginal
regions IV and V. However, Communal Areas realise limited benefits
because local authorities are unable to attract professional hunters through
whom the bulk of their revenue is derived and also as the export marketing
systems remain in the hands of the middlemen. The role of middlemen and
commodity sub-contracting was evident mainly in the horticultural sector,
while wildlife middlemen indirectly play a critical role through a system of
support services provision.

The incomes in Zimbabwe dollar terms realised by farmers through the
new land uses have grown during the 1990s, although in US dollar terms,
the growth has not been dramatic. But the new land uses realise more
income than older commodities due to the local wage-depressing effects of
the continued devaluation of the Zimbabwe dollar and inflation. Yet household incomes realised from horticulture are the fastest growing compared to
the Campfire wildlife disbursements among participating households.

Campfire data suggest that although more cash is immediately being
realised, the combined incomes of the Campfire project and other agricultural activities are still below Zimbabwe's rural poverty datum line of
Z$1,058.00 for seven people in a household and below the average earnings
of "capable" Communal Area (Z$1,500.00) families with access to good
arable land in other Mashonaland areas not far from Nyaminyami. This pattern begs the question whether resettling some of these families onto underutilised prime LSCF lands within Mashonaland would not yield better
results for them and Mashonaland West.

Conflicts over the distribution of income shares between Campfire projects and farmers or their households and between horticulture and ostrich
marketing agencies and farmers are an escalating problem. Racial acrimony
over alleged monopolistic and guildist forms of inputs and market control,
as well as over an uneven playing field in the policy and regulatory environment abound. Indigenisation has led to benefits for black elites in, for example, SSCF areas, in resettlement schemes and among those who control

water points in Communal Areas. But the unequal endowments which favour the mainly white LSCF is the main focus of conflicts emerging over the distribution of new land uses. The politics of mediating the uneven growth and distribution of the benefits of new land uses are, thus, the focus of the next chapter.

Chapter Five

Politics and Actors in New Land Struggles

5.1 The Politics of New Land Users

The new political economy of the land question in Zimbabwe is charac-terised by a broadening of increasingly interlinked state and non-state organisations which contest the ownership and use of land and natural resources, and compete over the material input and output markets related to land. These actors, which include state organisations engaged in regu-lating land markets, production processes and commodity markets, vie to structure the meanings and values of land and various land uses in their own images. The actors have evolved new and more complex organisational forms and strategies compared to their pre-ESAP approaches to policy advocacy.

Even the GoZ, in keeping with ESAP policies and trends in the economy, has been reorienting and restructuring its role and organisational strategies in land management and the regulation of related markets. This chapter examines the nature of the key actors engaged in new land uses and their strategic influences on related policies, including land reform policy.

The organisational map of new land use players reflects changing organi-sational responses and strategies with regard to the different ideologies espoused by the actors, emerging political realignments associated with the democratisation processes, and the new material benefits arising from em-erging land uses and related markets during the 1990s. Indeed, the new organisational strategies reflect new forms of external financing (aid, trade related support and lending), new conceptions of "development" based upon market forces, the changing character and capacity of the state at the local and central levels, and the spatial repartitioning of land control and its uses.

Our analysis of the emerging politics and political economy of the land question identifies six interrelated areas and issues which structure and motivate various land managers and players. These can be heuristically cate-gorised as follows:

i)   Spatial restructuring of the land question;
ii) Recolonisation of new land frontiers;
iii) Indigenisation and racial and cultural aspects of land struggles;
iv) Restructuring capital and commodity markets related to land;

v) Reallocating state finances and infrastructure, and privatising "natural" resources;

vi) Regional and global markets and influences.

Because of the importance of land-based economic development in Zimbabwe, the land question is a fundamental arena in which the above kinds of issues are contested leading to a reshaping of the the country's political economy. As we discuss further below, there are no simple organisational strategies for efforts to influence land policy, but rather a complex, differentiated and interconnected dynamic process of land policy advocacy among the different agencies. In this context, one major finding remains that the small farmers and the landless have been the main losers from the socio-economic "benefits" of the ESAP macro-economic, land sector and related policy reforms, as well as the least represented in current policy discourses because of the uneven playing field which epitomises the bi-modal agrarian structure of Zimbabwe. In this chapter, we now synthesize this process of unequal gains by first discussing the organisational map of the major new land use actors.

5.2 The Organisational Framework of New Land Uses

A wide spectrum of different types of organisations ranging from the governmental and the private to NGOs and community groups are central to the evolution of new land uses, and the consolidation of Zimbabwe's particular configuration of the land question (Table 5.2.1). These organisations provide a variety of services and functions, including policy analysis and lobbying, technical production, research extension and information, finance, marketing, community development activities, and the specific needs and concerns of members. The various organisations identified tend to be spatially and socially differentiated in the context of each of the three new land uses under study.

To begin with the state at central level, it has ten different agencies ranging from environmental, agricultural and financial to marketing and trade organisations (Table 5.2.1) involved with the three new land uses. At the local level, we found that in each district, at least three state-related structures, including the councils, ward and village committees were engaged in promoting or regulating new land uses. In addition, field officials of the 10 central agencies referred to above are represented locally. Our findings were that a dense and active organisational framework had been mobilised by the state towards these new land uses.

Table 5.2.1. *Organisational Map: New Land Use Actors*

Interest	Sector/Ministry Department	Examples	Functions
State	Agriculture	Agritex	Policy
	Lands/Water	Lands Department	Technical services
	Natural Resources	DNR	Regulation
	Parks	DNPWLM	Information
	Forests	Forestry Commission	Production
	Marketing	ADA	Finance
	State Firms	ZCT	Veterinary control
	Tourism	Zimtrade	Research
	Trade	AFC, Zimbank	
	Banks	Reserve Bank	
Private market Players	Banking	BOP, IBDC	Promoting markets
	Meat Processing	AAG	Providing inputs
	Hunting	Lewtawn Pvt	Finance
	Tour Operators	HPC	
	Exports Promotion	Olivine	
	Vegetable Oils Firms	HORTICO	
	Marketing Agents	Oilrich Investment	
		Cowbird Enterprises	
Farmers organisations/ Land users	LSCF Farmers	CFU, ICFU	Overall representation in policy
	CA Farmers	ZFU	and marketing land use
	Wildlife Producers	WPA	
	Ostrich Producers	TOPAZ	
	Small Ostrich Producers	SHOC	
NGOs Intermediators	Wildlife	Zimtrust	Technical assistance
	Biodiversity	CASS	Mobilising wildlife
	Biotechnology	Campfire Ass.	district councils
		ENDA	
Local Authority	Local Government officials and elected committees	Mutoko Council	Organising communities,
		WARDCO	controling land,
		VIDCO	licensing, infrastructure
		Natural Resource Committees	
Communities Land users	Villagers	Various CBO's	Production Resistance
Donors	Financial	USAID	Funding, technical assistance,
		CIDA	loans

Source: Various.

Zimbabwe has a variety of different types of land users and related private sector interest groups (see Annex for their profiles). In the main, they are divided between those which represent white, large scale formal sector hunters, market agents and farmers, including the CFU, BOP, WPA and so forth, and those which represent black ("indigenous") smaller scale and more informal land user sector activities such as the ICFU, SSCF, IBDC, IBWO, Campfire Association, OCCZIM, AAG, and ZFU. The latter group has allies among various mass-based, mainly black organisations, such as the labour movement (ZCTU), the university students, and numerous smaller indigenous associations which operate on a more sub-sectoral and regional scale. Similarly, NGOs exhibit sharp racial and class divisions, with the high profile NGOs engaged in policy advocacy and lobbying tending to be externally, and to some extent, white-dominated, while the mass-based Community Based Organisations (CBOs) and popular NGOs are black and rural-based.

However, the substantive basis for interest group differentiation reflects the historical but continued racially unequal structure of ownership, control and access to land and other rural productive resources, as well as control over capital and commodity markets. Indeed, even the national scale representativity of economic lobby organisations varies racially. The black organisations tend to canvass a wider population base, particularly the small farmers in "Communal Areas", and to seek policy support from urban workers, while the CFU and other sectoral farmer associations represent a smaller white population in LSCF areas. Within this spatial and institutional framework of policy lobbying, most black NGOs claim to articulate the development and policy requirements of the rural poor, a constituency which various NGOs and the state compete to influence. These differences are reflected in differing values held on land control and use, as well as in the nature of land policy changes sought by the various organisations.

This multiplicity of and division among interest group organisations reflect a long political history dating to the colonial period when most of the white policy lobbies were consolidated. Many studies of SAP reforms and land policy processes, however, tend to give superficial recognition to this racial and class differentiation of land user associations, and consequently to the political-economic interests which underlie and inform the evolution of land policy in Zimbabwe. Moreover, there are exceptions and overlaps in the membership and interests of lobby organisations, which caution us against an over-simplified approach to the racial and sectoral categorisation of interest groups. Thus, within the HPC, WPA, CFU etc., we found extremely large-scale multinational and Zimbabwean conglomerates which occupy dominant vertically and horizontally-integrated positions in the economy.

Some large-scale, land-using parastatals are members of the CFU, HPC and WPA simultaneously, as well as of the CZI. The CFU is also the *de facto* legal representative of about 500 black farmers, although about 800 black large farmers are reportedly also members of the ICFU. Many of these large black farmers occupy top political and bureaucratic posts in government. Thus, private and state domestic and external interests interact within seemingly homogenous interest groups. By and large, however, populist parlance treats the formally white-dominated organisations as representing only white "have alls", and those representing "indigenous" black people as representing the black "have nothings" or "have littles" (*Herald*, 1995, 1996), this in spite of the emergence of black landed capitalists.

While the Government of Zimbabwe does maintain regular dialogue with various formal interest groups, it has been observed rightly that the "white" lobbies retain more relative autonomy and policy influence than the black lobbies (Skålnes, 1995). Black lobbies are considered to have been generally repressed (Sachikonye, 1991) or to have been coopted or restricted by the state, partly because they compete for the same popular constituency with the government (Bratton, 1989; Skålnes, 1995). Meanwhile, NGOs have been found to be mostly subsidiary to government activity albeit increasing their policy dialogue with the state (Moyo, 1995). Indigenous economic associations tend to be weak, scattered and under-represented in policy making processes (Grierson, Moyo and Stegan, 1993).

The enigma, therefore, is how the Zimbabwean state manages to secure compliance with ESAP liberalisation and the limited redistribution of land and resources, given the declining quality of life among the majority black population, and the implications of this for democratisation.

Some commentators suggest that state rhetoric and promises to redistribute, for instance, land resources, are merely electioneering tactics used every five years among the poor because racial ideology has a premium in Zimbabwe's electoral politics. This perspective suggests that the poor are politically oblivious and that the redressing of land grievances is neither a rational nor legitimate and democratic policy demand. At any rate, such black majoritarian demands are categorised as only making "political sense" as opposed to the purely "economic sense", which the CFU land policy lobby is said to reflect (Skålnes, 1995). Thus, the GoZ is seen as pulling rhetorical wool over an apparently unconscientised rural populace's eyes. But the land occupations, land use diversification, and formal and underground natural resources market struggles we found, suggest otherwise and point to the fact that the formal policy pronouncements of the GoZ dovetail with popular concerns and struggle even it its actions do not match its rhetoric.

Moreover, this approach fails to see how the GoZ has consciously broken ranks with the World Bank's ESAP policy framework at various points in time in relation to critical popular demands, through state intervention such as legislation to expropriate land, drought-related food relief subsidies, and agricultural inputs subsidies for small farmers in Communal Areas. While these non-market and budget deficit-inducing state interventions do yield votes for the ruling party and sustain political compliance with GoZ policies, their credibility depends upon them having a social basis in Zimbabwe's body politic and the policy arena.

At the same time, the GoZ retains a strong hand over partisan political policy demands by undermining opposition parties, especially through co-opting their predominantly elitist leaderships. The Zimbabwe constitution's excessive, centralised and closed accountability structures and procedures (Makumbe, 1996) enable the GoZ to sustain that. Furthermore, "indigenisation" lobby groups (e.g. AAG, Boka) have been provided space to articulate and mobilize for "radical" redistributive policies up to a given threshold while being controlled politically and coopted financially. This scenario has not only restricted the level at which redistributive policies have been implemented, but has produced a somewhat distorted form of liberal democratic practice in general, and in land policy-making in particular.

The unique feature of Zimbabwe's so called "societal corporatism", therefore, is thus not that it allows "democratic space" for interest groups to influence policy, but that historically, it has created the conditions for narrowly-based, class and racially-founded commercial land user associations and their allies to continuously derive the major economic gains from macroeconomic, sectoral and land policy changes.

5.3 The Issues Raised by New Land Uses

As is evident from the above, the multiplicity of organisations which are engaged in promoting the development of new land uses or in struggles for land and related market control yields a variety of ideological, material and organisational conflicts and horse-trading. The politics of Zimbabwe's land struggles is, therefore, increasingly about settling particular ideological and material scores through a variety of strategies which we discuss next.

5.3.1 Spatial and Territorial Restructuring of the Land Question

The new political economy of the land question has an important spatial and territorial dimension. Zimbabwe's land resource base had, prior to 1980, been divided in terms of territoriality or simply spatially according to three main criteria. First, agro-ecologically on terms (natural regions) of the potential cropping intensity of land under rainfed conditions. State planning structures and academics retained this spatial framework or organisation in land policy discourses. Second, administratively in terms of districts and provincial governance zones whose boundaries reflect colonial ethnic symbols or metaphors of power, such as presumed "tribal" power configuration (Mashonaland, Manicaland etc.). These administrative or governance regions underlay a structure of indirect rule, through particular chiefdoms (coterminous with specific "Tribal Trust Lands" or "Communal Lands"), under white District Administration, rather than in a transcultural politico-administrative spatial framework. Thirdly, through "land tenure" categories denoting the spatial partitioning of land according to race, tribal community and state control and use of land. Unequal tenure structures yielded Zimbabwe's current spatial mosaic of land allocations under freehold, leasehold, communal and state forms of tenure.

As we have seen, private LSCF or freehold land also dominated Zimbabwe's prime lands (N.R.I and II) under natural conditions of production, as well as being located within areas with the most developed infrastructure and markets, while being administratively relatively autonomous from the central GoZ and separate from Communal Area administrations until the late 1980s. This pattern of land allocation among various land users which was consolidated by the Land Tenure Act (1969) was to remain until land redistribution and local government reforms began in the early 1980s. This agro-ecologically based division of land ownership and control had been based upon dryland farming conditions which assumed relatively static technological progress (for instance, no real leaps and bounds in irrigation and greenhouse technologies) and a narrow perspective of commodity markets based upon land use in terms of agriculture proper rather than the new land "outputs" we find today (Annex 5.3.1).

Since the 1970s, as we saw, there has been a tremendous growth, escalating during the mid-1980s, of water technologies, new more intensive methods of crop production, new types of crops (especially horticulture), new animals to husband (wildlife and ostriches), new markets (tourism, hunting, leather skins, low cholesterol meat, flowers etc.) and new forms of marketing commodities in a globalised world. The "enforced" deregulation of domestic markets and trade, particularly since the mid-1980s, was merely intended to enhance these new "opportunities". Altogether, these changes provided new criteria and an impetus for the spatial and territorial reconfiguration of land use and land values, as well as the restructuring of political and economic struggles and conflicts over land control, mere access to it and use rights.

We saw how the valuation of land which had previously been considered suitable only for wild animals and "evicted" blacks whose land had been alienated right up to the 1960s in the peripheral perimeter of Zimbabwe where most communal lands are (in the "outer" and "buffer" zones of our "onion ring" structure of land struggles outlined in Chapter Four), had changed especially since the late 1980s. Land which was rejected because of poor soils and rainfall, mosquitoes and tsetse flies which made it uninhabitable and not desirable to settlers, and towards which wildlife had been forced by land colonization in the core areas of the country, had now become a major site of land struggles. New land investors, black and white, multinational and domestic, elite and community-based were all found to have gained interest in wildlife land uses and land control in these "marginal" zones while continuing the struggles for prime agricultural lands through a variety of land accessing strategies. But there were pockets of resistance to wildlife programmes, and an uneven capacity among small and large, black and white, as well as state and community land users to capitalise on and optimise on the new land uses and markets.

According to Alexander and McGregor (forthcoming) in Matabeleland North the mention of "Campfire" was enough to provoke threats of violence from the residents of the Gwampa Valley in Southern Nkayi and Lupane

Districts in the mid-1990s. During this time councillors that were associated with the Campfire programme were afraid to travel to the valley and a lot of anger and feeling of betrayal was reflected on the part of the villagers. Although elsewhere in the world Campfire had been hailed for its participatory approach and its innovative strategies for confronting the developmental and environmental problems of some of the most marginal rural areas, in Zimbabwe this was not the case. Campfire was cast as a means of overcoming the legacies of colonial development initiatives that focused on technical prescription, coercive implementation and undermined the people's controle over their environment through a battery of rules and regulations.

The power struggles which emerged from this restructuring of land uses pose critical queries about the practice of local government as well as land policy, and the legitimacy of not only LSCF or private land holdings but also of various state organs.

For instance, since the late 1980s, the Forestry Commission had become notorious among local communities who suggested that its so-called "resource sharing" public rhetoric and donor-funded strategy was aimed at reinforcing the land shortage and alienation problems for its own beneficial entry into the new land uses (see Box 5.3.1). The cost-benefits of such land uses to the FC vis-à-vis redistribution to local communities had, indeed, also been queried even by the World Bank (Bojo, 1992).

5.3.2 Recolonisation of the New Land "Frontier"

Some analysts (Murombedzi, 1991) have viewed the Campfire programme as a new state instrument of recentralizing development management through the creation of community organisational structures which become subservient or dependent on the state. Thus, in those "economically marginal" areas where the state, and, to a lesser extent. NGOs and donors had little direct control over communities, because they were isolated by poor infrastructure and social services and slow economic growth, a form of "recolonisation" had begun through wildlife management and the growing tourist markets within a global market context.

However, the "recentralisation thesis" which rests on broad notions of community autonomy and local control (ibid) tends partly to be somewhat idealistic in its search for not merely decentralisation but also the promotion of a string of autonomous but weakly resourced community structures led by traditional authorities. But the territorial reconfiguration of various land tenure categories reflects a form of expanded reintegration of small farmers and poor communities into the "new" land-based markets which carry the day during this era.

Thus we see that tourism, environmentalism and related markets have created a new land frontier in Zimbabwe's perimeter, and that various "stakeholders" be they local, district, provincial, national and international, or private, state, NGO and community, are engaged in land struggles over the newly found land frontier. "Exploration" for new forms of biodiversity and the methods of their economic and social exploitation, as well as the touting of "indigenous technical knowledge" as virtuous, are a regular aspect of "technical assistance" and "research" in these "outer" and "buffer" zones among local and international NGOs and research organisations, various multilateral agencies and private firms. The frontier is being opened with questionable "participatory approaches to sustainable development" which have become the buzzword of government, NGOs, donors and the private sector in a land zone now cleared of tsetse flies with donor funding.

5.3.3 Indigenisation, Racial and Cultural Determination, and the Realignment of State and Private Interests

But the key national land struggle of the day remains the ideology of "indigenisation" or "affirmative action". This essentially argues against a racially determined legacy of privilege and relatively better capacities to exploit Zimbabwe's land resources within the framework of new commodity and capital markets arising from the growth in tourism, environmentalism and globalisation. At the ideological level, the new land uses have generated a distorted form of cultural determinism, wherein it has been argued by white-led NGOs and experts, as well as some middle class blacks (see Campfire and related literature) that blacks are not interested in the environment (Moyo, 1991, 1992) and have a wrong attitude towards nature and wildlife. In particular, they allegedly have little ecological sense. Numerous equally narrow and culturally deterministic academic responses to this essentially racial ideology have attempted to "prove" the efficacy of black or "indigenous technical knowledge systems" (see Otzen and Gumbo, 1994; Matowanyika 1991; and others). These discourses point, however, to a narrow new "anthropology" which not only idealises local systems of natural resources management but also neglects the fundamental material struggles in the new political economy of land.

To say blacks have no real interest in the material gains that natural resources can bring is highly misleading and this is attested to by the interests among elites and communities. As has been argued earlier, what meeds, however. to be remembered is that land alienation, the ruthless enforcement of local labour into the development of state and private plantations (Mtisi, forthcoming), and compulsory soil conservation measures (Beinhardt, 1984.) predicate black attitudes to environmentalism. Moreover, it is the association of living with wildlife as a form of banishment into the wilds and memories of wildlife management as a coercive practice which led to its extermination during the 1930s (Alexander and McGregor, ibid) that underlies the suspicion with which "environmentalism" and wildlife land uses and

Box 5.3.1. *Forestry Commission and Land Resources Sharing*

The Forestry Commission plays a key role in the Gwampa Campfire Project and holds. and holds jurisdiction over the Gwampa and Lake Alice forests as well as the forested land in Lupane and Matabeleland North. The Commission's interests are not in the development of the Communal Areas, but in establishing a buffer zone around its forests and restraining the poaching of game and other forest resources, There are several aid agencies that are involved and wield tremendous influence by right of their control over resources. When these aid agencies endorse a project, and agree to fund it, the project gains a momentum which it would otherwise lack. Beside providing funds for projects, the aid agencies often have personnel on the ground who facilitate implementation of the development project.

In Lupane, lengthy and acrimonious negotiations between the Forestry Commission and local councillors and MPs who had tried to prevent evictions reached an uncomfortable and temporary impasse by 1995. The Forestry Commission favoured excising a strip of infertile land neighbouring the Communal Area, redesignating it as communal land, and using it for resettling tenants and squatters, but it agreed to hold off on evictions until further land for resettlement can be found. The Lupane Council deemed the excised land unsuitable for human settlement, and unsuccessfully lobbied the Ministry of Local Government for alternative land. During that time forest settlers were prohibited from making repairs or improvements to homes or schools, and had their grazing land drastically reduced.

Though the Gwampa Valley Campfire programme was justified in term of benefit to local communities as well as fulfilling conservation goals, it also served other purposes. The Forestry Commission saw it as a step towards resolving its on-going battles over incursions from the Communal Areas. The council saw it as a way to raise revenue, and was impressed by the large sums of money pledged by donors. In the rush to develop and agree to the proposal, very little stakeholder consultation took place at the local level. When local communities were subsequently asked to endorse the project at a meeting, they adamantly refused.

Source: Alexander J. and McGregor J. "'Our Sons Didn't Die for Animals'. Wildlife and Politics of Development in Zimbabwe", *Development and Change*, forthcoming.

production are treated. Indeed, the current unequal gains so far realised from the growth of this land use are a self-evident bone of contention.

The politics of the indigenisation of land has, thus, seen a shift from interest in the entry into large commercial farming *per se* (see Moyo, 1995) towards the organised interest in capturing the most lucrative land-based export markets such as those in tobacco, horticulture, ostriches, timber, wildlife and nature-based eco-tourism. Large black landed and commodity trade interests, such as that of the tobacco merchant Mr. Boka (Boka Tobacco Auction Floors) and others such as black owned new merchant banks, have publicly called for the "setting aside" of operating licences, state and private capital as well as other markets associated with tobacco, fishing, ostriches, parks chalets etc., for indigenous actors. One of the strategies associated with this is that middle to large scale black land users should gain state support for black empowerment through the redistribution of white held land and associated resources within a framework of autarky from, or of parallel development alongside, the minority white-dominated land markets.

A competing indigenisation strategy, which is increasingly being promoted through various donor funded "enterprise development programmes" (e.g. USAID, NORAD, etc.), is the linkages strategy (see also Mead and Morrison, 1995). This strategy, which opposes indigenous autarky and structural redistribution, instead attempts to forge "linkages" between dominant mainly white and transnational business interests with those of smaller black businesses in various sectors. While this strategy, which uses "subcontracting", "franchising" and "set-aside" approaches involving exchanges of information, market requirements, capital and technology (ibid), has not been well articulated in the formal agricultural and land policy discourses, it has, in practice, been increasingly implemented within the various land sectors.

As we saw in Chapter Four, organisational and producer linkages through interactions involving physical marketing, finance and technology (e.g. inputs such as seeds, chemicals, ostrich birds, guns, surveying etc.) are many in the horticulture, ostriches and wildlife sectors, as they have also become in the tobacco and oil seeds land use sub-sectors. GoZ and NGOs such as the DNPWLM, Zimtrust, BESA (Business Advisory Services), WPA, TOPAZ, etc. are all involved in promoting these linkages, as are individual land owners and marketing agencies. The business "linkages" strategy of indigenisation and small enterprise development is, in fact, most advanced in the land-based sectors rather than in the industrial and mining sectors.

5.3.4 Re-allocating State Finances, Infrastructure and Privatising "Natural" Resources

The politics of "linkages", which is partly financed by private sector agencies is thus also an effort to counteract radical redistribution lobbies like those of lobby organisations such as SHOC, AAG, IBDC and ICFU, and the activities of community land occupation and poaching "movements". The aim is to realise a collaborative "win-win" strategy to benefit large and small black and white landed interests. The GoZ has been positive towards this strategy as it relieves the state of the political balancing and financing burdens of the former strategy which various black lobbies and leading politicians demand from it. Thus, the growing racial politics of conflict over land and related markets is based upon both concrete material grievances and competition over resources, as well as upon control of the ideological terrain of the land question and the role of the state in it. Zimbabwe's fiscal crisis of the 1990s has merely reinforced the importance that competition for economic opportunities from land and natural resources, which most blacks consider to be an indigenous and "natural" good, has gained so far. This is because the redistribution of these resources requires mainly "political will" rather than large scale public expenditure.

The restructuring of GoZ fiscal and monetary policies has gradually reduced the level of state subsidies to agricultural parastatals, as well as the real expenditures on social, infrastructural and other agricultural services (UNICEF, 1996) to local authorities which implement or coordinate "development" programmes. The allocation of direct GoZ subsidies to aid indigenous organisations and the poor has, thus, diminished, and the latter have less money to spend, except to capitalise their revenues and livelihoods from the available land and natural resources. Meanwhile, the focus of most political and economic struggles has been redirected to competition for major access to GoZ tenders and the limited assets it still holds. These include GoZ "markets" to supply various services and construct various infrastructures, licences where regulation remains justified by environmental, health and other "non-market" factors, and in the areas of social services and drought relief. The privatisation of parastatals has, so far, been too slow in terms of the ESAP benchmarks, and has yet to benefit many indigenous blacks.

The land and natural resources sectors offer numerous opportunities for such tenders including land surveying, consultancies, food relief, drought recovery inputs, food supplies to government institutions, marketing agrarian products to parastatals, managing parks and chalets, timber concessions, supplying state hotels, etc. In the growing land use and related industry, indigenisation efforts have targeted these tenders for preferential allocation to blacks and to break white "monopolies" in them at both central and local government levels, and among the parastatals. Elite blacks also struggle to legitimise their current and expected control in various land tenure sectors and among the various new land uses and their markets, parallel to community struggles for the same resources.

The evolution of growing and diverse markets in wildlife resources, and the process of converting land use under ESAP and SAP-type conditions in the last decade, has led to a variety of conflicts. In the wildlife land use sector, for instance, heated public policy debates reflecting a moral political query, focus mainly on what some consider to be the privatisation or transference to individuals from the public domain of a public heritage or "common property", and the artificial creation of wildlife markets based upon the dispossession of the rights of the majority over wildlife resources. Some of the trends in the evolution of wildlife resource markets which drive this politics were presented in Chapter Four and are further elaborated below.

Public controversy has also been stirred by some local politicians, including the provincial Governor of Masvingo and the Vice-President (*Herald,* 1995; Muzenda, 1996), who together with some traditional leaders, focus on the more parochial issues of seeking ways in which people from neighbouring Communal Areas (and it seems some indigenous elites from the area) can also be "given" shares by the Save Conservancy. But statements from what are considered a "rival faction" of politicians in the Masvingo province suggest that the conservancy notion is welcomed and that they do not want the issue to become "over politicised". Local communities are, therefore, expected to cooperate because of the employment and development benefits that tourism in the conservancy will bring.

Policy concern is also growing over popular discontent in Communal Areas with the emergence of the issue of problem animals that has been occasioned by their natural growth and increased commercial wildlife land uses. For example, about 100 people were killed by marauding elephants and buffaloes in Kariba in the period between 1980 and 1994 (Mr Mungate, District Administrator), and all efforts to ward off the animals from residential areas failed while calls to erect electric fences by the member of parliament have been ignored. In Beitbridge, wildlife managed by Jalukanga and Ehashi villagers was destroying canals and up-rooting trees planted in the irrigation schemes. Citrus trees that were planted under an agroforestry programme designed to raise money for villagers to maintain their schemes were being trampled upon (*Herald,* November 1995; *Herald,* 14/04/94).

The role of poachers and the cross-border diplomatic conflicts that this also raises continues to be a problem. For example, recently dozens of animals were dying daily in the game sanctuaries of Nyamandlovu in Matabeleland North Province following the poisoning of several water holes by suspected poachers. The dead animals included 30 monkeys, 25 baboons, 20 warthog, 30 guinea-fowls, 15 vultures, one buck, one jackal and scores of other smaller species of animals and birds. Two domestic suspects were apprehended by police on their way to Bulawayo to sell warthog and guinea-fowl meat. Thus, between the small time domestic poaching activities of poor small farmers who seek food for themselves (poaching for the pot) and the growing small-scale commercial poachers, on the one hand, and, on the other hand, the large scale domestic and international poachers or illegal appropriators of rights to control wildlife on private property, the GoZ faces a stiff policy challenge of regulating the growing underground and legal wildlife markets.

But these wildlife market conflicts become most problematic when it is suspected or reported that elements within the state, including the GoZ and Zambia's security forces, have become actively interested in these markets. For example, it is reported that senior Zambian military and police officers were involved in ivory poaching in the Zambezi valley through a large syndicate involving military and police officers, including a retired general and a colonel (*Parade Magazine*, 1997). Thus the Zambia/Zimbawe Joint Permanent Commission on Defense and Security has recently resolved to increase cooperation in combating poaching along the two countries' border. But it has been reported that Zimbabwean security forces and GoZ officials within the environment sector have, themselves, been involved in underground interactions with the growing wildlife resources markets (*Parade Magazine*).

Moreover, small and LSCF farmers, and their respective representatives, seem to be increasingly locked in competition and conflict over the control of export markets and other inputs associated with the new land uses. In the ostrich industry, for instance, one of the small holder producers' organisations (SHOC) has been demanding that the power to authorise export quotas which the GoZ had vested in TOPAZ should be taken away from that association as this was inconsistent with the general drive to "indigenise" the Zimbabwean economy. They want the power to be vested in the DPWLN or with SHOC itself (George Chiromo, SHOC Chairman, 1995; *Herald*). However, the GoZ Management Plan of Ostriches of 1992 (DPWLM) had been encouraging all ostrich producers to become members of TOPAZ since it had been given powers of "self-regulation and control".

Moreover, Topaz is seen as an extension of the white-dominated CFU. For example, a postal referendum recently undertaken to assess whether the majority of the members of TOPAZ wanted to join the CFU was seen by SHOCH as a political move. However the leader of TOPAZ argues that: "TOPAZ needed the CFU for its expertise, its lobbying skills and its clout in international marketing for our long-term future" (TOPAZ Chairman, Hammy Hamilton: *Herald*, 12/02/95).

SHOC argues that TOPAZ had, over the years, failed to involve smallholders in the mainstream of ostrich production: "The (GoZ) plan entrenches a retrogressive monopoly to TOPAZ in the regulation, control and administration of export quotas ... to raise revenue .... It is imperative for SHOC to regulate, control and administer its own export quota and raise revenue to procure adult breeding birds..., and invest in ancillary services" (G. Chiromo, SHOC Chairmen, report and proposals 02/04/93). But the Parks Director, Dr. Nduku had said export permits already given could not be withdrawn without good reasons as the permit holders could sue the government and he encouraged small farmers to apply for their quota "... you cannot demand cancellation of export quotas already given without indications of crime having been committed by permit holders" (Nduku, 1995).

Belatedly, however, the GoZ's DPWLM has given conditionalities to TOPAZ in exchange for its control over the exportation of the birds. The Parks Department now requires that for every five quality birds exported, TOPAZ should give smallholders one export quality bird for breeding in the rural areas. Apparently in response to this, TOPAZ has offered 300 three month-old chicks at a subsidized price of $800.00 to small farmers.

5.3.5 Restructuring Capital and Commodity Markets Related to Land

But the indigenisation movement has also sought to restructure private domestic capital markets, particularly banks (e.g. Barclays Bank, Standard Bank and various merchant banks) which through their financing traditions and patterns of credit allocation, impinge upon the social and economic patterns of entry into new land uses and markets. Given that the new land uses have become lucrative both in local and foreign currency terms to banks themselves, capital markets have become a high profile site of political struggles. The black lobbies have thus sought government pressure on the banking sector through banking policy reforms, efforts at influencing their top level staff appointments, regulations and legal actions which restrain banks from seizing indigenous peoples' family properties over loan repayment problems, and caps on the accumulated levels of interest payable (GoZ, High Court rulings, 1994, 1996). This struggle is basically for the increased allocation of credit (not only cheap credit) to indigenous businesses, including those involved or interested in the new lucrative land uses and markets. But, indigenous peoples have also set up three merchant banks of their own, most of which finance trade in land-related products, as well as numerous small credit schemes through local and international NGOs, many of which have a bearing on shifts in the land-based economy.

Thus, the need for efficiency and the competitiveness of capital markets have been deployed as arguments by indigenous organisations arguing the case for speedier reform within a context of enhancing their entry into new land uses and related markets. As we saw in Chapter Four the issue of private credit, donor funding, state finance and credit recurred among most schemes aiming to develop small and large black farmers in the new land uses, while linkages with LSCF farmers and agro-industrial firms to finance such land uses had begun to take root.

Many of these trends in the restructuring of capital markets, changing commodity markets, new "linkages", the spatial rezoning of land potentials and struggles about access to and use of land, reflect a realignment of power relations contingent upon economic and political liberalisation, and specifically in relation to the impacts of such reforms in shaping the changing use and exchange values embodied in land. Moreover, high inflation rates during the 1990s have hardened land prices, turning speculation in land and the use of land markets into a veritable vehicle for accumulation and source of investment in various economic sectors.

5.3.6 Regional and Global Markets and Influences

But some of these land use related restructuring processes have gained a clear regional or Southern African dimension, especially with regard to the spatial, financial and management integration of the tourist related land uses (parks etc.) and in associated industries (hotels, airlines etc.). As we saw, specific cross-border management of parks is high on the agenda. Formal regional cooperation schemes under the SADC tourism, trade, environmental and agricultural sectors, as well as in infrastructure interconnections, have been critical in fomenting such a "regional identity" (ADB, 1994; Chipeta, 1996). The growth of regional NGOs, trade unions and regional business associations (e.g. Tourism Council etc.), has begun to more formally shape the regional development strategy and ideologies, albeit on the basis of racially uneven and polarised policy resources, and with the under-representation of the poorer informal sectors in rural and urban areas.

But regional conflicts over poaching and the competition to extract and exploit shared natural resources, such as water, have also escalated as the intensification of land use through irrigation or through nature parks has been spreading in the region (see Moyo, 1997). Similarly, Zimbabwe's land policy model of gradual or limited land redistribution has been "exported" into the region (especially in Namibia and South Africa) through a false policy critique which pretends that radical land redistribution processes are in progress, that the cost-benefits of the resettlement programme are low and that the Land Acquisition Act of 1992 is unjustly being used (Palmer, 1997; Moyo, 1995a). Thus the ideological and market shifts occasioned by shifting land uses and values in those countries in the region with highly developed land and export markets are becoming structured into a regional development framework. But the absence of equitable trade relations in a region dominated by South Africa means that there is a tendency for countries such as Zimbabwe to evolve into more intensive primary producers based upon new land uses. This, at any rate, is the corner stone of the export model of development which underlies ESAP's global agenda. But the national implications of these new land use trends for future land reform need further examination.

5.4 Summary Remarks

The chapter identified numerous state, private, NGO and community organisations which are engaged in shaping the operationalistion of ESAP in the three land use sectors examined in Chapter four. Their organisational strategies and concerns were assessed leading to the conclusion that policy influence resources are uneven by spread among white and black interest groups. The latter however, are increasingly influential on the GoZ policy process, especially as they get better organised, articulate more specific demands for state support to enter the new land uses, and begin to control critical platforms in the marketing and financial sectors of the Zimbabwean economy. In overall perspective, the land question has resulted in new geographic, spatial and territorial sites of struggle emerging with new actors dominated by the indigenisation backlash against white monopoly controls of the land, capital and natural resources markets. The regional replications of such uneven racial control of resources and of poverty suggest a trans-national shift in the land question of Southern Africa.

Chapter Six

Concluding Remarks

This study examined the emerging political economy of Zimbabwe's land question during the SAP-type macro-economic reforms undertaken from the mid-1980s. Empirical evidence and secondary sources of information were used to trace the emerging material, political and ideological changes in land values and uses, and the land question in general. Case studies which focused upon struggles for the control of the prime lands of the "Mashonaland" provinces were examined within the wider framework of Zimbabwe's land tenure and agro-ecological system.

The point of departure was that, although land redistribution was a key political and economic demand of the liberation wars, official GoZ land policy had been to restrain private or community "self-provisioning" of land, and to pursue a slow redistribution programme. Less than 15 per cent of Zimbabwe's land, half of which was held by the LSCF and the state had been redistributed by 1990 to about 6 per cent of the rural population, while the government hesitantly sought to transform the land tenure system and promoted improved production and commercial markets among less than 10 per cent of the mainly black smallholder farmers (Moyo, 1995). This result was not politically satisfactory and did not promote sustained economic growth.

To sustain such a programme of "land reform with little redistribution", while "alleviating poverty", ameliorating measures to avoid the risk of drought, promoting employment and investment growth through an essentially land or natural resources based economic development strategy, the GoZ had gradually embarked upon SAP-type agricultural, financial and trade reforms during the mid 1980s. The full-blown ESAP adopted in 1990 also aimed to correct monetary and fiscal "imbalances" and other ineffi-ciencies emanating from centralised domestic markets and trade regulations. The agricultural and tourism sectors were key components of the ESAP development strategy aimed at optimising the use of available land, natural resources and cheap labour.

A key influence on the shifting land policy of these macro-economic and land relevant sectoral policy reforms was the explicit privileging of export-oriented land uses. This was achieved through particular monetary policy reforms, fiscal support, trade de-regulation, domestic market liberalisation, as well as other administrative reforms related to land and natural resources control and use. These policy shifts were cumulatively and gradually adopted by the GoZ as a result of various sources, levels and forms of influences.

Land acquisition and land market policies during the 1990s were also changed to allow the GoZ greater ease of access to land for redistribution, although this instrument only began to be used in late 1997. Land taxation was promised but not implemented, while land sub-divisions were encouraged without much formal fanfare about the underlying and *de facto* policy shift which the sub-divisions meant for the evolving land market. This trend allowed for increased private transfers of small sized freehold lands with almost a standstill in official land redistribution.

The slow pace of land redistribution among poorer communities seemed, in turn, to lead to increased unofficial "illegal" and "underground" land occupation and natural resources poaching activities. During this period, so called "squatting" by the rural and urban poor was spreading within all the land tenure regimes of the study as our related study shows (Moyo, forthcoming). A tough but ambiguous "squatter policy" was consolidated, it failed to stem the land "self-provisioning" strategies of the poor. This suggests that there were real benefits being derived from this process by local elites and land administrators, and that local power structures were increasingly gaining strength and autonomy vis-à-vis central government, particularly in matters related to land administration and law enforcement at the local level.

The 1990s saw deepening contradictions in land policy and related discourses within various levels of the GoZ's organisations and the ruling party, between governmental and other local power structures concerned with land. Organisational conflicts over land increased at the local level among traditional authorities, community-based associations, NGOs, and the indigenous elites, as well as between the latter groups and white landholders (see Chapter Three and four). But a key land policy thrust apparently desired by most formal organisations representing landholders and various government agencies remained the promotion of land use "diversification" into high value commodities, particularly for export. Indeed, government agencies were themselves deeply engaged in converting state land uses towards the new exports.

As a result of these land and related policy processes, there was a shift in the financial returns to export land uses, in the organic use and exchange value of land, the viability of alternative land use strategies and techniques, as well as in the relative importance of "economies of scale" to land use. There was an increase even in the utility of formerly marginal lands and of natural resources which, hitherto, had had insignificant markets. These outcomes generated greater struggles for access to and control of land.

The key trend was a shift in land use patterns in the form of a reallocation of lands which had mainly been unused and underutilised, as well as land which had formerly been allocated for household and domestic markets, towards new export oriented land uses. This pattern occurred among private, state and community landholders whose land management practices and endowments are drastically varied. This led to an overall shift in the macro-level spatial patterning of land values and struggles and shifting micro-level land use enterprise combinations.

There was a noticeable shift in production relations underlying land use with new practices such as land subletting, farmer subcontracting of production, new commodity marketing procedures and new organisational strategies and policy demands among a growing and complex profile of landed interests. New forms of "business linkages" around these changing land use patterns emerged. More transnational corporations entered the marketing and land use fray. Large farmers evolved new land ownership strategies through the introduction of extremely large scale shareholding combinations. Tourism operators grew in number and had begun to own and sublet land from other land users including the state, Communal Area and LSCF organisations.

The racial aspect of the social relations of production also changed. A variety of elite indigenous black export land users and related commodity brokers also entered the fray. Large white farmers increased the practices or started reforms of sub-contracting the production or buying of land-based commodities from small black farmers. Various state organisations entered or doubled up their role in promoting and benefiting from the new land uses among all types of land owners. And, more donors, local banks and international capital were drawn into financing the land use conversion process.

Thus, new political alliances coalescing around an export-led land use ideology and material gains were consolidated. This exposed qualitatively new conflicts, trade-offs and contradictions expressed through reconfigured but in essence old racial, spatial, administrative, agro-ecological and social contradictions.

The growth of new land uses and financial gains from it was, as expected, unequally achieved among the different land users. The mainly white-dominated large scale commercial farm sector and state land users such as ADA, the Parks Authority, and the Forestry Commission were the main beneficiaries. A small number of black elite large and small scale landholders gradually entered horticultural and ostrich production, while less than 5 per cent of the Communal Area farmers were engaged in wildlife and related land uses. Altogether, by 1996 close to 30 per cent of the entire LSCF (about 1,500 of the farms) had become engaged in one or more of the new land uses, albeit in combination with older cropping enterprises.

This suggested a major land use shift in the LSCF sector since the late 1980s. This was mainly at the expense of maize and cotton production, a trend which had taken root during the early 1980s as peasants began to compete effectively in producing those crops. But that shift coupled with another shift away from beef production was consolidated during the 1990s by conversion of land uses towards the three new land uses. But this reflected more the bringing in of wildlife and nature related land uses on the formerly underutilized LSCF lands. Land use intensification and extensification into new export commodities were a key trend in both prime and marginal LSCF land regions. It appeared that the LSCF was beginning to create the illusion that full productive use of all their lands was becoming the norm by also using prime lands for wildlife and tourism enterprises. But politicians, policy analysts and the black land owners incessantly voiced doubts about this claim.

Just as the land use cost-benefit superiority of wildlife and nature land uses over Communal Area household mixed farming had been found to be questionable by political analysts, the underlying socio-economic impacts of the adoption of the new land policy and land uses were not felt in terms of substantial employment and incomes growth in Communal Areas. Nor was this so in terms of greater food security as the negative effects of the droughts and resulting food relief programmes showed. And over 65 per cent of rural peoples continued to live below the poverty datum line (CSO, 1996). Instead, demands for land redistribution and conflicts over access to land increased over the period.

However, as we found, the politics of macro-economic and land policy reform remained circumscribed by the various conceptual shortcomings and political distortions of the SAP programme. In particular the class, race and region based influences on the design of ESAP had shaped the differentiated and uneven responsiveness of the various actors, including the small and larger farmers, black and white, the landed and landless, and marginal and prime land owners to the market and political liberalisation process. This was to be expected in the highly polarised agrarian relations of production typical of a society such as Zimbabwe.

The associated emergence of a multiplicity of state, private, farmer, NGO and community organisations lobbying for various specific policy changes, while on the surface introducing a form of pluralism in Zimbabwe's struggles and encouraging greater "policy dialogue", did not change the substantive ideological and material lines of cleavage in the society. In this sense, ESAP encouraged the emergence of greater income disparities and poverty, and had temporarily restrained the land redistribution agenda only for a populist land acquisition process to be forced upon the government by strong elements in the rural party around 1997.

To understand this unequal outcome of the SAP process, we need to broaden our analytic framework of the politics of economic reform. The prospects for democratisation and egalitarian land reform in Zimbabwe have increasingly diminished since economic reforms were adopted in 1990. Indeed, the ESAP macro-economic and sectoral economic policy reforms not only influenced the evolution of land policy towards an elitist agenda, but also reinforced a broadly undemocratic policy making practice. This outcome reflects the uneven organisational map and resources for policy influence which is a legacy of the racial and class structure of Zimbabwe.

The Zimbabwean land reform experiences discussed in this monograph reflect the polarised institutional and spatial framework within which land policy under ESAP has evolved. Unequal control over land and access to capital and infrastructure, as well as the prevalence of monopsonistic factor markets, are the substantive material differences and interests underlying the struggles for the maintenance of privilege by white and black elites against the redistributive demands of the rural poor. New export-oriented land uses, while contributing somewhat to a shaky but improved current account, have not necessarily impacted positively on livelihoods among rural small landholders. This reinforces the long standing agrarian inequalities and the depressed incomes levels of rural Zimbabwe.

This pattern of racially configured uneven development has held under different macro-economic and political regimes over numerous decades. It was consolidated during the so-called colonial "open economy" and under the sanctions regime, as well as during the majoritarian rule's protectionist economy of the 1980s such that uneven development was sharpened even with the cooperation of a few elite blacks. Then, during the current neo-liberal ESAP policy regime, the later expansion of markets for new land uses was further developed through new alliances among dominant local white and foreign capital and a few black elites, leading to a reproduction of the same unequal agrarian structure.

What is exceptional indeed in the Zimbabwean case study of the impacts of ESAP on the land question is the capacity of the state to secure relative political compliance and relative peace in spite of the pitiful land redistributive policy measures implemented so far. The absence of comprehensive land redistribution in Zimbabwe is a fundamental measure of the GoZ's relative success in containing popular demands albeit by ignoring the self-evident fact of the growth of some land occupations. The close scrutiny, support and lobbying of large scale landed domestic and external financial interests has been crucial to this model of land reform with little land redistribution.

But as our related work will show, increasing land occupations for self-provisioning, as well as dramatic government efforts to show progress towards compulsorily acquiring land for redistribution are symptoms of growing popular pressures for land reform exerted upon a government with waning popularity. As a result of increased urban and rural poverty under ESAP, and as the channels for accumulation among indigenous elites are narrowed down to the sphere of land and natural resources, the burning land question remains high on the Zimbabwean political agenda.

This trajectory of the development of Zimbabwe's land question suggests that neither the extreme market led strategy for land policy change as propounded by the World Bank (1991) under ESAP, nor an evolutionary theory of land rights reform (see Platteau, 1996, for details of this theory) which is akin to the reforms recommended by Zimbabwe's Land Tenure Commission (LTC, 1994) are empirically or socially relevant to the Zimbabwean land reform experience. The neo-liberal evolutionary theory of land rights (ETLR) which presumes that increased commercialised agricultural and population growth lead to intensive land uses, and, thus, increased demand for exclusive land rights among communal land tenure arrangements (Platteau, 1996), is not correct in predicting increased evolutionary demands for private property rights in Zimbabwe under economic liberalisation.

Rather our case study shows that worsening conditions in an inegalitarian agrarian system with underutilized lands now being redirected towards external markets and with low employment and income, lead instead towards "radical" strategies of community led self-provisioning of land, continued and increased land conflicts amongst white and black elites against the rural poor, and increased transaction costs in the land markets. As a result, there has been increased pressure on the state to intervene radically in the land markets in order to correct unequal patterns of landholdings and of access to productive forces such as capital and technology.

Moreover, our study shows how indigenous agrarian interest groups and other economic associations have grown in number, scale and purpose, and in terms of effectively articulating their demands for land and related assets, inputs and services from the state vis-à-vis the white LSCF sector. Rather than being repressed, it seems the GoZ has, indeed, encouraged such interest groups and their indigenisation case, and perhaps even leaned on them for political and economic capital. Nor has central government managed to repress community led land occupation strategies (Moyo, 1998).

Instead, the state has continued to successfully trade off the interests of indigenous elites against white elites vis-à-vis those of the rural poor. The government strategy has been to offer a little bit of land and related resources to the black interest groups, and continually threaten to implement large scale radical land transfer albeit doing this in practice only on a small scale and at a gradual pace. The higher commodity-specific financial returns at the micro level from new land uses have, indeed, simply increased the appetite of larger segments of the population for access to land since only a few white and black elites have been visible beneficiaries of this ESAP export-oriented development strategy.

Bibliography

ADA (1996) "Tenant Farmer Programme Plans". Mimeo. Harare.

Adams, J.M. (1989) "Female wage labour in rural Zimbabwe" Cambridge University. Faculty of Land Economics. Unpublished paper.

African Development Bank (1994) "Financial structures, reforms and economic development in Africa", in *African Development Report*. Abidjan, Côte d'Ivoire.

Agricultural and Rural Development Authority (1995) *Annual Report for the Financial Year 1993/94* Mashonaland East Fruit and Vegetable Project, Project No. 7 Zim. 016.

Alexander, Joselyn (1993) "The Unsettled Land: The Politics of Land Distribution in Matabeleland, 1980–1990", in *Journal of Southern African Studies*, Vol. 17, No.4, Oxford: Oxford University Press.

Alexander, J. (1994) "State, Peasantry and resettlement in Zimbabwe" in *Review of African Political Economy*. Vol. 21, No.61 pp. 325–345.

Alexander J. and McGregor J. (forthcoming) "'Our Sons Didn't Die for Animals'. Wildlife and Politics of Development in Zimbabwe", in *Development and Change*.

Anonymous (1995) "The Land Answer", in *Zimbabwe Review*, (Review of Moyo, S: *The Land Question in Zimbabwe*, by Anonymous referred to as: An Economist Working for an International Development Organisation).

Baland, J.M., and J.P. Platteau (1996) *Halting Degradation of Natural Resources: Is There a Role for Rural Communities*. Oxford: Clarendon Press.

Bates, R. (1983) *Essays on the Political Economy of Rural Africa*. London: Cambridge University Press.

Bates, R. (1981) *Markets and States in Tropical Africa: The Political Basis of Agricultural Policies*. California: University of California.

Beinart, W. (1984) "Soil erosion, conservationism and ideas about development: A Southern African Exploration 1900–1960", in *Journal of Southern African Studies*, 11(1):52–83.

Berdegue, Julio, A. and German Escobar (1997) *Markets and Modernisation: New Directions for Latin American Peasant Agriculture*. Gatekeeper Series No 67. International Institute for Environment and Development, Sustainable Agriculture Programme. United Kingdom.

Bojo, J. (1993) "Economic valuation of indigenous woodlands" in Bradley P. N. and McNamara K. (eds.) *Living with Trees: Policies for Forestry Management in Zimbabwe*. World Bank Technical Paper No. 210. Washington D.C

Bond, I. (1993) "The Economics of Wildlife and Land Use in Zimbabwe: An Examination of Current Knowledge and Issues", in *WWF Multi Species Animal Production Systems Project*, No. 36. Harare: WWF.

Brand, V., Mupedziswa, R. and P. Gumbo (1995) "Structural Adjustment, Women and Informal Trade in Harare" in Gibbon, P. (ed.) *Structural Adjustment and the Working Poor in Zimbabwe. Studies on Labour, Women, Informal Sector workers and Health*. Uppsala: Nordiska Afrikainstitutet.

Bratton, M. (1984) *Draught Power, Draught Exchange and Farmer Organisations*. Working Paper No. 9. Harare: Department of Land Management, University of Zimbabwe.

Bratton, M. (1986) "Farmer Organisation and Food Production in Zimbabwe", in *World Development*, Vol. 14, No. 3.

Bratton, M. (1989) "The Politics of Government-NGO Relations in Africa", *World Development*, Vol. 17, No. 4.

Bratton, M. (1994) "Land Redistribution 1980–1990", in Eicher and Rukuni (eds.). *Zimbabwe's Agricultural Revolution*. Harare: University of Zimbabwe.

Buchan, A.J.C. (1989) *An Ecological Resource Survey of Chisunga Ward, Guruve District, with Reference to the Use of Wildlife*. Project Paper No. 7, Project No. 3749. Harare: WWF

Campbell, B.M., Vermeulen, S.J. and Lynam, T. (1991), *Value of Trees in the Small Scale Farming sector of Zimbabwe*. Ottawa: IDRC.

Campfire Programme Strategy Workshop (1992), *Workshop Report: Conference held between 29 September–2 October 1992, Hunyani Hills Hotel, Lake Chivero*, conducted by the Campfire Association, Harare.

Campfire Programme: *The Nyaminyami Project and Other Campfire Initiatives. Project Completion Report for the Period 1989 to 1994*. Harare: Zimtrust.

CFU (1995) "Survey of Current Input Cost and Recent Input Cost Increases". The Economics and Inputs Department. Harare.

CFU, (1990) "Land Policy Proposals", CFU Congress Paper. Harare.

Chachage, C.S.L. (1997) *The Land Policy Paper and the Tenure in National Parks, Game Forest Reserves*. Dar es Salaam: Department of Sociology and Anthropology, University of Dar es Salaam.

Chegutu Rural District Council, (1995) "Illegal Settlers, Chief Ngezi's Area (Mupawose)", Chegutu Rural District Council minutes.

Chichilnsisky, Graciela, (1994) "North-South Trade and the Global Environment", *The American Economic Review*, Vol. 84, No. 4, pp. 851–874.

Chichilnisky, Graciela (1996a) "Trade Regimes and Gatt: Resource Intensive vs. Knowledge Intensive Growth", *Journal of International and Comparative Economics*, pp.20, 147–181.

Chichilnisky Graciela, (1996b) "The Economic Value of the Earth's Resources", in *Trends in Ecology and Evolution*, Vol. 11, No 3, pp. 103–144.

Chichilnisky, Graciela (1997) *Development and Global Finance: The Case for an International Bank for Environmental Settlements*. Discussion Paper Series. Office of Development Studies, UNDP.

Child, B. (1990) "Assessment of Wildlife Utilisation as a Land Use Option in the Semi-Arid Rangelands of Southern Africa" in Kiss, A. (ed.), *Living with Wildlife: Wildlife Resource Management with Local Participation in Africa*. World Bank Technical Paper No. 130. Africa. Technical department series. Washington D.C

Child B. (1993) "A Perspective from Zimbabwe: The Elephant As a Natural Resource", in *The African Point of View*. March/April.

Chinhoyi Municipality (1995) "Squatter Returns in Urban Areas", minutes of the Chinhoyi Municipality.

Chipeta, C. (1996), *Rural Industries*. 08.02.02 Doc. Rural industries in Malawi. Harare: SAPES books.

Chiromo, George F. (1994) "Executive Report: An Executive Report Submitted to the Parliamentary Indigenous Sub-Committee to Indigenise the Ostrich Industry in Partial Fulfilment of an Affirmative Action to Indigenise the Zimbabwean Economy", paper presented by SHOC to the parliament of Zimbabwe.

Chiromo, G. (1995) "Financial Statements", Jobs Farming (Private) Ltd., January 31 and March.

Chisvo, M., Kulibaba N. and Associates (1997) "Regional Activity to Promote Integration through Dialogue (RADIO) in SADC", Agriculture Sector Stakeholders' Survey Report, SADC/USAID, Gaborone, 15–17 May.

Cliffe, L. (1988) "Zimbabwe's Agricultural Success and Food Security", in *Review of African Political Economy*, No. 43, pp. 4–25.

Cousins, C. (1991) *Hundred Furrows: The Land struggle in Zimbabwe 1890–1990.* Education Series, Book 1. Harare: TADG. Working Groups Coop.

Cousins, B., Amin N., and D. Weiner (1993) *The Dynamics of Social Differentiation in the Communal Lands of Zimbabwe.* Harare: CASS, University of Zimbabwe, 1988.

CSO (1994) *Quarterly Digest of Statistics.* March. Harare.

CSO (1996) *Quarterly Digest of Statistics.* March. Harare.

Cumming, D.H.M. (1990) *Wildlife Products and Market Place: A View from Southern Africa.* Project Paper No. 12. Multi-species Animal Production Systems Project, Harare: WWF.

Cumming, D.H.M. (1990) *Developments in Game Ranching and Wildlife Utilisation in Eastern and Southern Africa.* Project Paper No. 13. Multi-species Animal Production Systems Project. Harare: WWF.

Cumming, D.H.M. (1991) *Multispecies Systems and Rural Development in Southern Africa: Opportunities, Constraints and Challenges.* Project Paper No. 19. Harare: WWF.

DDF-Water (1996) "Inventory of Dams, Shamva District".

Deloitte and Touche, (1997) "Issues Paper Trade Protocol Rapid Project". Mimeo. Tohamatso International.

Department of National Parks and Wildlife Management (1992) *Research Plan 1992.* Harare.

Disch, A. (1995) "Public Expenditure and Poverty Reduction". Draft mimeo undertaken under the World Bank Harare Office.

District Development Fund (1996) "Report on Squatters on State Land (Model A Schemes)". Resettlement Division.

DNR (1995) *Desertification and Poverty Alleviation Through Rural small Landholders: Participation in Ostrich Production and Complementary Project Proposals.* Ministry of Environment and Tourism.

DNR (undated) "Draft Desertification and Poverty Alleviation through Rural Small Land Holders Participation in Ostrich Production and Complementary Projects", Project Proposal.

Dold, D., G.F. Chiromo, and T. Mapingure, (undated) *Ostrich Husbandry Manual 1.* Rural Ostrich Development Programme. Pilot Scheme for Curriculum Development.

Drinkwater, M. (1991) *The State and Agrarian Change in Zimbabwe.* London: Macmillan.

DSCC (1996) "Minutes of the District Squatter Control Committee (DSCC) Meeting Held at the DA's Office, Shamva, on the 27th of February".

Eicher, C. and M. Rukuni (eds.) (1994) *Zimbabwe's Agricultural Revolution.* Harare: University of Zimbabwe.

Eicher, C.K. (1995), "Zimbabwe's Maize Based Green Revolution: Preconditions for replication", in *World development*, Vol. 23, No. 5, pp. 805–818. May.

Englund, H., (1996) "Waiting for the Portuguese: Nostalgia, Exploitation and the Meaning of Land in Malawi–Mozambique Borderland", in *Journal of Contemporary African Studies*, 14:2, pp. 157–172.

FAO (1991) *A Review of Wildlife Utilization in the SADCC Region.* Harare.

Foggin, C.M. (1996) *Quarterly Research Report (Wildlife, Ostriches, Crocodiles)* Veterinary Department.

Galtung, Johan (1997) *Globalisation and Its Consequences.* Institute of Sociology, Academia Sinica, Taipei.

Gereffi, Gary (1994) "The Organisation of Buyer-Driven Global Commodity Chains: How U.S Retailers Shape Overseas Production Networks", in Gereffi, Gary and M. Korzeniewicz (eds.) *Commodity Chains and Global Capitalism*. Westport, Conn: Greenwood Press.

Gibbon, Peter (ed.) (1995) *Structural Adjustment and the Working Poor in Zimbabwe. Studies on Labour, Women, Informal Sector workers and Health*. Uppsala: Nordiska Afrikainstitutet.

Gibbon, P. and A. Olukoshi (1996) *Structural Adjustment and Socio-Economic Change in Sub-Saharan Africa: Some Conceptual, Methodological and Research Issues*. Research Report No. 102. Uppsala: Nordiska Afrikainstitutet.

Gore, C., Katerere, Y. and Moyo, S. (1992), *The Case for Sustainable Development: Conceptual Problems, Conflicts and Contradictions*. Harare: ENDA Zimbabwe and ZERO.

Gibbon P., P.O. Pedersen and P. Raikes (1997) "Economic Restructuring in Africa in a Gobal Context", Research Programme Proposal. Mimeo.

GoZ (1986) *Chelliah Commission Report*. Harare.

GoZ (1990) *Zimbabwe: A Framework for Economic Reform*. Harare: Government Printers.

GoZ (1990) *ESAP policy document*. Harare: Government Printers.

GoZ (1992) *Land Acquisition Act*. Harare: Government Printers.

GoZ (1994) *Report of the Commission of inquiry into the appropriate agricultural land tenure systems*. Under the Chairmanship of Professor Mandivamba Rukuni. Volumes 1, 2 and 3. Harare: Government Printers.

GoZ (1996) *Value for money project*. Comptroller-Auditor General. Harare.

Green, R. and Khadhani, X. (1986) "Zimbabwe: Transition Economic crisis 1981–1983, Re-Prospect and Prospect", in *World Development*, Vol. 14, No. 8, pp 1059–1083.

Grierson, J., Moyo, S. and Stegan, F. (1993) *Issues in Small and Medium Scale Enterprise Development*. NORAD, Harare.

Gunliffe, R.N. (1992) *An Ecological Resource Survey of the Communal Lands of Centenary District*. Project Paper No. 26. Harare: WWF.

Gunliffe, R.N. (1994) Assessment of the Wildlife Resources of Nyatana Wildlife Management Area, Project Paper No. 41. Harare: WWF.

Gunliffe, R.N. (1991) An Ecological Resource Survey of the Communal Lands of Hurungwe District with Reference to the Use of Wildlife, Project Paper No. 21. Harare: WWF.

Havnevik, K. (1997) "Outline of an Interdisciplinary Research Programme on the Land Question in East- and Southern Africa". Uppsala: University of Agricultural Sciences, Department of Rural Development Studies.

Herbst, J. (1990) *State and Politics in Zimbabwe*. Harare: University of Zimbabwe Press.

Herbst, J. (1991) "The Dilemmas of Land Policy in Zimbabwe", in *Africa Insight*, Vol. 21, No. 4, pp. 269–277.

Heri, S.T. (1995), *Marketing of fresh produce: The Zimbabwean experience*. HPC, Harare.

Hirst, Paul and Grahame Thompson (undated) "Globalization in Question", Policy Press, The International Economy and the Possibilities of Governance.

Holt-Biddle, (1994) "Campfire, An African Solution to an African Problem", (unnamed journal), Vol. 2. No. 1, pp. 33–35.

IBDC (1993) "Conference", in *SSE News* Vol. 3, No. 2. July.

ILO (1994) *Employment and SAP in Zimbabwe*. ILO Working Paper. Geneva: ILO.

ILO (1994) "Social Clauses in Trade: Protecting the rich or helping the poor", in *Courier*, No. 145, pp. 95. May–June.

Irfan-ul-Haque, I., M. Bell, C. Dahlman, S. Lall and K. Pavitt (1995) *Trade, Technology, and International Competitiveness*. EDI Development Studies. Washington D.C.: World Bank.

Jackson, J.C., P. Collier and A. Conti (1988) *Rural Development Policies and Food Security in Zimbabwe: Part II*. Geneva: ILO.

Jansen. D, I. Bond and B. Child (1992) *Cattle, Wildlife, Both or Neither: Results of Financial and Economic Survey of Commercial Ranches in Southern Africa*. Multispecies Animal Production Systems Project, Project Paper No.27. Harare: WWF.

Jourdan, Paul and Ketso Gordham (1996) *Spatial Development Initiatives (Development Corridors): Their Potential Contribution to Investment and Empowerment Creation*, Harare: Ministry of Trade and Industry, DBSA.

Kothari, Ashish (1997) *Conserving India's Agro-Biodiversity: Prospects and Policy Implications*. Gatekeeper Series, No 65. International Institute for Environment and Development, Sustainable Agriculture Programme. United Kingdom.

Kreater, P. and Workman (1992) *The Comparative Economies of Cattle and Wildlife Production in the Midlands of Zimbabwe*. Project Paper No.31, Harare: WWF.

Maast, M. (1996) "The harvest of independence: Commodity boom and socio-economic differentiation among peasants in Zimbabwe". Unpublished Ph. D. Thesis in International Development Studies at Roskilde University, Denmark.

Machingaidze, V.E.M. (1980) "The development of settler capitalist agriculture in Southern Rhodesia with particular reference to the role of the state, 1908–1939." Unpublished Ph. D. thesis, School of Oriental and African studies, University of London.

Mackie, C. (1993) *Aerial Census of Herbivores in Western Dande Communal Land (Kanyurira Ward) 1990–1992*. Project Paper No. 35, Harare: WWF.

Mackie, C. (1993) *Aerial Survey of Large Herbivores in Northern Mukwishe Communal Lands and Southern Chewore Safari Area*. Project Paper No. 34. Harare: WWF.

Madondo, B.B.S. (1996) "A review of Policy Interventions on Gender Isues in the Irrigation Development of Zimbabwe". Mimeo. Harare.

Mamdani, M. (1996) *Citizen and Subject: Contemporary Africa and the Legacy of Late Colonialism*. Princeton, N.J.: Princeton University Press.

Mandaza, I., and L.M. Sachikonye, (eds.) (1991) *The One Party State and Democracy: The Zimbabwe Debate*. Harare: Sapes Trust.

Masters William, A. (1994) *Government and Agriculture in Zimbabwe*. Westport Connecticut and London: Praeger.

Matowanyika, J.Z. (1991) "Indigenous Resource Management and Sustainability in Rural Zimbabwe: An exploration of concepts in commonlands". Unpublished Ph. D. thesis. Department of Geography, University of Waterloo, Canada.

Mbiba, B. (1995) *Urban Agriculture in Zimbabwe: Implications for Urban Management and Poverty*. Aldershot: Avebury.

Mead, D. and Morrison, C. (1996) "The Informal Sector Elephant", in *World Development*, Vol. 24, No. 1.

Ministry of Water Development (1996) "Dam Inventory for Mt. Darwin District, Rushinga, Centenary, Guruve, Mazowe", Government of Zimbabwe.

Ministry of the Environment, Water Resources and the Legal Amazonia Secretariat for the Coordination of Amazonian Affairs, (1997) "Agenda 21 for Amazonia", Brasilia, Brazil.

Mkandawire, T. (1984) "Home Grown Austerity Measures in Zimbabwe". Mimeo. ZIDS working paper, Harare.

Mkandawire, T. (1995) "Fiscal Structure, State Contraction and Political Responses in Africa", in Mkandawire, T., and A. Olukoshi (eds) *Between Liberalisation and Oppression: The Politics of Structural Adjustment in Africa*. Dakar: Codesria.

Mkandawire, T. and A. Olukoshi (eds.) (1995) *Between Liberalisation and Oppression: The Politics of Structural Adjustment in Africa*. Dakar: Codesria.

Moyo, Jonathan (1992) *Voting for Democracy*. Harare: University of Zimbabwe.

Moyo, Sam (1986) "The Land Question", in Mandaza, I., (ed.), *Zimbabwe: The Political Economy of Transition, 1980-1986*. Dakar: Codesria.

Moyo, S. (1989) "Institutional Issues for Appropriate Technology Development: Rural NGO's in Zimbabwe" Harare, ZERO, 1989. International symposium on appropriate technology and International Cooperation, Tokyo. 8–9 December, 1989.

Moyo, Sam (1990) *Agricultural Employment Expansion: Smallholder Land and Labour Capacity Growth*. ZIDS Monograph Series No. 2. Harare.

Moyo, S. and Ngobese, P. (1991) *Issues of Agricultural Employment Development in Zimbabwe*. Working Papers no.15. ZIDS, Harare.

Moyo, Sam (1993) "Economic Nationalism and Land Reform", *SAPEM*: October.

Moyo Sam (1995a) "Development and Change: NGOs in Zimbabwe". Unpublished Monograph.

Moyo, Sam (1995b) *The Land Question in Zimbabwe*. Harare: Sapes Trust.

Moyo, Sam (1996) "Environment Policy Research Programme: Inter-State Management of Natural Resources", a Draft Research Programme Proposal for the Period 1997–2001.

Moyo, Sam (1994) "Land Tenure Bidding among Black Agrarian Capitalists in Zimbabwe", *SAPEM*, May.

Moyo, Sam (1992) "The Politics of Economic Reform". Mimeo. NORAD.

Moyo, S., and J. Nyoni (1996) "Agricultural Development in Zimbabwe by 2020". Mimeo presented to GoZ, Vision 2020 Programme; National Economic Planning Agency, Harare.

Moyo, Sam (1997) "Environmental Security in Southern Africa". Research Proposal, SARIPS Southern African Inst. for Policy Studies.

Moyo, S., Matondi, P. and Marongwe, N. (1998) "Land Use Change and Communal Land Tenure Under Stress", in Masuko, L. (ed.) *Economic Policy Reforms and Meso-Scale Rural Market Changes in Zimbabwe: The Case of Shamva District*. Harare: Institute of Development Studies. University of Zimbabwe.

Moyo, Sam (1998) "Political Economy of Land Redistribution in the 1990's", seminar on Land Reform in Zimbabwe: *The Way Forward*. London, 11 March.

Mtisi, J. P. "Stirring times: Labour on tea estates in Zimbabwe" forthcoming.

Mudzi Rural District Council (1995), Mudzi Rural District Council Campfire Report, April 1995–August 1995.

Muir, Kay (1993) *Economic Policy and Wildlife Management in Zimbabwe*. Environment Department Working Paper. Wahsington D.C.

Muir, K. and Blackie, M. (1994) "The Commercialization of Agriculture" in Eicher and Rukuni (eds.) *Zimbabwe's Agricultural Revolution*. Harare: University of Zimbabwe.

Muir, K. (1994) "Agriculture in Zimbabwe", in Eicher and Rukuni (eds.).

Murombedzi, J. (1991) *Decentralising Common Property Resources Management: A Case Study of the Nyaminyami District Council of Zimbabwe's Wildlife Management Project*. Issues Paper. No. 30. IIED Dryland Network Programme. International Institute for Environment and Development. London.

Murphree, M. (1992) *Ivory Production and Sales in Zimbabwe, Branch of Terrestrial Ecology*. Department of National Parks and Wildlife Management, Government of Zimbabwe.

Myers, G.A. (1996) "Democracy and Development in Zanzibar? Contradictions in Land and Environmental Planning", *Journal of Contemporary African Studies*, 14, 2, pp. 221–245.

Nayyar, Deepak (1995) "Globalisation: The Past in Our Present", Seventy-Eighth Annual Conference Indian Economic Association Chandigarh.

Nayyar, Deepak (1996) *Free Trade: Why, When and for Whom?*, New Delhi, India: Centre for Economic Studies and Planning School of Social Sciences, Jawahalal Nehru University,

ODA (1994) *Whose Eden: An Overview of Community Approaches to Wildlife Management*. International Institute of Environment and Development. Nottingham: Russell Press.

ODA (1996) *Report of ODA Land Appraisal Mission to Zimbabwe: 23 September–4 October*. British Development Division in Central Africa.

Oden, Bertil Morten Boas and Fredrik Söderbaum, (1995) *Regionalism in Southern Africa: South Africa, the Benign Hegemon?*. Working Paper No. 7, the Southern Africa Programme, Uppsala: Nordiska Afrikainsitutet.

Oden, Bertil (1996*) Southern African Futures: Critical Factors for Regional Development in Southern Africa*. Discussion Paper 7. Uppsala: Nordiska Afrikainstitutet.

Ohlsson, Leif (1995) *Water and Security in Southern Africa*. Publications on Water Resources: No. 1. Gothenburg: Department of Natural Resources and the Environment, University of Gothenburg.

Otzen, O. and Gumbo, D.J. (1994) *Facilitating Sustainable Agricultural Development in Zimbabwe: Key factors and necessary incentives*. Berlin/ Harare: GDI/ENDA,.

Palmer, R. (1977) *Land and racial denomination in Rhodesia*. Heinemann Educational.

Palmer, R. (1997) *Contested lands in Southern and Eastern Africa: A literature survey*. London: Oxfam.

Pankhurst, D. (no date) *Constraints and Incentives in "Successful" Zimbabwean Peasant Agriculture: The Interaction between Gender and Class through the Relations of Production and Reproduction*. Discussion papers in development studies, No. 9005. Manchester: University of Manchester.

Parks and Wildlife Board (1991) *Management Plan for Ostriches in Zimbabwe*. Harare.

Penzhorn, B.L. (1994) *Wildlife Monograph No. 1: The Future Role of Conservation in Africa*. Du Toit Game Services (Pvt) Ltd.

Peterson J.H. (jr) (1991) *Campfire, a Zimbabwean Approach to Sustainable Development and Community Empowerment through Wildlife Utilization*. Harare: CASS, University of Zimbabwe.

Platteau, J.P. (1996) "The Evolutionery Theory of Land Rights As Applied to Sub-Saharan Africa: A Critical Assessment", in *Development and Change*, Vol. 27, No. 1, pp. 29–88.

Price Waterhouse (1992) *The Role of Wildlife in Land Use*. Background Papers, Vol. 3. Wildlife Management and Environmental Conservation Project. Prepared by Price Waterhouse and Environmental Resources Limited.

Provincial Squatte Control Committee (1995) "Minutes of the Provincial Squatter Control Committee meeting held on 23 July 1995 at Provincial Administrator's Office".

Provincial Squatte Control Committee (1995) "Mashonaland West Provincial Squatter Control Meeting, 6 June".

Robinson, P. B. (1996) "Potential Gains from Infrastructural and Natural Resource Investment Coordination in Africa", draft paper for a seminar on Regional Economic Integration and Global Economic Cooperation: The Case of Africa, 7–8 February, Forum on Debt and Development.

Roth, H.H. (1966) "Game utilization in Rhodesia in 1964", in *Mammalia*, 30, pp. 397–423.

Roth, M.J. (1990) "Analysis of Agrarian Structure and Land Use Patterns in Zimbabwe", background paper for the Zimbabwean Agriculture Sector Memorandum for the World Bank. LTC. Wisconsin.

Ruigro, Winfried and Rob van Tulder (undated) *The Logic of International Restructuring*. London and New York: Routledge.

Sachikonye, L.M. (1991) "Wages, Prices and the cost of living since independence". paper to a conference organised by EMCOZ and Friedrich Naumann Foundation. Harare. April.

Sachikonye, L.M. (1995) *Democracy Civil Society and the State: Social Movements in Southern Africa*. Harare: Sapes Trust.

Save Valley Wildlife Services Ltd. (1995) "Eighth Draft", August.

Scoones, I. (1997) "Landscapes, Fields and Soils: Understanding the History of Soil Fertility Management in Southern Zimbabwe", in *Journal of Southern African Studies*, Vol. 23, No. 4, pp. 615–643.

SHOC (undated) *Rural Ostrich Development Programme*. Harare.

Shopo, T.D. (1985) *The Political Economy of Hunger in Zimbabwe*. ZIDS Working Papers No. 2. Harare.

Singh, Ajit (1997) *Global Unemployment, Long Run Economic Growth and Labour Market Rigidities: A Commentary*. Cambridge: Faculty of Economics, University of Cambridge.

Skålnes, T (1995) *The politics of economic reform in Zimbabwe: Continuity and change in development*. London: MacMillan Press.

Stoneman, C. (ed.), (1988) *Zimbabwe's Prospects: Issues of Race, Class Capital in Southern Africa*. London: MacMillan.

Stoneman, C. (1992) "The World Bank Demands Its Pound of Zimbabwe's Flesh", *Review of the African Political Economy*, No. 53, pp. 94–96. March.

Strasma, J. (1991) "Alternatives for Land Tax Reforms in Zimbabwe", Zimbabwe Agricultural Sector Memorandum, World Bank, Washington D.C.

Swatuk, Larry, A. (1996) "Environmental Issues and Prospects for Southern African Regional Cooperation", paper for presentation at the international meeting, *South Africa and Africa: Environmental Policy Frameworks*, Johannesburg, South Africa.

Takavarasha, T. (1994) "Agricultural Pricing Policy" in Eicher and Rukuni (eds) *Zimbabwe's Agricultural Revolution*. Harare: University of Zimbabwe.

Taylor R.D. (1991) *Ecologist's Report for 1990. Nyaminyami Wildlife Management Trust Annual General Meeting*. Project Paper No. 28. Project No. 3749. Harare: WWF.

Taylor R.D. and C.S. Mackie (1993) *Aerial Census of Elephant and Other Large Herbivores in the Sebungwe and Western Pande* Project Paper No. ZW0007. Harare: WWF.

Taylor R.D. (1993) *Elephant Management in Nyaminyami District, Turning a Liability into an Asset*. Project Paper No. 33. Harare: WWF.

Taylor R.D. and D.H.M. Cumming (1993) *Elephant Management in Southern Africa*. Project Paper No. 40. Harare: WWF.

Taylor R.D. and D.H.M. Cumming (1988) *Aerial Census of Large Herbivores in Pilot Project Areas*. Project Paper No. 4. Harare: WWF.

Taylor, R.D. (1989) *Aerial Census of Large Herbivores in Pilot Project Areas*. Project Paper No. 11. Harare: WWF.

TOPAZ (undated) *Economics and Management Systems of Ostrich Farming in Zimbabwe*. Harare.

ULG Consultants (1994) *Midterm planning and assessment of Zimbabwe component*. Pp 690–721, Southern Africa Regional Project of the USAID. Harare: USAID.

UNICEF (1996) *Economic and Social Survey for Africa*. Addis Ababa.

Weiner, D., Moyo, S., Manslow, B., and Okeefe, P. (1985) "Land Use and agriculture productivity in Zimbabwe", in *Journal of Modern African Studies*, Vol. 23, No. 2.

Weiner, D. (1988) Land and Agricultural Development", in Stoneman (ed) *Zimbabwe's Prospects: Issues of Race Class and Capital in Southern Africa*. London: Macmillan.

White, S. (1990) "The Technical Costs and Benefits of Agroforestry to the Catchment as a Whole. Upstream-Downstream relations", in Prinsley R.T. (ed.) *Agroforestry for Sustainable Production: Economic Implications*. London: Commonwealth Science Council.

World Bank (1991) *Zimbabwe: Agriculture Sector Memorandum: Vol I and Vol II*. No. 9429—Zim. Washington

ZFU, (1994) "Zimbabwe Country Paper", paper presented at the International Federation of Agricultural Producers' Conference, Harare.

Zimbabwe National Committee of Large Dams (1993) "Register of Large Dams in Zimbabwe".

Annual and Quarterly Reports

AD, Spearheading Zimbabwe's Future.

AFC (1994/95) *Annual Report*.

AFC (1992/93) *Annual Report*.

AFC (1990) *Annual Report*.

AFC (1995) *Agricultural & Economic Review*.

AFC (1993/94) *Annual Report*.

AFC (1991) *Annual Report*.

AFC (1992) *Annual Report*.

AFC (1996) *Agricultural & Economic Review*.

COPRO (1994) *Ostrich Quarterly Review*, Vol. 1 No. 2, August.

COPRO (1995) *Ostrich Quarterly Review*, Vol. 2 No. 3, October, magazine.

COPRO (1995) , *Ostrich Quarterly Review*, Vol. 2 No. 2, June, magazine.

COPRO (1994) *Ostrich Quarterly Review*, Vol. 2 No. 3, November, magazine.

CSO 1994 *Quarterly Migration and Tourist Statistics*, Court Printers, Harare.

Veterinary Department, *Annual Report*, October 1994 to September 1995.

Information Booklets and Brochures

AFC in Perspective Information Booklet.

Africa Resources Trust, Africa Resources Trust Brochure.

Agricultural Development Authority Consultancy Services, (Brochure).

Campfire Brochure, Zimtrust: Campfire in Zimbabwe. An Introduction.

Commercial Farmers Union of Zimbabwe, Wildlife Producers Association, Information Booklet.

Constitution of the Zimbabwe Ostrich Producers Association.

Zimbabwe Trust, Zimtrust Brochure.

Zimbabwe Investment Centre, Zimbabwe: Key Economic and Business Para.

Zimbabwe Ostrich Producers Association (1996) Presentation on Formation of Provincial Committees.

Magazines and Newspapers

Financial Gazette (Various Years), various letters, articles and reports.
Herald (1992, 1993, 1994, 1995, 1996), various letters, reports and articles.
Parade Magazine 1997.
Sunday Mail (Various Years), various articles.
The Farmer, Vol. 66 No. 7, February 22, (Magazine).
The Farmer, Vol. 66 No. 6, February 15, (Magazine).
The Zimbabwean Farmer/Murimi/Umlimi, (1995) Feb., (Magazine).
The Farmer, Vol. 66 No. 6, February 8 (Magazine).
The Zimbabwean Farmer/Murimi/Umlimi (1996) Vol. 3 No. 1 February (Magazine).
The Zimbabwean Farmer/Murimi/Umlimi (1996) Vol. 2 No. 12, December 95/January, (Magazine).
The Zimbabwean Farmer/Murimi/Umlimi (1996) March, Vol. 3 No. 2, (Magazine).

Newspaper and Magazine Articles

Jean-Raymond Bulle (1997) "Adventurer's Quest for Zaire's Glittering Prize", *The STAR*, South Africa 21 May.
The Economist (1997) "Stored Health", 3 May.
The Economist (1997) "Theme Park", 3 May.
Zimbabwe Independent (1997) "Proposed Land Tax a Potential Minefield", 9 May.
Chenje Munyaradzi (1997) "Ivory Trade Ban Usurps Power of Communities", *Sunday Mail Magazine*, 16 March.
Arenstein, J. (1997) "Water floods Mpumalanga", *Mail and Guardian*, 9–15 March.
Day Jim (1997) "Riots Over Border Dispute blamed on ANC", *Mail and Guardian*, 9–15 March.
Adelzadeh, A. (1997) Agriculture Slips out of Gear", *Mail and Guardian*, 9–15 March.
Hammond (1997) "Making Money out of Africa", *Mail and Guardian*, 9–15 March.
Karras (1997) "Environment on Agenda at Last", *Mail and Guardian*, 9–15 March.
Grove R. (1997) "Going Green Brings about Better Coorporate Profits, *Mail and Guardian*, 9–15 March.

Annexes

Annex 1.0 Profile of Researcher, Research Assistants and Persons Interviewed and Case Studies

Annex 1.1.1. Profiles

Principal Researcher: Prof. Sam Moyo: Currently Principal Director (Studies and Training) at SARIPS

Prof. Moyo holds a Doctorate in Environmental Management undertaken in England at the University of Northumbria, Newcastle. He is also a holder of a Masters Degree in Economic Geography from Ontario, Canada. Teaches rural, agricultural and environmental courses at the University of Zimbabwe and has presented lectures on land, small scale enterprises, and the environment at a number of fora.

He has published extensively on land issues, agrarian reform, environmental policy, rural development, NGOs, cooperatives and development cooperation for a period spanning 17 years. His publications both national, regional and international, have meant that he has effectively and efficiently utilised his professional assets i.e. academic qualifications, teaching experience and research capabilities in the socio-economic development of his country whilst also contributing immensely to higher education.

He has been actively involved in the formation, management and promotion of NGOs involved in policy advocacy for land reform, rural transformation and environmental sustainability. He has also been awarded a number of scholarships such as the Commonwealth Scholarship, and the Canadian International Development Agency (CIDA) award while studying at universities. He is a board member of a government environmental department and an African research institution.

Research Assistant: Edward Mabaya

A former student of the University of Zimbabwe 1992–1994 in the Department of Agricultural Economics. Now a Masters Student in Agricultural Economics at Cornell University in the State of New York, United States of America. His main focus of research is on horticultural marketing.

Research Assistant: Nelson Marongwe

He is now working as a Research Fellow with ZERO, a regional environment organisation based in Harare. He completed his Masters Degree in Environmental Policy and Planning in the Geography Department at the University of Zimbabwe in 1995 and immediately joined the research team. He intends to enroll for a PhD programme focusing on wildlife/ostriches in relation to the land question.

Research Assistant: Prosper B. Matondi

He worked as a Research Assistant in the Environmental Unit of SARIPS based in Harare (until January 1998). He completed his Masters Degree in Environmental Policy and Planning in the Geography Department at the University of Zimbabwe in 1995 and immediately joined the research team. Worked with the principal researcher as a research assistant 1993–1997. Has enrolled for a Ph D degree with the Swedish University of Agricultural Sciences and his research focus will be on horticulture production and the land question.

Annex 1.1.2. List of People Interviewed

National Level—Harare

Name of person	Organisation	Occupation	Subject
Nontokozo Mema	Africa Resources Trust	Information Officer	Campfire and wildlife issues
Mr. Gotoza	DNPWLM—Govt.	Training Officer	Wildlife issues.
Mr. Gatawa	DNPWLM—Govt.	Provincial Warden	Wildlife issues
Mr. G. Chiromo	Small-holder Ostrich Cooperative (SHOC)	Managing Director	Ostriches
Mr. D. Munemo	Department of Natural Resources	Director	Ostrihes
Mr. Shoko	Resources	Acting Chief Resources Planning Officer	Resources
Mr. Mathambo	Zimbabwe Ostrich Producers Association	Director-Munhumupata	Business machines
Mr. D. Utete	Agritex		Horticulture
Mr. Marwisi	Agritex		Horticulture
Mr. B. Mawonera	ZFU		Horticulture
Mr. Matao	ADA (Mash. East)		Horticulture
Mr. P. Macqueene	Zimtrade		Horticulture
Mr. S. Heri	HPC		Horticulture
Mr. C. Karimanzira	HPC		Horticulture
Mr. Tandi	Chesa Ostrich Project	Afgate Engineering	Horticulture
Mrs. Langster	CFU	Wildlife Department	Wildlife
Mr. J. Makunyere	ZIMTRUST	Regional Manager Zambezi Valley	Wildlife
Mr. Mupezeni & Mr. Pedzisai	Harare City Council	N/A	Squatters
Mr. E.P. Nyakunu	ZATSO	ZATSO	ZATSO
Mr. Shamu	ADA	Land Planner	ADA Wildlife and Ostrich Project
Mrs. Hove	ADA	Livestock Specialist	Livestock and wildlife issues
Mr. Katsande	Water Department	Irrigation Specialist	Horticulture and water provision
Mrs. Ndiweni	Water Department	Planning Engineer	Horticulture
Mr. Masheneke	Campfire Association	Director	Campfire Projects
Mr. G. Lopez	Ford Foundation	Head	New land uses in Zimbabwe
Mr. B. Kinsey	Private Consultant	-	New land uses in Shamva District

Mashonaland East Province

Name of person	Organisation	Occupation	Subject
Dr. J.E. Jackson	Horticulture Research Centre	Officer in Charge	Horticulture
Mr. Makaya	Agritex	Provincial Horticulturist	Horticulture
Mr. Mutingi	MLGRUP	Provincial Administrator	Horticulture, wildlife, squatting, ostriches
Mr. Shumba	MLGR	Senior Executive Officer	Horticulture wildlife, squatting, ostriches
Dr. Hoggins	Vet. Department, Wildlife Unit	Principal Vet. Research Officer	Wildlife activities
Mr. Gwenzi	DDF Resettlement	Senior Resettlement Officer	Squatters in resettlement
Mr. Chaeruka	Department of Physical Planning	Provincial Planning Officer	Consolidation and sub-division
Mr. Mazingi	DNR	Provincial Natural Resources Officer	Ostriches and resources land uses
Mr. Mashengi	National Affairs	Provincial Head	Ostriches, horticulture and cooperatives
Mr. Chimambo	Kushinga Pikelela Institute	Acting Vice Principal	Ostriches, horticulture and wildlife

Mashonaland West Province

Name of person	Organisation	Occupation	Subject
Mr. O. Svubure	Agritex	Provincial Agronomist	Squatters in Resettlement
Mr. Mudzingwa	DDF-Resettlement	Provincial Head	Horticulture and ostrich projects
Mr. Muchiya	National Affairs	Provincial Head	Horticulture
Mr. Ndando	DDF-Water	Senior Field Officer	Wildlife and ostriches
Dr. Muponda	Vet. Department	District Vet. Officer	Horticulture
Mr. Mundota	CIDA (National Affairs)	Training Officer	Horticulture
Mr. Mavhiya	DNR	Provincial Natural Resources Officer	Natural Resources
Mr. Borerwe	DNR	Deputy Provincial Natural Resources Officer	Role for ZFU
Mr. Manyerere	ZFU	Provincial Organiser	Sub-division and consolidation
Mr. Chiwanga	DPP	Provincial Planning Officer	AFC support to new land uses
Mr. Sithole	AFC	Loans Manager, Commercial Division	AFC in CA and RST
Mr. Chindove	AFC	Loans Manager, Development Division	

Mashonaland Central Province

Name of person	Organisation	Occupation	Subject
Mr. Munyoro	MLGR	Provincial administrator	Squatting, horticulture ostrich and wildlife
Mr. Chega	Vet. Department	Chief Animal Health Inspector	Ostriches and wildlife
Dr. Nyika	Vet. Department	Provincial Vet. Officer	Ostriches and wildlife
Mr. Magaya	Department of Physical Planning	Provincial Planning Officer	Sub-division and consolidation
Mr. Munyayi	DNR	Acting Provincial Natural Resources Officer	Ostriches and natural resources
Mr. Mvere	Agritex	Acting Provincial Agronomist	Horticulture
Mr. Towindo	DDF-Water	Provincial Field Officer	Horticulture and water resources
Mr. Chigumwe	National Affairs	Officer-Women and Community Development	Ostriches, horticulture and cooperatives
Mr. Jaji	DA—MLGR	Assistant DA Shamva	Squatters
Mr. Zendera	Chaminuka Rural District Council	Chief Executive Officer	Squatters
Mr. Gumunyu	Agritex	Agritex Officer	Ostriches, wildlife, horticulture
Mr. Munyuru	Chaminuka RDC	Chairman	Squatters
Mrs. Mavudzi	Hortipac	Vice-Chairperson ZFU-Horticulture	Horticulture
Mr. Nherera	ICFU	President	Land redistribution
Mr. L. Mawowa	DAPP	Manager—River and Park Estate	Communal to commercial farmer scheme
Mr. A. Morckel	Zimproduce	Director	Horticulture

Case Studies of Wildlife Projects: Campfire

Name of project	District	Province
Chiweshe Campfire Project	Mazowe	Mash-Central
Guruve Campfire Project	Guruve	Mash-Central
Muzarabani Campfire Project	Muzarabani	Mash-Central
Shamva Campfire Project	Shamva	Mash-Central
Nyami-Nyami Campfire Project	Kariba	Mash-West
Hurungwe Campfire Project	Hurungwe	Mash-West
UMP Zvataida Campfire Project	UMP Zvataida	Mash-East
Mudzi Campfire Project	Mudzi	Mash-East
Chipinge Campfire Project	Chipinge	Manicaland
Chiredzi Campfire Project	Chiredzi	Masvingo
Mwenezi Campfire Project	Mwenezi	Masvingo
Bulalima-Mangwe Campfire Project	Bulalima-Mangwe	Mat. North
Beit Bridge Campfire Project	Beitbridge	Masvingo
Gwanda Campfire Project	Gwanda	Mat. North
Tsholotsho Campfire Project	Tsholotsho	Mat. South
Binga Campfire Project	Binga	Mat. South
Nkayi Campfire Project	Nkayi	Mat. South
Lupane Campfire Project	Lupane	Mat. South
Bubi Campfire Project	Bubi	Mat. South
Gokwe North Campfire Project	Gokwe North	Midlands
Gokwe South Campfire Project	Gokwe South	Midlands

Case Studies of Safari Areas

Name of safari area	District	Province
Chipinge Safari Area	Chipinge	Manicaland
Malapati Safari Area	Chiredzi	Masvingo
Doma Safari Area	Makonde	Mash-West
Chewore Safari Area	Binga	Mash-West
Sabi Safari Area	Chiredzi	Mash-West
Hurungwe Safari Area	Hurungwe	Mash-West
Charara Safari Area	Kariba	Mash-West
Umfuli Safari Area	Hwange	Mash-West
Dande Safari Area	Guruve	Mash-Central
Umpfurudzi Safari Area	Shamva	Mash-Central
Umzingwane Safari Area	Umzingwane	Mat. South
Matetsi Safari Area	Hwange	Mat. North
Chirisa Safari Area	Binga	Mat. North
Chete Safari Area	Binga	Mat. North

Case Studies of ADA Wildlife Farms

Name of farm	District	Province
Vungu Ranges	Gweru	Midlands
Mkwasine Ranges	Chirdezi	Masvingo
Battle Fields	Kadoma	Mash-West
Sesombi	KweKwe	Midlands
Marula Ranges	Bulawayo	Mat-North

Case Studies of Wildlife Game Parks

Name of game park	District	Province
Imire Game Park	Hwedza	Harare/Mash-East
Pamuzinda Safari Lodge	Zvimba	Mash-West
Mhondoro	Chegutu	Mash-West
Chipangali Game Park	Gwanda	Mat-South
Gwanda-West Nicholson Area	Gwanda	Gwanda
Valley Voughan Game Park	Bindura	Mash-Central
Catolina Wilderness Centre	Beatrice	Mash-East
Bushy Park Game Section	Chiredzi	Masvingo
Sipura Ranch	Chiredzi	South-Est Lowveld
Humani Ranch	Chiredzi	Masvingo, South
Lone Star Ranch	Chiredzi	East-Lowveld

Case Studies of Wildlife Conservancies

Name of conservancy	No. of farmers	District	Province
Chiredzi River Conservancy	12	Chiredzdi	Masvingo
Bubiana Conservancy	8	Chiredzi	Masvingo
Save Valley Conservancy	21	Chegutu	Masvingo
Marirangwe Conservancy	–	Hurungwe	Mash-West
Mutorashanga Conservancy	–	Kwekwe	Mash-West
Munyati Black Rhino Conservancy	–	Kwekwe	Midlands
Sebakwe Black Rhino Conservancy	–	Kwekwe	Midlands
Zzimrhicon Conservancy	–		

Case Studies of Horticultural Producers

Name of producer	District	Province
Uzumba Horticulture Producers Association	UMP Zvataida	Mash-East
Murehwa Horticulture Producers Association	Murehwa	Mash-East
Chinamhora Horticultural Producers Association	Goromonzi	Mash-East
Parirewa School	Goromonzi	Mash-East

Case Studies of Ostrich Projects

Name of project	No. of farmers	District	Province
Chesa-Nyajenje	11	Mt. Darwin, Chesa SSCF	Mash-Central
Musengezi Ostrich Syndicate	15	Zvimba, Musengezi SSCF	Mash-West
Makumbirofa Project	–	Chirau Communal Lands	Mash-East
Chiwanzamarara	–	Chihota Communal Land	Mash-East
Mhondoro (proposed)	–	Kadoma, Mhondoro Ngezi C.L.	Mash-West
Mudzi Ostrich Project	20	Mudzi	Mash-East
Domboshawa Training Centre	State project	Goromonzi	Mash-East
Mutoko Ostrich Syndicate	11	Mutoko	Mash-East
Mutoko Rural District Council Project (proposed)		Mutoko	Mash-East
Mlezu Agricultural Institute	–	KweKwe	Midlands
Chibero Agricultural College	–	Zvimba	Mash-West
Stowe Philip's Ostrich Farm	1	Zvimba	Mash-West
Beit Bridge Council Ostrich Project	–	Beit Bridge	Masvingo
George Chiromo (Tynwald Plot)	1	Harare	Harare
George Chiromo	1	Murehwa, Chitowa SSF	Mash-East
H. Mukurazhizha	1	Murehwa, Murehwa Communal Lands	Mash-East
ADA's Battle Fields Range	Parastatal	Kadoma	Mash-West
ADA's Vungu Ranges Farm	Parastatal	Gweru	Midlands
Hwedza Ostrich Project	2	Hwedza Communal Lands	Mash-East
Guruve Ostrich Project		Guruve, SSCF	Mash-Central

Case Studies of Irrigation Schemes

Name of scheme	No. of farmers	District	Province
Ngezi/Mamina	144	Kadoma	Mash-West
Makwavarara	28	Kadoma	Mash-West
Takainga	30	Kadoma	Mash-West
Madzongwe	21	Chegutu	Mash-West
Johannadale I	7	Chegutu	Mash-West
Johannadale IIA	19	Chegutu	Mash-West
Hamilton Hills	5	Chegutu	Mash-West
Sharmrock	41	Chegutu	Mash-West
Mukadzimutsva	19	Zvimba	Mash-West
Negonde	30	Kariba	Mash-West
Gatshe Gatshe	39	Kariba	Mash-West
Chirimudombo	17	Hurungwe	Mash-West
Chimhanda	40	Rushinga	Mash-Central
Tsakare	32	Mt. Darwin	Mash-Central
Rukunguse	–	Mazowe	Mash-Central
Principe	6	Shamva	Mash-Central
Mufurudzi	proposed	Shamva	Mash-Central
Mudotwe	–	Bindura	Mash-Central
Tsunda	–	Bindura	Mash-Central

– No data at the time of the research.

Case Studies of Squatter Settlements in Resettlement Schemes

Name/place	No. of squatters (households)	District	Province
Mupfurudzi Resettlement	13	Shamva	Mash-Central
Hoyuyu Resettlement	69	Mutoko	Mash-East
Macheke Wenimbi	11	Marondera	Mash-East
Ngezi Resettlement	227	Kadoma	Mash-West
Sashuru Resettlement	129	Kadoma	Mash-West

Case Studies of Irrigation Schemes in Mashonaland East

Name of scheme	District	Ward	No. of farmers
Nyadire 10	Mutoko	Nyadire Res.	20
Hoyuyu V53	Mutoko	Hoyuyu Res.	20
Murara	Mutoko	Murara	36
Mahusekwa	Marondera	Nyandoro	36
Nyamhemba	Hwedza	Chigodora	36
Mudungwe	Hwedza	Goto	30
Chihowa	Hwedza	Mubaiwa	20
Nyamatanda	Mudzi	Nyamatanda	110
Shinga	Mudzi	Shinga	21
Nyangande	UMP	Uzumba	23
Nyahuni	Chikomba	Nyahoni	37
Sadza	Chikomba	Sadza	15

Case Studies of Squatter Settlements outside Resettlement Schemes

Name/place	No. of Squatters (Households)	District	Province
Gambuli Farm	147	Makonde	Mash-West
Kasvisva Squatter Camp	721	Kariba	Mash-West
Marove	189	UMP	Mash-East
Masingandima River Bank	19	UMP	Mash-East
Leleza	19	Chikomba	Mash-East
Mwoyowamira Grazing Scheme	361	Shamva	Mash-Central
Maskum Farm	91	Mt. Darwin	Mash-Central
Summerset Farm	50	Mazowe	Mash-Central
Mwemba Farm	500	Makonde	Mash-West
Omay	200	Kariba	Mash-West
Chiridzangoma	40	Kadoma	Kadoma

Annex 2.0 Methodological Framework and Study Area

Annex 2.2.1. Specific Research Questions

The major research questions investigated in this study include:

1. What is the history of wildlife management, ostrich production and horticultural production in the district? When did farmers move into each of the sectors and what prompted this shift in land-use from the traditional crops to these new land-uses?
2. What it the legal framework that controls wildlife, ostrich and horticultural production and what is the impact of this on the LSCF, SSCF and Communal areas at the sub-regional level?
3. What are the policy and market incentives arising from ESAP for those engaged in wildlife management, ostrich production and horticultural production?
4. What were the previous land-uses before diversification?
5. How are wildlife, ostrich and horticultural products marketed (on the spot, approved buyers, representative organisations Contracts), local/international markets?
6. Who is involved in ostrich, wildlife and horticultural production (race, sex, ethnic and social status)? What is the level of entrance into these sectors by blacks? Which class or racial processes affect entry into these sectors?
7. What type of land is used for horticultural, ostrich and wildlife production? What percentage of prime land in the LSCF and SSCF is occupied by these users. Are wildlife, ostrich and horticultural production mutually exclusive land-uses vis-à-vis traditional crop production or livestock rearing?
8. What is the relationship between wildlife management, ostrich production and horticultural production? Are there any conflicts in land-use between these forms of production and how are they resolved?
9. What new forms of inputs and investments for production are being used for the new land uses? (infrastructure: electricity, water, roads, feeds, horticulture bypro-ducts, stock-feed—type, quantity, cost—veterinary services)?

10. What are the negative impacts of ESAP on ostrich, wildlife and horticultural production? (fluctuation of prices, retrenchment of farm labourers, and regulations and incentives).

11. What has been the government's response to the growth in horticulture, ostrich and wildlife production, especially the use of prime agricultural regions? Has land redistribution or subd-ivision for sale been encouraged for these new land uses?

12. What new forms of marketing (e.g. sub-contracting arrangements) between communal, SSCF and LSCF farmers involved in horticulture, ostrich and wildlife production have emerged? What are the benefits of such contractual arrangements? What are the inter-linkages between the various participants of the wildlife, ostrich and horticultural sub-sectors? (middle men and kinds of arrangements existing between producers, processors, transporters and marketers).

13. What it the structure of the wildlife, ostrich and horticultural sub-sectors in the district? Where are the various sub-sector participants located? To what extent is production affected by nature of farm i.e. LSCF, SSCF, resettlement farmers, Communal Area farmers?

14. What is the labour input into wildlife, ostriches and horticulture? (decreasing absolute labour numbers and increased specialist skills, the wage trends)?

15. What are the by-products from wildlife, ostriches and horticulture and how are they marketed?

16. Where do farmers get the information on wildlife, ostrich and horticultural production? TV/newspapers/radio, representative organisation, government, other farmers and others (specify).

17. What are the future prospects of wildlife, ostrich and horticulture industry? What are the major problems hindering the viability of these types of production?

18. What are the impacts of wildlife, ostrich and horticultural production on the environment? Positive and negative impacts, destruction of natural vegetation)?

Ostriches, Wildlife and Horticulture Questions

OSTRICHES

1. How productive is ostrich farming vis-à-vis other crops and livestock? (returns per hectare—incomes and quantity employment generation etc).

2. What kind of ostrich management is being done in the district? Intensive farming, semi-intensive, and extensive. What are advantages of the preferred type of ostrich farming?

3. What is the ideal area required for ostriches?—Climatic conditions, vegetation requirements and water requirements.

4. To which organisations are farmers affiliated? (TOPAZ, SOPAZ, SHOC and Others: What benefits are derived by member)?

5. How difficult is entry into ostrich production? (Purchasing of ostriches, Marketing and Financing).

WILDLIFE

1. What is the current wildlife population in the Mashonaland farms and what is their rate of increase per year?

2. What are the most popular breeds and types of game that attract tourists in the district?

3. How do the farmers control wildlife poaching, capture and translocate animals? Where do they get the animals?

4. What is the level of trade in animals? Are farmers involved in wildlife-based tourism? What kind of tourism are farmers engaged in–consumptive and non-consumptive tourism?

5. Who organises hunting safaris and who benefits?

HORTICULTURE

1. How has horticultural production affected food security under the different farming categories?

2. What has been the impact of horticultural production on the environment? Are new chemicals being used?

Annex 2.4.1. Land Productivity by Agro-Ecological Region

Region	Area extent (million ha)	% of total land area	Rainfall (annual)	Agricultural productivity
N.R. 1	0.62	1.6	<1000mm	Suitable for dairy farming, forestry, tea, coffee, fruit, beef and maize production
N.R. II	7.31	18.8	750–1000mm	Suitable for intensive farming based on maize,tobacco and cotton and livestock production
N.R. III	6.85	17.6	650–800mm	Semi-intensive farming region. Severe mid-season dry-spells are common. Suitable for livestock pro-duction, together with the production of fodder crops and cash crops under good farm management.
N.R. IV	12.84	33.0	450–650mm	Semi-extensive region. Subject to periodic seasonal droughts and severe dry spell during the rainy season. Suitable for farming systems based on livestock production and drought resistant fodder crops. Forestry, wildlife/tourism.
N.R. V	11.28	29.0	>450mm	Extensive farming region. Suitable for extensive cattle ranching or game ranching. Zambezi Valley is infested with tsetse flies. Forestry, wildlife/tourism

Source: CSO, Agritex.

Annex 2.4.2. Provincial Areas by Natural Region

Province	NRI	Percentage NRII	NRIII	NRIV & NRV
Manicaland	17.0	5.3	42.4	35.3
Mash East	–	31.5	40.9	27.6
Mash Central	–	42.1	18.2	39.7
Mash West	–	36.9	34.0	29.1
Midlands	–	–	64.2	35.8
Masvingo	–	–	14.9	85.1
Mat. North	–	–	6.2	93.8
Mat. South	–	–	–	100.0

Source: Roth, 1990.

Annex 2.4.3. LSCF Land Use Efficiency Utilisation

Province	Total area (000 ha)	Arable land (000 ha)	Arable land (%)	Crop area planted (000 ha)	Cropping Efficiency (%)	Net arable land (000 ha)	Net cropping efficiency (%)	Adjusted crop area (000 ha)	Adjusted crop efficiency
	A	B	C = B/A	D	E = D/B	F	G = D/F	H	I = H/F
Mash-West	1,886.0	760.6	40.3	184.6	24.3	650.3	28.4	270.2	41.6
Mash-East	957.8	522.1	54.5	97.6	18.7	446.4	21.9	139.1	31.2
Mash-Central	732.6	307.3	41.9	105.4	34.3	262.7	40.1	152.7	58.1
Total	3,626.4	1,590.0	43.8	387.6	24.4	1,359.4	28.5	562.0	41.3

Annex 3.0 Policy and Institutional Context

Annex 3.2.1. Export Promotion Incentives

Policy	Details	Year Of Start	Year End	Group affected
Devaluation of Z$	Massive depreciation of the Zimbabwean dollar against major currencies. This increased the value of imports and exports in local currency terms	1982	On going	LSCF
Foreign Currency Scheme Export Promotion Programme (EPP)	Z$140 million allocated to Agricultural Sector between 1987 and 1989. For use as follows on imports – 25 per cent for chemicals and fertilizers – 20 per cent for spare parts – 15 per cent for livestock	1987	1991	LSCF
Export Retention Scheme (ERS)	Exporters entitled to retain part (5–7%) of their earnings from exports. Retained foreign currency earnings could then be used to import freely any goods (for consumptive use or input procurement).	1991	1994	LSCF
Export Revolving Fund (ERF)	Scheme allows exporters to retain 25 per cent of increases in export earnings. Established in 1983 for manufacturing industry only and expanded in 1987 to include agriculture and mining.	1987	On going	LSCF
Export Incentive Scheme	Was designed to increase value added exports. Gives exporters of processed and semi-processed commodities a 9% rebate on the FOB value of exports.	1982	1994	LSCF
Open General Import License (OGIL)	Imported goods placed under OGIL could be imported directly. Made input procurement easier and cheaper.	1990	–	All
Commodity Import Programmes (CIPS)	Made easier the importation of specific commodities (mainly inputs)j	1983	1991	LSCF
Transport subsidies	Government subsidized north bound flights for Affretair to increase cargo capacity which was short.	1985?	1994/95	LSCF

Source: Moyo, 1995.

Annex 4.0. Changing Land Uses and Reconstructing the Land Question

Annex 4.2.1. Location of National Parks, Sanctuaries, Safari Areas, Botanical Gardens and Reserves and Recreational Parks within Zimbabwe

Province	District	Name	Year	Activity	Land area (ha)	Water area (ha)
Manicaland	Chimanimani		Chimanimani		1953	National park
	Nyanga	Nyanga	1965	National park	33,000	0
	Chipinge	Chipinge	–	Safari area		–
				Botanical garden and reserve		
Masvingo	Chiredzi	Bangala	1975	Recreational park	2,800	1,133
	Chiredzi	Manjirenji	–	Recreational park	3,400	2,023
	Masvingo	Mutirikwi	–	Recreational park	16,900	9,105
	Chiredzi	Malipati	–	Safari area	0	–
		Manjini	–	Pan	–	0
	Chiredzi	Gonarezhou	1968	National park	505,300	–
	Chiredzi	Sabi	–	Safari area	–	0
Midlands	Kwekwe	Sebakwe	–	Recreational park	5,800	580
Mash West	Kariba	Mana Pools	1968	National park	219,600	
	Chegutu	Ngezi	–	Recreational park	–	0
	Karbia	Doma	–	Safari area	–	0
	Binga	Chewore		Safari area	–	0
	Hurungwe	Hurungwe	–	Safari area	–	0
	Kariba	Charara	–	Safari area	–	0
	Kariba	Matusadona	1963	National park	–	0
	Zvimba	Lake Chivero	–	Recreational park	–	2,630
	Zvimba	Lake Darwendale	1952	Recreational park	–	0
	Chinhoyi	Chinhoyi Caves	1955	Recreational park	–	0
	Kariba	Lake Kariba	1961	Recreational park	283,000	283,000
Mash Central	Muzarabani/Dande Gunwe		–	Safari area	–	0
	Shamwa	Umfurudzi	–	Safari area	–	0
Mash East	Goromonzi	Ewanrigg	–	Botanical Garden	–	0
	Harare	National Botanical Garden	–	Botanical Garden	–	0
Mat. South	Umzingwane	Umzingwane Lake Cunningham	1968	Safari area Recreational park	1,233	456
Mat. North		Umfuli		Safari area	–	0
	Hwange	Matetsi	–	Safari area	–	0
	Hwange	Kuzuma		Pan	–	3,130
	Hwange	Hwange	1928	National park	1,465,000	0
	Kariba	Chizarira	1963	National park	191,000	0
	Binga	Chirisa	–	Safari area	–	0
	Binga	Chete	–	Safari area	–	0
	Victoria Falls	Victoria Falls	1952	National park	2,34	0
	Matobo	Matopos	1952	National park	42,400	0

– Indicates that no data was available at the time of the research.

Source: Constructed from various GoZ records and literature.

Annex 4.2.2. Financial Returns of Crop Enterprises (1994/95 Season) per Hectare

Crop	Yield	Total revenue (Z$)	Variable total costs (Z$)	Gross margin (Z$)	Returns to variable cost
Horticulture					
Tomatoes	35,000	22,750	8,339	14,411	1.73
	45,000	29,250	8,552	20,698	2.42
	55,000	35,750	8,766	26,984	3.07
Green Mealies	24,000	7,800	3,122	4,678	1.49
	40,000	13,000	3,140	9,860	3.14
Green Beans	3,000	15,000	5,821	9,179	1.57
	4,000	20,000	6,206	13,794	2.22
Paprika	2,000	20,000	10,193	9,807	0.96
	3,000	30,000	10,299	19,701	1.91
Michigan Red Beans	4,000	14,040	3,226	10,814	3.35
	6,000	21,060	3,251	17809	5.47
Sweet Corn	12,000	12,000	4,824	7,176	1.48
	15,000	15,000	4,834	10,166	2.10
Sugar Beans	2,000	13,000	5,876	7,124	1.21
	2,500	16,250	5,983	10,267	1.71
Other Field Crops					
Tobacco	2,400	38,400	20,182	18,218	0.90
	3,300	52,800	27,621	25,179	0.91
Soyabeans	2,000	4,700	2,098	2,602	1.24
	2,600	6,110	3,068	3,042	0.99
Wheat	5,200	9,100	4,822	4,278	0.89
	5,500	9,625	5,075	4,550	0.90
Groundnuts	3,000	9,900	7,127	2,773	0.39
	4,000	13,200	8,376	4,824	0.58
Sorghum	2,000	2,300	2,762	(462)	(0.17)
	4,000	4,600	2,892	1,708	0.59
Cotton	1,800	9,000	4,418	4,582	1.04
	2,800	14,000	5,727	8,273	1.44
Maize	3,500	4,025	2,892	1,133	0.39
	6,500	7,475	4,274	3,201	0.75

Source: Muzenda, H. (unpublished).

Annex 4.3.1. Profile of Horticultural Producers by LSCF Agricultural Province (1994/95)

Province	Total no. of farmers	No. of hort. farmers	% of hort. farmers	Citrus	Flowers	Vege-tables	Tropical fruit	Deciduous fruit
Midlands	355	109	30.7	23	14	58	8	6
Makonde	972	172	17.7	35	31	76	22	8
Marondera	562	187	33.3	26	35	83	16	27
South West Mash.	292	120	41.1	37	12	47	17	7
Mash. Central	1,260	583	46.6	81	112	287	73	30
Eastern Districts	361	277	76.7	42	38	77	39	81
Masvingo	253	70	27.7	23	4	34	7	2
Matabeleland	554	121	21.8	57	5	23	23	13
Totals	4,609	1,639	35.6	324	251	685	205174	

Source: Horticultural Promotion Council.

Annex 4.3.2. Land Use on Commercial Farms: Areas under Horticulture (In Hectares)

As at Sept. 30	Fruit			Other		
	Large scale	Small scale	Total	Large scale	Small scale	Total
1970	5,626	2	5,628	3,000	829	87,982
1971	5,538	2	5,540	3,000	1,137	83,710
1972	5,841	2	5,843	3,000	1,307	83,514
1973	6,189	10	6,199	3,000	874	82,636
1974	5,983	279	6,262	3,000	4,592	82,184
1975	5,359	341	5,700	3,000	4,558	80,573
1976	5,228	288	5,516	3,000	4,333	84,168
1977	4,752	243	4,995	3,000	3,777	72,611
1978	4,275	216	4,991	3,000	3,401	70,864
1979	4,864	–	–	3,000	–	–
1980	3,663	_	–	3,000	–	–
1981	4,005	314	4,319	3,000	2,846	59,828
1982	3,679	206	3,885	3,000	2,153	53,709
1983	3,543	160	3,703	3,000	1,964	54,168
1984	4,062	–	–	3,000	–	–
1985	3,415	–	–	3,000	–	–
1986	–	–	–	–	–	–
1987	4,051	–	–	6,952	–	–
1988	5,710	258	5,968	9,380	2,373	11,753
1989	5,885	121	6,006	9,514	2,423	11,937
1990	6,426	110	6,536	9,561	2,707	12,268
1991	7,339	809	8,148	9,576	2,478	12,054
1992	7,270	487	7,757	8,989	1,908	10,893
1993	9,064	–	–	10,995	–	–

Note: Fruits = Include citrus fruits like oranges, grapefruit, deciduous fruits including strawberries, tropical fruits like mangoes, bananas, avocados and tree nuts. Others = Includes edible dry beans, sunhemp, nyimo, sweet potatoes, potatoes, onions, peas, tomatoes, other unspecified vegetables, green flowers, shrubs, seedlings and planted pastures grown commercially.

Source: Central Statistics Office, 1994.

Annex 4.3.3: Area under Fruit And Vegetables: 1994/95 Season (Hectares)

Crop	1994/95
Mangetout pea	261,817
Sugar snaps	57,224
Chillies	58
Beans (runner)	53
Beans (fine)	19
Baby corn	88
Carrots	22
Sweet corn	5,277
Passion Fruit	26,648
Citrus—Highveld	2,000
Citrus—Lowveld	1,500
Mangoes	400

Source: Horticultural Promotion Council.

Annex 4.3.4. Area of Cutflowers in Zimbabwe (Hectares)

Crop	1989/90	1990/91	1991/92	1992/93	1993/94
Protean	150	200	240	280	312
Roses	30	45	120	150	198
Asters	–	20	35	40	45
Chrysanthemums	–	–	20	23	28
Molucella	–	–	20	26	32
Bupleurum	–	–	15	10	18
Hypericum	–	–	–	11	18
Ammi Majus	–	2	40	8	38
Liatris	–	–	50	12	12
Summer Flowers	–	175	225	180	232
Total		442	765	740	933

– Indicates that no data was available at the time of the research.

Source: Horticultural Promotion Council.

Annex 4.3.5. Horticultural Producers In Mashonaland (1995)

Mash. East	No. of farmers	Citrus	Flowers	Mush-rooms	Vege-tables	T-Fruit*	D-Fruit*	Potato	Plant
Bromley	182	10	18	7	37	5	6	8	3
Headlands	40	2	5	0	3	3	4	2	1
Macheke	76	2	3	0	10	0	1	1	2
Marondera	190	8	7	2	30	8	14	9	5
Wedza	73	4	2	0	3	0	2	3	0
Gadzema	1	0	0	0	0	0	0	0	0
Total	562	26	35	9	83	16	25	23	11

Mash. West	No. of farmers	Citrus	Flowers	Mush-rooms	Vege-tables	T-fruit	D-fruit	Potato	Plant
Battlefields	21	1	0	0	3	1	1	2	0
Chakari	25	1	1	0	1	1	0	1	0
Chegutu	62	5	3	0	13	3	1	7	3
Gadzema	23	4	0	0	1	3	1	1	0
Kadoma	87	16	7	2	18	3	4	9	3
Selous	39	5	1	0	5	2	0	6	1
SuriSuri	35	5	0	0	4	4	0	0	3
Total	292	37	12	2	47	17	7	26	10

Mash. West	No. of farmers	Citrus	Flowers	Mush-rooms	Vege-tables	T-fruit	D-fruit	Potato	Plant
Ayshire	93	5	1	0	5	5	9	1	2
Banket	77	1	1	1	3	2	1	1	0
Chinhoyi	122	2	2	0	11	1	0	6	0
Doma	85	3	3	0	1	0	0	1	0
Karoi	183	8	6	2	7	5	0	1	0
Tengwe	62	1	1	0	0	1	0	0	0
Trelawney/Dar	139	4	19	0	4	2	1	1	2
Umbee	38	1	0	0	8	1	0	1	0
Bromley	183	10	18	7	37	5	6	8	3
Total	972	35	51	10	76	22	17	20	7

* T-Fruit = tropical fruits, D-Fruit = deciduous fruits
Source: HPC.

Annex 4.3.6. Total Value of Horticultural Production

	1983	1984	1985	1986	1987	1988	1989	1990	1991	1992
Commercial sector veget. (Z$ million)										
Dry beans	491	190	123	101	231	867	1,062	598	706	1,495
Potatoes	5,388	6,567	7,770	7,819	9,829	12,647	16,985	17,605	21,748	28,627
Onions	1,665	1,509	3,365	3,890	3,919	4,432	4,600	6,028	5,844	6,000
Peas	331	394	633	804	419	1,095	863	1,152	1,815	2,304
Tomatoes	4,426	5,966	5,106	6,466	5,514	3,884	7,377	5,560	10,076	22,827
Other vegetables	3,026	332	3,031	3,670	4,886	7,210	7,628	9,611	21,718	20,255
Flowers & gardens plants	581	574	1,000	806	1,484	3,332	10,734	15,726	27,583	39,525
Total	15,908	18,532	21,028	23,556	26,282	33,467	49,249	56,280	89,490	121,033
Commercial sector fruits (Z$ million)										
Citrus	4,096	5,161	5,454	5,750	6,219	9,091	10,265	12,597	15,965	13,358
Deciduous (inc. berries)	3,866	3,737	4,273	55,169	5,656	4,211	6,104	6,741	12,688	16,258
Tropical	1,261	1,543	1,482	1,964	2,465	3,299	6,367	8,317	11,073	9,852
Fruit trees	126	75	74	97	269	208	212	281	1,687	2,110
Total fruit	9,349	10,518	11,283	12,980	14,609	16,809	22,948	27,936	41,413	46,362
Total commercial fruit & veg. (Z$ million)	25,257	29,050	32,311	36,536	40,891	50,276	72,197	84,216	130,903	167,396
% growth		15	11	12	22	22	43	16	55	28
Communal sector Beans, fruit & vegetables (Z$ thousand)	17,464	21,385	23,774	27,289	31,369	38,804	39,829	47,179	59,104	101,149
% growth		22	11	14	14	11	14	18	25	71

NB: Figures include estimates of vegetables consumed. Figures on commercial fruit do not include sales of canned fruit.

Source: CSO in The Agricultural Sector of Zimbabwe: Statistical Bulletin.

Annex 4.3.7. Zimbabwe's Horticultural Exports

Year	Flowers		Produce		Citrus		Total		Growth per annum %
	Tonnes	Gross value (US$'000)	Tonnes	Gross value (US$'000)	Tonnes	Gross value (US$'000)	Tonnes	Gross value (US$'000)	
1985/86	338.00	1,554.80	396.00	1,188.00	2,272.00	772.48	3,006.00	3,515.28	
1986/87	593.00	2,727.80	610.00	1,830.00	5,026.00	1,708.84	6,229.00	6,266.64	78.27
1987/88	1,326.00	6,099.60	748.00	2,244.00	7,352.00	2,499.68	9,426.00	10,843.28	73.03
1988/89	2,411.00	11,090.60	1,413.00	4,239.00	7,848.00	2,668.32	11,672.00	17,997.92	65.98
1989/90	2,872.00	13,211.20	2,823.00	8,469.00	8,780.00	2,985.20	14,475.00	24,665.40	37.05
1990/91	3,722.00	17,121.20	4,215.00	12,645.00	6,300.00	2,142.00	14,237.00	31,908.20	29.36
1991/92	4,757.70	21,885.41	4,354.27	13,062.81	8,929.85	3,036.15	18,041.82	37,994.37	19.04
1992/93	5,206.00	23,947.60	3,998.56	11,995.68	9,000.00	3,060.00	18,204.56	39,003.28	2.68
1993/94	5,769.73	36,540.76	5,202.27	15,606.81	15,000.00	5,100.00	25,972.00	47,247.57	21.14
1994/95	9,095.44	41,839.02	8,989.04	36,967.12	20,000.00	6,800.00	38,084.48	75,606.14	60.02
1995/96	12,278.84	56,482.68	12,135.20	36,405.61	24,000.00	8,160.00	48,414.05	101,048.29	33.65
1996/97	16,576.44	76,251.62	16,382.53	49,147.58	32,000.00	10,880.00	64,958.96	136,279.20	34.87
1997/98	22,378.19	102,939.69	22,116.41	66,349.23	45,000.00	150,000.00	89,494.60	184,588.92	35.45
1998/99	302,210.56	133,968.58	29,857.15	89,571.46	64,000.00	21,760.00	124,067.71	250,300.04	35.60
1999/00	40,784.26	187,607.58	40,307.16	120,921.47	84,000.00	28,560.00	165,091.41	337,089.05	34.67
2000/01	55,058.75	253,270.24	54,414.66	163,243.98	100,000.00	34,000.00	209,473.41	450,514.22	33.65
2001/02	74,329.31	341,914.32	73,459.79	220,379.38	1,330000.00	45,220.00	280,789.10	607,514.19	34.85
2002/03	100,344.57	461,585.01	99,170.72	297,512.16	158,000.00	53,720.00	357,515.29	812,817.16	33.79
2003/04	135,465.16	623,139.76	133,880.47	401,641.41	182,000.00	61,880.00	451,345.64	1,086,661.17	33.69
2004/05	182,877.97	841,238.67	180,738.63	542,215.90	200,000.00	68,000.00	563,616.61	1,451,454.58	33.57

Source: Horticultural Promotion Council.

Annex 4.3.8. Management Committee of the Irrigation Scheme (Tsakare, 1996)

Name	Position	Status/Feature
Chairperson	Stanlake Chimanikire	Organise internal and external meetings
Vice Chairman	Mrs. Fidius Chibondo	Assist the chair
Secretary	Kingstone Chakanyuka	Minuting at meetings
Vice Secretary	James Chiuye	Assisting the secretary
Treasurer	Chinyandura	Handling financial matters
Maintenance Committee	1. Chanaka Chikuape	Maintenance and procurement of equipment
	2. Richard Bandamira	
Production Committee	1. Kudakwashe Masawi	Marketing and surveying
	2. Mrs Magina Karonga	
Ordinary Committee	1. Frick Karonga	Traverse all the positions (advise)
	2. Sherpard Chipadze	
	3. Mrs Nyamuzhanda	
	4. Mrs Mabhidhori	

Source: Field interviews, 1996.

Annex 4.3.9. Principle Irrigation Scheme Cropping Patterns

Name of farmer	Crops produced	Amount produced	Cost of crop
Mr. E. Gatsi	Tomatoes	250 crates/month	$25/crate
	Onions	700 bundles	$5/bundle
	G/mealies	600 dozen	$10/dozen
	Okra	60 crates	$45/crate
V. Chiwara	Baby corn	2,200 cobs	16c/cob
	Green beans	3 x 50 kg	$9/dozen
	Sweet potatoes	gallons	$35/gallon
Chihuri	Green beans	5 tins	$150/tin
	Sweet potatoes	4 tins	$35/tin
	Green mealies	500/dozen	$50/dozen
Mrs. Dimba	Tomatoes	300 to 400 crates/month	–
	Green vegetables	20 bundles/day	$2/bundle
	Green mealies	–	–
Mr. Kagogoda	Tomatoes	20 boxes/week	$10–15/box
	Vegetables	300–400 bundles/month	$5/bundle
	Butternut	0.5–1 tonne	–
	Okra	4–7 boxes	$30–45/box
	Cucumber	3–4 sacks (90 kgs)	–
Mr. M Mhako	Tomatoes	15 boxes/week	$15–30/box
	Vegetables	300 bundles/month	%5/bundle
	Okra	6 boxes/harvest	$45/box
	Cucumber	5–7 sacks	$30/sack
Mrs. Manyara	Tomatoes	100 boxes/week	$10–30/box
	Vegetables	40–50 bundles/day	$5/bundle
	Okra	8 boxes/month	$35–45/box
Mr. Makuvatsine	Tomatoes	30 boxes/day	$15–30/box
	Vegetables	500 bundles/day	$5/bundle
	Butternut	400 heads/day	–
	Okra	6 boxes/month	$30–45/crate
	Cucumber	–	–
	Cabbages	500 heads/day	$2/head
Mr. Mwanga	Tomatoes –	–	$30–35/box, $800/day
	Vegetables	700–800 bundles/day	$5/bundle
Mr. Kasusu	Tomatoes	75 boxes/day	$30–45/box
	Vegetables	700 bundles/day	$5/bundle
	Nyimo	–	–
	Cucumber	50 boxes/crop season	–

Annex 4.3.10. Tsakare Dryland Resettlement Scheme

History

Established in November 1982, the farm was bought by the Government from Edwards Love to resettle people without land from Madziwa, Dotito, Mt. Darwin and Rushinga. However, even people from as far as Chinhoyi settled on the resettlement scheme. 10 to 15 families settled on the farm in November 1982, when it was suggested that the first settlers would come in 1983. This demonstrates the level of land shortages that was being experienced then in the Communal Areas.

There were too many wild animals and they destroyed crops. The wildlife population was greater than the cropped area. Most people came in 1983 and the problem of wildlife gradually ceased as more land was cleared. The major constraints were lack of draught power and labour shortages because children remained in the Communal Areas. In 1984, a plan was produced for a grazing scheme. Members were asked to contribute $25.00 per person for the procurement of fencing material. 125 people raised the money and it was managed by the VIDCO. Donors were by then not forthcoming to provide finance for paddocks, and the resettlement officer recommended a border fence, with finance mainly from Government.

A new problem cropped up, fence vandalism by people from Mupfure and Chihuri communal lands. These people felt that the resources on the farm belonged to everybody (blacks) and were the new fruits of independence. They wanted to benefit as well, from the grazing scheme. The fence was completely destroyed and the project ceased to operate. The problem of resource poaching (grass, firewood, poles, and crops) still continued and failure to develop Communal Areas equitably means that such problems will continue for the unforeseeable future.

The 1991/92 drought had a devastating impact as production on the thriving re-settlement went down completely. AFC loans were not repaid and AFC threatened to attach property. The tillage system was affected as the oxen were sold during the drought and farmers are still to recover from the effects of the drought on draught power. On the other hand the DDF is failing to provide tractors to the farmers who desperately need these.

Land tenure status

Farmers on the resettlement scheme, are resident according to the permits given by DERUDE. Each member is allocated 5 ha for arable cropping and 0.5 ha for residence. Some farmers have benefitted from the 0.5 ha for irrigation.

Crop production

Major crops produced on the scheme are maize, cotton, tobacco and some traditional crops such as nyimo (round nuts), nyemba, groundnuts which are retained for family consumption. Farmers produce maize crops ranging from 200 to over 500 bags (90kgs) of maize in a good year, and they get cash incomes of $10,000 to $15,000 per season. For cotton, they harvest from 10 to 50 bales and realise incomes of between $8,000 and $15,000 per season. Tobacco is sold to the Harare Tobacco Auction Floors. In the last season the crop fetched badly as it could only be sold for $1 per kg tumbling from $4.00 to $5.00 when the crop was first sold in May.

Land problems

Currently there are 136 people who are plot holders, but a "lot" of young people do not have any land and it is illegal to sub-divide the land set aside for the plot holders. Authorities on the have approached government about the land shortages and it has promised more.

Impacts of ESAP

A combination of ESAP and drought has had a devastating impact on crop production on the scheme. Expensive inputs and water shortages have reduced the farmers cash incomes. The buying prices by dealers and Government is not equitable to the buying of inputs by the farmers. Without money for the farmers there is nothing positive to say about ESAP, because prices of commodities are rising. The marketing of crops particularly maize has generally improved as farmers can now bid for prices favourable to themselves. Private buyers come with their own transport and packs. In some instances some farmers have gained whilst others have been crooked. But so far no farmers have complained and at times they just do not notice because they sometimes need cash desperately so they overlook some of the losses they make to these companies.

Agritex role

Agritext officers at the resettlement scheme provide extension services to farmers in the scheme on proper and current information on crop production. Advice is not enforced on people, but some farmers who do not follow instructions later turn back for advice when they see the success of some farmers. The officers go on refresher courses, but they lack of information on critical detail horticultural issues.

Agritex would like to work hand in hand with lobby organisations such as ZFU, but none of the farmers are affiliated to any of the representative bodies.

Source: Field interviews, observations and GoZ Records

Annex 4.4.1. Land Area(km²) Used For Wildlife Conservation and Utilisation in Zimbabwe

Year	National parks km²	(ha)	Safari areas km²	(ha)	Forest areas km²	(ha)	CAs km²	(ha)	LSCF km²	(ha)	Total km²	(ha)	% of Zimbabwe
1930	17,500	1,750,000	0	0	0	0	0	0	?	?	17,500	1,750,000	4.48
1940	10,583	1,058,300	0	0	0	0	0	0	?	?	10,583	1,058,300	2.71
1950	11,075	1,107,500	0	0	0	0	0	0	?	?	11,075	1,215,000	2.83
1960	11,800	1,180,000	0	0	0	0	0	0	350	35,000	12,150	1 ,215,000	3.11
1970	26,073	2,687,300	7,494	749,400	0	0	0	0	30,000	3,000,000	63,567	6,356,700	16.26
1980	22,799	2,279,900	18,576	1,857,600	5,541	554,100	3,356	335,600	30,000	3,000,000	80,272	8,027,200	20.54
1990	22,799	2,279,900	18,576	1,857,600	4,963	496,300	12,806	1,280,600	27,000	2,700,000	86,144	8,614,400	22.04

Source: Cumming ,1990, p.15; Jansen, 1992.

Annex 4.4.2. Parks and Wildlife Estate of Zimbabwe, 1995

Estate	Number	Area (ha)		Facilities
National park	11	2.7m	6.8%	Visitors accommodation / Nature protection
Safari area	16	1.9m	4.8%	Recreational hunting and non-hunting safaris, hiking / More freedom than parks
Recreational parks	15	–	–	Large impoundment around water bodies / Natural features and rural atmosphere are presented with a variety of recreational activities
Sanctuaries	6	18,500	–	Protection of individual animals, bird and plant species
Botanical reserves	14	1,500	–	Protect plant communities
Botanical gardens	3	–	–	

Annex 4.4.3. Safari Establishments in All Mashonaland Provinces, 1995

Name	Province	Where located	Infrastructure/ game	Facilities offered
Fothergill Safari Lodge	Mashonaland West	Matusadona national park	Electricity, 14 thatched en suite, 28 beds hot/cold running water.	Drives and walks, boat and fishing trips, platforms.
Katere Safari Lodge	Mashonaland West	5km west of Bumi Hills Kariba Lake shore	16 twin beded lodges and 1 suite, brick built under thatch, electricity laundry and swimming pool, hot/cold running water, bath sower, toilets.	Game viewing in open vehicles, bird watching, fishing.
Pamuzinda Safari Lodge	Mashonaland West	Private estate in Selous Chegtu	Plain game species including elephants, giraffe and rhinocerous. Thatched bungalows.	Game viewing.
Mwanga Safari Lodge	Mashonaland Central	Private Bally Vaughan	Buffalo, giraffe, sable, eland, lion, leopard, hyena and elephant, 16 en suite A-Frame chalets, dining complex.	Game viewing.
Sijarira Camp	Mashonaland West	Lake Kariba	7 open-fronted, wood, reed and thatch chalets en suite with twins beds.	Fresh water fishing and the famous fighting tiger fish.
Kaburi Wilderness	Mashonaland West	Near Kariba	Big game species, buffalo elephants and big cats.	Game viewing.
Matusadona Sky Safari	Mashonaland West	Matusadona National Park	Game viewing.	Big game viewing and exploring scenic Sanyati Gorge.
Lower Zambezi Mana Pools Safari and Beef Eater Canoeing	Mashonaland	Mana Pools	World Heritage site, Ruckomechi Camp with thatched chalets over- looking the Zambezi river.	Fishing with game viewing, canoeing, adventure and safari.
Lake Kariba Safari	Mashonaland West	Kariba	Individual chalets.	Game viewing by kind of water. Fishing.
Snake Park and Larvon Bird Garden	Mashonaland West	Outskirts of Harare on highway to Bulawayo Zvimba RDC	Hundreds of species of exotic birds. Venomous and non-venomous snakes —cobras boom- slangs and mambas.	Snake viewing and bird watching
Lion and Cheetah Park	Mashonaland West	Off-Bulawayo– Harare road in Zvimba FDC	Well staked game which include rhino, giraffe, etc.	Viewing of rare and nocturnal species
Bally Vaughan Game Park	Mashonaland Central	Outside Harare	Species include lion, leo- pard, hyena and elephant.	Viewing of game and watching of birds.
Kariba and Victoria Falls Sky Safari		Bumi Hills, Forthergill Island and Spurwing	Nature sanctuary and crocodile farm.	Game viewing by vehicle or water.

Source: Zim-Sun Hotel Brochures & UTC Brochures.

Annex 4.4.4. Case of LSCF Conservancies

a) Membership of The Chiredzi River Conservancy

Ranch	Owner	Area (ha.)
Spear Grass	C. Holden	1,808
Nyamadindiza	C. Holden	1,866
Melrose	A, Davies & D. Nesbitt	1,816
Glen Devon	G. Southwood	1,825
Dawlish Estate	D. Nesbitt	5,678
Seabenani	B. Van Aarde	3,655
Oscro	T. Sarpo	3,010
Chiredzi Ranch South Lot 2	I. Rukatcha (leased by T. Sarpo)	5,104
Mungwezi	T. Ballance	5,038
Crown Ranch East	Hein Family (leased by Dombodema Ranching)	9,307
Buffalo Range	Style Family	17,000
Rware	A de la Rue	32,375
Total		89,482

Source: Price Waterhouse, 1993.

b) Membership of The Bubiana Conservancy

Ranch	Owner	Area (ha)
Sovelele	N. York	36,075
Peregwe	P. Abbot	17,261
Dwala	N & R Rosenfels	9,444
Mkashi	D. Rochat	14,974
Barberton	G. Barber	10,680
Ladi	J.M. Rorke	10,320
Drummond Ranch	K. Drummond	28,792
Total		127,546

Source: Price Waterhouse, 1993.

c) Save Valley Conservancy

Ranch	Owner	Area (ha)
Matendere	Redco (Pvt) Ltd.	13,123
Gunundwe	B. Gous	11,374
Mapari	H. Vorster	23,153
Chishakwe	D. Henning	9,977
Msaize	Brooklands Ranching (Pvt) Ltd.	16,340
Chapungu	Zimbabwe Sun Limited	12,976
Savuli	Savule Syndicate	5,529
Makore	D. Duckworth	7,451
Bedford Block	Dunmow (Pvt) Ltd.	12,215
Humani	Humanio Estates (Pvt) Ltd.	41,158
Angus	Zimbabwe Hunters Association	15,792
Mukazi River	R. Cunningham	11,457
Mukwasi	P. Wenham	12,549
Senuko	Senuko (Pvt) Ptd.	24,120
Masapas	P. Henning	15,437
Levanga	J. Otterson	13,040
Mkwasine	L. Engels	12,547
Impala	J. Naude	8,097
ARDA (potential)	ADA	12,146
Chanurwe	PASDT Holdings (Pvt) Ltd	44,348
Mkwasine	Mkwasine Limited	3,502
Total		326,331

Source: Save Valley Wildlife Services Limited, Eighth Draft, August 1995.

Annex 4.4.5 Mashonaland Individual LSCF Wildlife Ranching

Case 1: Valley Voughan Game Park owned by Robin and Peter McIntosh is located 40km from Harare along Shamva road, in Mashonaland Central. The size of the farm is 1,600 acres.

- The farmer has developed eco-tourism which has proved popular with foreign, regional and local visitors alike. Though comparatively smaller than most game parks with an acreage of 1,600 acres, the Park is probably the most concentrated game farm in the country.

- Species at the Park range from spring duiker and impala to bigger game like giraffe, elephants, lions and leopards and all the species are breeding.

- It is expensive to run the park, for example, each of the 2 adult lion that form the foundation of the Park, needs 2kg of meat per meal, and a leopard, which was captured after killing 49 cattle in the surrounding farms, eats a cattle leg every day.

- Six chalets, named the Mwanga Lodge, have been developed at the Park and since being formed, have retained a 50% bed occupancy that is expected to improve.

Case 2: Catolina Wilderness Centre owned by Dave Thomlison. The size of the Game Park is 2,700 ha, located on the 20km peg along Beatrice Road.

- Once a tobacco stronghold, the farm, 20km from Beatrice, has turned into a wildlife sanctuary carrying over 10 different non-predatory species. The species include the Lichtentein's hartebeest, which is one of the most endangered species in Zimbabwe. There are only 37 left in the country and 16 of them are at the Catolina Wilderness Centre, where he keeps them in trust for Parks.

- Most of the hartebeest were shot in the early 1960s during a campaign against foot and mouth disease, but were reintroduced in the Lowveld in 1970 but continued to dwindle in numbers and were later brought to the Highveld and Carolina Wilderness volunteered to give them sanctuary.

- It started in 1987 and employs 4 game scouts.

Source: Field Observations, *Sunday Mail*, 9/02/95, 16/10/94.

Annex 4.4.6. Location of Campfire Projects by Province and District

Province	District	Year	Activity
Mashonaland Central	Chiweshe	1993	Safari hunting
	Guruve	1989	Photographic safari
	Rushinga		Fishing
	Muzarabani		
	Shamva	1995	
Mashonaland West	Nyaminyami	1989	Safari hunting
	Hurungwe	1993	Photographic safari
			Fishing projects
Mashonaland East	UMP Zvataida	1994	Tourism and fisheries
	Mudzi	1994	
Manicaland	Chipinge	1993	Safari operations
			Eco-tourism
Masvingo	Chiredzi	Early 1990s	Safari operations
			Photographic safari
			Forestry
	Mwenezi	Early 1990s	Eco-tourism
Matabeleland	Bulilima Mangwe	Early 1990a	Safari operations
	Beitbridge		Non-consumptive tourism
	Gwanda	Early 1990s	Eco-tourism
Matabeleland South	Tsholotsho	Early 1990s	Safari hunting
	Binga	1991	
	Nkayi	Early 1990s	
	Lupane	Early 1990s	Tourism
	Bubi	Early 1990s	Joint venture with forestry commission in timber exploitation
Midlands	Gokwe South		Safari operations
	Gokwe North		

Source: Zimtrust and Campfire Brochures.

Annex 4.5.1. Ostrich Land Use and Management Requirements

Management System	Area	Stocking Ratio	Stage of Growth	Feeding patterns/ requirements	No. of chicks produced
Rearing chicks	1–2 ha	1 foster parent 5–6 chicks	0–3 months	Zero grazing	–
Growers semi-intensive	20–40 ha	–	9–22 wks	1.5kg/day	–
Intensive breeding	0.5 ha (50mx50m)	1:2 or 1:1 (cock to hens)	breeding season	Zero grazing scheme: – lucerne – comery – carrot top – barna – rye grass	
Semi-intensive breeding	40 ha	1:1/1:2 birds run free	breeding season	Feed from natural vegetation	20–40 chicks per year
"–	20 ha	2 females	breeding	Supplementary feeding	"–
Intensive growing	1 ha	3:2 hens/cocks		Zero grazing scheme	Minimum of 5 chicks/hen

Source: Fieldwork, interviews.

Annex 4.5.2. Mutoko Ostrich Producers Syndicate (Proposed)

Member	Farm area (ha)	Proposed Area under ostriches (ha)
Mudzinganyama (use same farm)	170.8382	2.0
Hodzi	525.45	1.0
Masayi	101.0195	1.0
Taruvinga	89.7022	1.0
Chipunza	61.3506	1.0
Zinyemba	87.3839	1.0
Nhidza	225.0290	1.0
Jiri	183.8381	1.0

Annex 4.5.3. LSCF Ostrich Farmer

Case 1: A 350 acre farm owned by Stowe Philip located 90km from Harare, along the Mutorashanga Road was subdivided into 50-metre by 50-metre paddocks. In 1993, the farm had over 1,100 birds of varying ages, ranging from a few weeks old to five years. These comprised 750 chicks, 350 two-year old birds and 100 eighteen-month-old birds. The system of farming is such that two hens with their cock are put in one paddock and this means cock fighting is zero and there is more egg production. "This new system has seen each hen laying 100 eggs that have 98% fertility as opposed to about 40 eggs with 68% fertility in the past" (Mr. Philip, *Herald*, 14/02/93). Equipment at the farm include three incubators which can take 500 eggs each. The main problems are disease problems and the rampaging thieves who steal eggs and chicks which they later sell to neighbouring farms. "To my surprise, some neighbouring farmers are buying the stolen eggs and chicks, thereby promoting thefts" Mr. Philip (*Herald*, 14/02/95).

Source: *Herald*, 14/02/93.

Annex 4.5.4. Mudzi Ostrich Project

The project is located at Kudzwe Dam in Mudzi Rural District on a 13 ha. farm on the banks of Kudzwe Dam. The farm produces its own foliage, soya beans and maize to feed the 58 birds there. Eggs at the farm were being transported over long distances to hatcheries in Harare and Domboshawa for incubation but most of these were not producing any chicks despite their high fertility rate. Out of the 70 fertile eggs produced in the 1994/95 breeding season, only 35 chicks were hatched and it is believed the low production rate was associated with the long distances eggs were being carried before being placed in incubators. A hatchery building is currently under construction after Zimtrust donated $30,000 for the purchase of materials. Locals involved in the project would benefit through providing cash and employment and they provide inputs such as bricks, river sand, stones and labour. An incubator was provided under an $870,000 European Union grant that enabled project to take off but has been idle at the farm as there was no appropriate building to house it. One hatcher is operational and the farm expects to reach its capacity of 200 birds as more chicks would be produced. The services of a farm manager and a consultant, Mr. Evans Graham, have been secured and seconded to council by the New Zealand Volunteer Services.

Source: *Herald*, 21/03/96.

Annex 5.0 Politics and Major Actors in the New Land Struggles

Annex 5.2.1 Major Institutions Involved in New Land Use Struggles

A. Key Horticultural Organisations

Reserve Bank

The main role of the Reserve Bank of Zimbabwe as it relates to the horticultural sector is in foreign currency provision, through facilities such as the Horticultural Facility and the Export Retention Scheme, and, in monitoring export earnings and the authorisation of payment in foreign currency for the hire of charter aircraft.

Horticultural Research

The Horticultural Research Institute of the Department of Research and Specialist Services (DR & SS) operates three research institutes located in Marondera, Chiredzi and Nyanga and undertakes trials at the Chipinge and Matopos research stations, funded by the government and external donors such as the Kellog Foundation, the World Bank, Swedish Aid (SAREC), Cornell University, Rockefeller Foundation and Overseas Development Administration of the United Kingdom. Because of limited financial resources, little research can be conducted, targeting the smallholder farmers. The Agricultural Research Trust also carries out some horticultural researches usually on contract basis, while the University of Zimbabwe conducts researches under the Crop Science Department in the Faculty of Agriculture.

Extension Services

Extension on horticulture is provided by the Department of Agritex of the Ministry of Agriculture. It targets its extension at the smallholder sector with extension to the large scale commercial farms being provided only on request. Through a FAO funded programme called "Improvement and Expansion of Horticulture in Communal Areas of Zimbabwe", six Agritex employees were sent to U.K. to train as horticulturalists. These have further trained more than a hundred extension workers to specialise in horticulture. The extension workers, who advise smallholders on technical aspects of production and horticultural marketing (Agritex interview, 1995). Various private organisations such as input supply companies (e.g. chemical, fertiliser, seed companies) also provide some extension advice on various aspects of horticulture especially those that relate to services which they provide. The Commercial Farmers Union (CFU) also provides extension to its members on various aspects of horticultural production, processing and marketing.

Agricultural Development Authority (ADA)

ADA is a parastatal which has played a major role in horticultural promotion nationally, through its own production and promotional work. ADA implements a major European Community funded horticultural development project called the Mashonaland East Fruit and Vegetable Development Programme, which started in 1987 "... to promote fruit and vegetable production among smallholder farmers of Communal Areas of Mashonaland East" (Interview, Mangaer, Hunting Technical Services Ltd., 1992), through extension advice and, support for marketing and transportation. The main crops promoted are mangoes and tomatoes which it is hoped will take smallholders into the export market.

Farmer Associations

There are many informal horticultural producer groups which vary in terms of both size and operations. Producers of export fruit, vegetables and flowers usually belong to marketing cooperatives or are represented by export agencies. One big association is the Export Flower Growers Association of Zimbabwe (EFGAZ) which represents and is financed by flower growers. This is split into smaller groups such as the Rose Growers Association which in turn may be further split into smaller groups of farmers in the same location. These farmer groups also vary according to type of produce. There are some commercial farmers who are not members. There are however few such horticultural groups in the smallholder sector, as most operate independently and as such have no representation. The Zimbabwe Farmers Union (ZFU) has plans to promote associations for smallholder horticultural farmers.

Chart 1.0. Some Key Wildlife Organisations

Institution	Function
Zimbabwe Council for Tourism (ZCT)	Is the representative body of all the sectors which make up the Zimbabwe tourism products and is the spokesman for the industry. Aims to produce an enabling environment for the growth of tourism by encouraging development of a fiscal, legislative and physical environment favourable to tourism investment and growth.
The Zimbabwe Professional Hunters & Guides Association (ZPHGA)	Provides training courses at all levels: Learner exam course (January each year) Full exam refresher course (October each year) Practical courses at various times in: firearms, birds, trees, mammals, skinning and trophy preparation. Considers requests from the industry for specific training requirements e.g. a canoe course is currently being considered. Liaises with National Parks on examinations and assists where required. Runs a Bursary Fund to assist those not able to fund these courses from their own resources.
ZATSO (Zimbabwe Association of Tour and Safari Operators) 1989, 592 members	Supply of information on trade fairs, publications and participate in promotional activities such as the visits of foreign journalists and attending trade conventions. Take up members' problems with the relevant government departments and make representations on the industry's behalf regarding Park entry fees, trophy fees, documentation and other relevant matters. Facilitate members' access to the preferential Public Liability Insurance premium rates through brokers.
ITOZA (Inbound Tour Operators of Zimbabwe Association) 1989, 592 members	Package tours for overseas promotion. Arranging in-house courier training programme to provide suitably trained couriers and tour bus drivers for conducted tours. Liaison with airlines increase internal routes. Participate in internal industry discussions to regularise price systems and pursuing the provision of insurance. Cater for Inbound operators against the recent overseas E.C. consumer protection law provisions which enable a dissatisfied customer to sue for enormous damages. Assisting in participation of external trade fairs. Runs a Benevolent Fund to assist members injured during the course of their duties and who do not receive adequate compensation from other sources.

Bow Hunting Association	Consists of operators involved in bow-hunting activities. On-site training provided for tourists.
Wildlife Producers Association (WPA)	Promotion of sustainable utilisation of wildlife on members' properties, Communal Areas and within the Southern Africa region. Office bearers visit prospective members, attend farmers' Association and Intensive Conservation Area Meetings, hold field days and discussion groups, speak at universities, schools, financial institutions and other interested bodies. Visit members on their farms and ranches and give and receive members advice. Arranges for the capture and translocation of endangered species in collaboration with the endangered species committee and the Parks Department. Liaises with Parks Department for the setting up of breeding sanctuaries on farms and ranches for endangered species, and once numbers have built up, redistribute animals to areas where they once existed.
The Wildlife Society of Zimbabwe	An NGO established in 1923 for the purpose of preserving wildlife in National Parks and other sanctuaries.
The Zimbabwe National Conservation Trust	NGO
Crocodile Farmers' Association of Zimbabwe	Represents farmers' interests.
Zimbabwe Trust/Campfire Association	Coordinates policy, marketing and technical services of Campfire Districts

The Horticultural Promotion Council

The HPC is the umbrella organization for the horticulture industry in Zimbabwe, with particular emphasis on export production. Formed in the 1980s, its main objective is to create an environment within which the horticulture industry could develop. The HPC, through active liaison with the relevant Ministries of the Government of Zimbabwe, has created an awareness of the requirements of the industry for investment, foreign currency and transport. It is fully financed by the private sector in the form of both membership fees and levies on exported produce. It represents the interest of the horticulture industry as a whole, growers, exporters, wholesalers and ancillary industries, such as packaging, but draws most of its membership from individuals who are also in the Commercial Farmers Union. Its representation is therefore mainly in the Large Scale Commercial Farmers, even though there are current efforts to contribute money towards development of small scale horticulture.

Zimtrade

Zimtrade was established in 1991 as a joint venture between Government and the private sector to function as a national trade promotion organisation with the principal aim of expanding Zimbabwe's exports world wide. Horticulture and floriculture are key products of the Zimtrade business. It works closely with the Horticultural Promotion Council (HPC) in trying to facilitate and promote Zimbabwe's horticultural exports. While the HPC is more limited to the local industry and acts as a lobbying group, Zimtrade is more focused on international markets. It conducts local and international flower and horticultural shows, produces a Horticultural Newsletter on market intelligence, conducts market surveys and product research to identify markets and to find ways of improving competitiveness of its products, and provides market and price information to interested parties such as export agencies and other middlemen (Zimtrade Interview, 1995).

B. Wildlife Institutional Framework

The first government officers to be employed full-time on the protection and control of wildlife were appointed in the Forestry Department in 1928, followed later by staff of the Game and Fish Preservation Act in 1929, which were superseded by the creation of a Department of National Parks in 1950, when most of the 14 reserve areas which form the basis of today's major parks and safari areas, were proclaimed. Other key wildlife organisations are summarised in Chart 1.2 below.

The WPA promotes markets for wildlife ranchers through publicity work and linkages to the tourist market, it arranges for game captures in conjunction with government agencies and auctioneers, it monitors drugs use and conservation practices, licences producers and lobbies for appropriate policies. To achieve these tasks the WPC conducts its own on-farm extension work, through local level Intensive Conservation Area Committees to advise, monitor and receive advice from members. The WPA also conducts public lobbying to improve environmental awareness, promote wildlife management in Communal Areas and to exchange experiences within the Southern African region. The WPA also works closely with research organisations, various environmental NGOs and with wildlife commodity associations such as the ostrich and crocodile producer associations.

After the WPA was formed, about seven licenced game capture units were formed, five of which are commercial operations and two are part of the Department of National Parks and Wildlife Management. The licensing of these units is controlled by the Department of National Parks in conjunction with the WPA. Since 1985, more than 15,000 head of game have been captured and translocated in Zimbabwe, thus restocking areas that have long since been denuded of wildlife. WPA also seeks to promote wildlife based tourism and it has formed the Zimbabwe Safari Farms Co-op Limited which seeks to promote and market tourism on farms and ranches throughout Zimbabwe that can offer tourists unique tracts of bush and high standards of safari accommodation.

WPA also works closely with other government and non-governmental organisations in the conservation of wildlife and these include the Department of National Parks and Wildlife Management, Department of Veterinary Services—Wildlife Unit, Ministry of Environment and Tourism, Natural Resources Board and its Intensive Conservation Areas, the Zambezi Society, the Zimbabwe National Conservation Trust, Zimbabwe Trust/Campfire Association, Zimbabwe Association of Tourism and Safari Operators, and Zimbabwe Professional Hunters and Guides Association.

Chart 1.2. Zatso Membership Subscriptions: 1995

Activity	Amount ($)
Hunting:	
Big Game Operator	7,000
Plains Game Operator	3,000
Ranch Hunter	1,500
Photographic:	
Large Operator (over 20 beds/passengers)	7,000
Medium (11-20 beds/passengers)	3,000
Small (up to 10 beds/passengers)	1,500
Associate Member (Business related to tourism without actually running an operation i.e. taxidermist, agent etc):	
Foreign	US$50
Zimbabwean	Z$ 500

Crocodile Farmers Association (CFAZ)

The CFAZ was formed in 1978. This association had been tasked with the development of crocodile farming as a main stream agro-wildlife industry. The industry has expanded rapidly in the 1980s. In 1986 there were only 6 CFAZ members, and in 1990, there were, 66, of which 46 had crocodiles being raised for slaughter. In 1983 earning totalled US$300,000 and by 1989 had increased to US$ 2.6 million. The crocodile farming has remained a small entity, but a very lucrative sector in in Zimbabwe. Operations have mainly been restricted to the tourist resorts, particularly Victoria Falls and Kariba where consumption of crocodile meat is popular wih tourists. The export of crocodile skins and domestic use in the leather industry is also growing, particularly in the small family businesses.

Zimbabwe Trust

Zimtrust was established in 1980. The trust focuses on the development of representative community-based wildlife management institutions of an economic nature. The trust has been involved in the CAMPFIRE programme, were it is assisting communities to get appropriate authority status from central government. CAMPFIRE though directed by the DNPWLM in the Ministry of Environment and Tourism is engaged in the districts to develop the programme through institutional development and financial support. Zimtrust sold the CAMPFIRE concept to Nyaminyami and Guruve RDCs, these were the guinea pigs of the programme and as such most of the activities were carried by the trust. However, for all other districts the greater responsibilities were given to the local authorities and they are also required to identify financial resources for themselves. ZIMTRUST also receives donor funding, USAID has just released US$6.6 million to CAMPFIRE and ZIMTRUST. A further US$3 million is to be expected from the Netherlands. Workplan for the next 8 years has been done. The aim is to concentrate on institutional development and not capital assets as was the previous emphasis.

Campfire Association

The Campfire Association was established in 1989, after Guruve and Nyaminyami RDCs were granted Appropriate Authority (AA). The organisation has some community members on its board, seeks to establish and strengthen institutions at village level so that communities manage wildlife resources on a sustainable basis and manage the revenues derived from such self-reliance. The success of Campfire is measured by them from the fact that one third of the country's land is devoted to some form of wildlife conservation and management, whereas 13% is officially designated as such in the form of the protected areas. The main functions of the association are marketing of wildlife through its advisory capacity, institutions building and training of rural communities so that they make informed decisions, lobbying for RDC's and the rural constituencies in negotiations with various government departments. Information dissemination is also an important function of the association.

Department of National Parks and Wildlife Management (DNPWLM)

The DNPWLM sets the wildlife quota as a percentage of the wildlife stock assessed through regular counts, manages the Parks and Wildlife estate and services the wildlife resources outside the estate. But an apparent contradiction is that the Department has no jurisdiction on the land where wildlife resources are found, and has to liaise with other government departments such as Agritex so that its land use plan complement the major land use planning of Agritex.

District Councils

Central government delegates wildlife management authority to District Councils, who in turn approach interested communities. Councils and communities, councils and communities propose annual plans for the utilisation of wildlife to the DNPWLM. Revenues initially accrue to the council. According to guidelines, councils should not keep more than 15 per cent. Details of allocation are decided by the community and wildlife revenues can be used to compensate farmers for crop and livestock losses. Appropriate Authority (AA) power rests at the district level, but they do not own land. Land allocation is controlled by central government instead of the people.

Centre for Applied Social Sciences (CASS)

The Centre for Applies Social Sciences is an arm of the University of Zimbabwe, whose sole responsibility is research and publication on socio-economic issues. It is for this specific reason that CASS was drafted into the collaborative group. CASS is the research programme evaluating and monitoring the social, economic and cultural effects of CAMPFIRE. The centre also provides tertiary training in natural resource management.

World Wildlife Fund (WWF)

WWF works with the DNPWM to advise villagers on resource economics and the ecological aspects of wildlife management e.g. on how to deal with problem animals, how to set up exclusive wilderness areas, how to establish joint ventures with safari operators and how to count and monitor wildlife populations.

C. Ostrich Institutional Framework

Institutional Structures in the Ostrich Sector

The ostrich sector is made up of a number of institutions which are located both in the public and private sector. These include the Ostrich Producers Association of Zimbabwe (TOPAZ), the Commercial Ostrich Producers Trading Company (COPRO), the Small Holders Ostrich Co-operation (SHOC), the Department of National Parks and Wildlife Management, the Veterinary Research Institute in Ostrich Management and the various other private enterprises allied to the Ostrich Industry. The Department of the Parks allocates the export quota to the Ostrich industry which specifies the number of live birds and eggs for export whilst the local quota specifies the birds retained for local breeding to replenish exported birds.

The Small-Holders Ostrich Co-operative (SHOC) is an autonomous, non-political, developmental organisation dedicated to the improvement of the standard of living in the rural areas through ostrich production and marketing. SHOC was formed and registered as a cooperative in 1994 and seeks to implement the Rural Ostrich Development Programme whose target is to promote rural development through expanding the ostrich production base in rural areas thus enhancing the viability of the ostrich industry. SHOC identifies clients and then recommends them to AFC and credit worthy rural clients within categories of groups of farmers and established cooperatives, individual and small scale commercial farmers and any other approved persons are set to benefit from the scheme. SHOC consolidates inter-sectoral linkages with the relevant sectors by coopting their representatives in the SHOC Executive Board and the Board of Directors consists of representatives from the Ministry of Agriculture, Agricultural Finance Cooperation, Ministry of Finance, Ministry of Environment, COPRO and Big Bird Stock-feeds.

However, the lack of transparency in the day-to-day running of SHOC activities and its being centred on one man (the SHOC Chairman) have curtailed implementation of SHOC plans and its objectives as envisaged in the Rural Ostrich Development Programme. SHOC has no organisational structures and this has hindered its extension services into the rural areas and there is also a mixing-up between SHOC activities and the activities of Jobs Farming (Pvt) Ltd, a company wholly owned by the Chairman of SHOC. As a result one can conclude that there is no SHOC besides its Chairman. The board of SHOC relies heavily on representatives of the GoZ (see Table 5.2).

Chart 1.3. Board of directors of SHOC

Member	Organization
Dr. W. Madzima	
Deputy Director Veterinary Services	Ministry of Agriculture
Mr. N. Zambika	
Deputy General Manager (Development)	Agricultural Finance Corporation (AFC)
Mr. G. Chiromo	
Chairman	Small-Holders Ostrich Co-operative (SHOC)
Mr. M. Rogers	
Commercial Farmer/Funder Member TOPAZ	Big Bird Stockfeeds
Mr. C. Bradshaw	
Managing Director	Copro
Representative	Ministry of Finance
Representative	Ministry of Environment and Tourism
Representative	French Embassy

A new Ostrich Association, the Smallholder Ostrich Producers Association (SHOPA) was formed in 1996 as a commodity association of the Zimbabwe Farmers Union. The association is supposed to take over the national functions of SHOC. Sitting on the board of SHOPA is one of the Vice Presidents of the ZFU (livestock) and all provincial Chairmen, whilst the Representatives of ADA, Veterinary, Parks and Agritex are supposed to be co-opted.

There are at least five private sector organisations involved in the ostrich sector (Chart 1.4). These are engaged in training, marketing, policy advocacy and other promotional activities.

Zimbabwe Ostrich Producers Association (ZOPA)

ZOPA is a national organisation formed on the 30th of October 1995, to spearhead and co-ordinate the activities of rural small-scale farmers as well as the large commercial farmers who choose to join ZOPA. It was set up by the Ministry of Environment and Tourism, in consultation with the Ministries of Agriculture, Lands, Agricultural Finance Corporation and interested Indigenous Ostrich Producers, TOPAZ and ZFU.

The Director of Natural Resources is the head of the ZOPA Secretariat, and he facilitates meetings in various provinces. Two commercial farmers donated the initial funds to set up the association and were also assisting in setting up the provincial committees. ZOPA has no financial capacity to assist its membership and at this stage it can only recommend its members to various financial institutions who offer agri-business finance. ZOPA has no birds to give its members and is currently negotiating with the TOPAZ members to provide birds preferably at point of lay at subsidized prices to ZOPA membership. ZOPA will organise their membership who acquire birds to be provided with a short period of training on how to keep and feed the birds.

Chart 1.4. Private Institutions in Ostrich Production

Institution	Function
TOPAZ	Undertakes stimulates and supports research in the ostrich industry. Undertakes promotional activities in the development of the ostrich industry through platforms such as field days. Disseminates ostrich information to its officiated members.
COPRO	Provides co-ordination of live ostrich bird exports and fertile ostrich egg exports. Imports specialised ostrich equipment and management equipment. Supplies manuals on practical ostrich farming (e.g. the TOPAZ/Hallam Handbook). Exports ostrich hides and leather goods, egg shells, feathers and curios. Supplies goods including microchips, leg tags, dehumidifiers, air conditioners, under floor heating etc. to farmers engaged in ostrich farming.
LEWTAN (Pvt) Ltd.	Provides for the tanning and marketing of finished leathers. Purchases wet-salted ostrich and crocodile skins.
Dilrich Investments	Provides the largest domesticated ostrich flocks in Zimbabwe. Provides an extensive genetic pool of ostrich birds comprising offspring from various parts of Zimbabwe. Breeds quality ostriches for the local and export markets. Exports live ostriches and eggs within Africa and overseas. Gives basic training of incubator operation and chick-attendance to all their customers who purchase ostrich chicks. Gives advice on building, layouts and designs of chick-pens, ostrich paddocks etc.
Cowbird Enterprises (Pvt) Ltd.	Gives/provides the specialised tanning of the ostrich hide. Provides consultancy on all aspects of production, exports, marketing and tanning.
Bigbird Ostrich Feeds	Manufacturers specialist ostrich feeds for the birds at various stages of growth– starters, growers and finishers.

Annex 5.3.1. Actual Land Use Valuation Comparison

i)	Communal Farmers vs LSCF—1980s (small farmers in C.A. and Resettlement Areas vs large farmers).
ii)	Communal farmers vs Resettlement farmers—1984s (long established small farmers) vs new beneficiaries of land reform.
iii)	Small farmers vs Collective farmers—1984 (communal and resettlement small farmers vs resettled collectives).
iv)	Small communal farmers vs small scale commercial farmers—1982.
v)	Commercial ranching (LSCF beef enterprise) vs wildlife ranching—1985.
vi)	LSCF woodlands management vs livestock.
vii)	LSCF livestock ranching vs. Communal Area mixed farming—1983.
viii)	LSCF woodlands management vs LSCF cropping—1985 (wildlife and tourism).
ix)	Communal Area woodlands management vs C.A. mixed farming—1990 (Campfire programme: wildlife vs mixed cropping, livestock and woodlands).
x)	Specialised wildlife (e.g. ostriches) vs cropping in drylands—1991 (smaller scale areas devoted to wildlife vs cropping/cattle).
xi)	Communal Area woodlands management vs LSCF woodlands management—1990.
xii)	Traditional exports (tobacco etc) vs traditional crops (maize, cotton, small grains).
xiii)	Horticulture vs traditional exports (floriculture at a small scale in any tenure regime vs older export crops).
xiv)	Multiple land use alternatives compared (1992).

Source: Various studies, workshop debates and speeches by GoZ, farmers organisations and NGOs.

Annex 6.0 Questionnaires

Annex 6.1. Squatter Questionnaire

1. Where are squatter camps located?
1. Province......................................
2. District......................................
2. What is the history of the squatter camps?
1. Land ownership/tenure.........................
2. Previous use of the land......................
3. Current use..................................
3. What is the history of the squatter population?
How did they come there and when? ....
Original homes of the squatters by province or district?..
Why did they move to that place?..
How did they come to know that there was open land?..
4. What are the characteristics of the squatter population?
Average Age....................................
Sex Composition...............................
Employment Situation..........................
Levels of Literacy............................
Family Sizes..................................
Ethnicity.....................................
Religion......................................
Total numbers of squatters and how they have been growing?..
5. What are the economic activities that the squatters are engaged in? ....
Major sources of income for the squatters?
1. Farm Labourers
2. Gold Panning
3. Farming
4. Others (specify)............................
6. What infrastructural developments have been made on the land and what
assets do they own?..
7. What is the government's policy towards squatters and what is the government's response towards the
squatters problem?..
8. How do the squatters get their social services:
Health..
Water...
Schools.......................................
Shops...

Annex 6.2. Wildlife Questionnaire

Interviewer:..................................
Date of Interview:...........................
Questionnaire No:............................

General Information
Ranch Name(s):...............................
Company Name(s):.............................
Owner/Operator Name:.........................
Management:..................................
Interviewee(s):
(a)   Name:.............................
(b)   Position:.........................
District/ICA:................................

Section I: Land Base
1. How long have you been operating here? and what is the historical
background of your farm?..
2. What is the total farm area?

	Area (ha/ac)	Since
Self owned/purchased	....	....
Self owned/inherited	....	....
Family ownership	....	....
Company shareholding	....	....
Leased in	....	....

Leased out	....	....
Other (specify)	....	....

3. What do you do on your farm?...
4. From what do you earn most of your money?...
5. What is the total arable land on your farm?

	Area (ha/ac)
Dryland crops	....
Irrigated crops	....
Cultivated pastures	....
Other (specify)	....

6. What is the total land area devoted to game, ostriches and livestock?

Cattle only	....
Game only	....
Cattle and game	....
Sheep and goats	....
Ostriches	....
Other (specify)	....

Section II: Wildlife System
1. (a) Do you have any game?
      1. Yes
      2. No
If no, why not? ....
(b) When did you move into wildlife production?..
(c) What is the wildlife population on your farm?

Species	Initial no. 19--	Current No. 1996	Value each	Ave. hide price	Ave. Meat price
Buffalo					
Elephant					
Giraffe					
Lion					
Leopard					
Cheetah					
Nyala					
Hartebeest					
White Rhino					
Black Rhino					
Kudu					
Hyena					
Roan					
Sable					
Eland					
Waterbuck					
Zebra					
Wildebeest					
Tsessebe					
Reedbuck					
Klipspringer					
Bushbuck					
Impala					
Warthog					
Bushpig					
Duiker					
Steenbok					
Grysbok					

2. (a) What is the main reason for having wildlife at your farm?
      1. None
      2. Aesthetic
      3. Ecological
      4. Personal hunting
      5. Economic
      6. Other (specify).....................................
(b)From where did you get your animals?..
(c)What was the previous on-farm landuse before you entered in wildlife production and why did you decide to leave the previous land use?..

3. What are the main sources of revenue from wildlife (rank)?
   1. Safari hunting
   2. Non-consumptive safari
   3. Meat sales
   4. Hide sales
   5. Live animal sales
   6. Lease game user rights

4. What facilities and services do you provide.

(a) Hunting

	Camp Site	Board	Guides	Vehicles
Number				

Remarks: ....

(b) Non-Consumption

	Camp Site	Board	Guides	Vehicles
Number				

Remarks:..

5. What types of hunting are provided on your ranch?

Importance/Comment

1. Plains game
2. Lion/Leopard
3. Buffalo
4. Big game
5. Other

6. How do you provide hunting opportunities?
Importance/Comment
Provide hunts through/to:
1. Own safari operation
2. Self catering clubs
3. Concessionaires
4. Other

7. If you have your own operation, what areas do you use?

Areas used for Safaris	Hunting	Non-Consumptive
1. Owned private land	....	....
2. Leased private land	....	....
3. Communal land	....	....
4. State land	....	....

8. How do you market your hunting and non-consumptive Safaris?

(a) Advertising	Hunting	Non-Consumptive
1. Word of mouth	....	....
2. Commodity Association	....	....
3. Local/International Agent	....	....
4. Newspaper/Magazines	....	....
5. Own brochures	....	....
6. Other	....	....

(b) Markets used (quantity)	Hunting	Non-Consumptive
1. Zimbabwe	....	....
2. South Africa	....	....
3. Other countries in Africa (specify)	....	....
4. North America	....	....
5. Other	....	....

(c) What are the advantages and disadvantages of local and international markets for wildlife products?

Local markets	International markets
Advantages:	Advantages:
1.	1.
2.	2.
3.	3.
Disadvantages:	Disadvantages:
1.	1.
2.	2.
3.	3.

(d) What problems do you encounter in marketing Safaris?...

9. (a) To whom do you market your game products?
1. Live animals   ....
2. Game meat   ....
3. Game hides   ....
What problems do you face in marketing these game products?...
Year........................

(b) Live Animal Sales and Purchases

Specie	Live animal purchase		Live animal sales		Related cost	Comments
	No.	Price	No.	Price		
Buffalo						
Elephant						
Giraffe						
Lion						
Leopard						
Cheetah						
Nyala						
Hartebeest						
White Rhino						
Black Rhino						
Kudu						
Hyena						
Roan						
Sable						
Eland						
Waterbuck						
Zebra						
Wildebeest						
Tsessebe						
Reedbuck						
Klipspringer						
Bushbuck						
Impala						
Warthog						
Bushpig						
Duiker						
Steenbok						
Grysbok						

Year....................

10.   What game management do you practise? (Census Animals)
       1. Casual Counts   ....
       2. Spot counts   ....
       3. Strip counts   ....
       4. Sex/Age ratios   ....
       5. Other   ....

Section III: General

1. What do you see as the major problems being faced by the wildlife industry?
    1. Poaching
    2. Veld Burning
    3. Water shortage
    4. Others (specify)

2. What do you think government or any other organisation should do to help the wildlife industry?..

3. Are you a member of any organisation, why, yes or no?
WPA   ....
ZATSO   ....
ZPHGA   ....
ITOZA   ....
Wildlife Society of Zimbabwe ....
Zimbabwe Farmers Union ....
CFU   ....
Bow Hunting Association ....

4. What problems does wildlife cause you? How do you feel about buffalo? Do you want buffalo on your land (why yes or no)?...

5. What is the value of your land?
    1. With wildlife $...............................
    2. Without wildlife $...............................
    3. Arable $...............................
    4. Irrigated $...............................

6. (a) Are there any conflicts in landuse between agriculture (cropping) and wildlife production?
....
(b) How are you resolving these conflicts?
....

7. How difficult is the entry into the industry?
(a) Purchasing of animals?
....
(b) Marketing of animals and animal products?
....
(c) Financing?
....

8. Where do you get the information on wildlife production?
a. TV/Newspapers/Radio
b. Representative organisation
c. Government
d. Other farmers
e. Trade fairs
f. Private consultancy
g. Others (specify).......................................

9. What has been the government's response to your orientation towards wildlife production, given that your land is in the prime agricultural region?..

10. (a) Are there any sub-contracting arrangements between communal and large commercial farmers involved in wildlife production?..
(b) What are the benefits of such contractual arrangements?..

11. What has been the impact of ESAP on the wildlife industry?
a. Fluctuation of prices
b. Retrenchment of farm labourers
c. Diversification to meet the challenges of ESAP
d. Forex—availability or non-availability
e. Others (specify).......................................

12. What do you see as the impacts of wildlife production on the environment?

<u>Positive Impacts</u>   <u>Negative Impacts</u>
....

13. How is the industry affected by drought and what mitigatory measures have you set in place?
a. Shortage of water...

b. Drying of vegetation and horticultural crops...
c. Vulnerability of crop production..
d. Others (specify)..

Section iv

(a) Employment

Description	Number of employees			Total	Approx. val. salaries and benefits	Comments
	Cattle	Game	Other			
Wage labour						
Cattle hands						
Game guards						
Tracker/skinner						
Other safari						
General Labour						
Other						
Sub-total wage labour						
Salaried employees						
Cattle managers						
Game managers						
Hunters						
Office/admin.						
Secretarial						
Other						
Sub-total salaried employees						
Total employees						

(b) Capital and Assets

No.	Description of item	Year acquired	Value	Allocation to ventures			Forex	Duty
				Cattle	Game	Other		

Codes:
1.   Land (veld, irrigated)
2.   Buildings (dwellings, shores, sheds)
3.   Safari Camp (building, furniture)
4.   Fencing
5.   Dips/spray races
6.   Motor vehicles (tractors, boats, aircrafts)
7.   Water supplies (dams, pumps, boreholes, pipelines)
8.   Power supplies (ZESA, Solar)
9.   Butchery/refrigeration
10.   Rifles
11.   Purchased animals

c) Wildlife Costs

Cost item	Cost Z$	Per cent Forex	Comments
Purchase of trophies Lease/camp fees			
Homegrown feed Purchased feed Supplements			
Agents commission Trophy handling Advertising			
Fuel and lubricants: Diesel Blend Other			

Repairs & Maintenance: Motor Vehicles Tractor/Farm Equipment Other machine/Equipment Water supplies Fencing Buildings Safari Camp/Equipment Roads Others			
Hired Transport Ammunition Capture/Culling Aircraft Expenses Electricity Water Consumable Stores			
Wages Salaries			
Other			
Total			

Annex 6.3. Ostrich Questionnaire

Interviewer:.................................
Date of Interview:...........................
Questionnaire No:............................

General Information
Ranch Name(s):...............................
Company Name(s):.............................
Owner/Operator Name:.........................
Management:..................................

Interviewee(s):
(a) Name:....................................
(b) Position:................................
District/ICA:................................
Section I: Land Base

1. How long have you been operating here? and what is the historical background of your farm?
....

2. What is the total farm area?

	Area(ha/ac)	Since
Self owned/purchased	....	....
Self owned/inherited	....	....
Family ownership	....	....
Company shareholding	....	....
Leased in	....	....
Leased out	....	....
Other (specify)	....	....

3. What do you do on your farm?..

4. From what do you earn most of your money?..

5. What is the total arable land on your farm?
Area (ha/ac)
Dryland crops   ....
Irrigated crops   ....
Cultivated pastures   ....
Other (specify)   ....

6. What is the total land area devoted to game, ostriches and livestock?
Area (ha/ac)
Cattle only   ....
Game only   ....
Cattle and game   ....
Sheep and goats   ....

Ostriches   ....
Other (specify)   ....

Section II: Ostrich Production

1. When did you move into ostrich production and why?...

2. What is the main reason for having/entering into ostrich production?
1. None
2. Aesthetic
3. Ecological/Conservation
4. Economic
5. Other (specify).......................................

3. Where did you get your birds?
a. Other farmers (specify)
b. TOPAZ/SHOC or other organisations (specify)
c. Others (specify)

4. What incentives are there from buying from representative organisations such as SHOC, TOPAZ?
1. Delayed repayment
2. Availability of loans
3. Ensuring birds
4. Other incentives (specify)...........................

5. i) What was the previous on-farm land-use before you entered ostrich production?
ii) Why did you decide to leave your former enterprise?

6. What is the ostrich population at your farm?

	Initial No. 19---	Current No.	Value each	Ave. hide price	Ave. meat price
Males					Local....................... International................
Females					Local....................... International................
Chicks					Local....................... International................

7. What type of ostrich production are you engaged in and why?
a. Intensive ostrich production
b. Semi-intensive production
c. Extensive production

8. How do you market your ostriches and other ostrich products?
1. On the spot
2. Approved buyers—COPRO
3. Representative organisations (specify)
4. Contracts
5. Others (specify)......................................

9. i) To whom do you market your ostrich products?
1. Ostrich meat
2. Ostrich feathers
3. Ostrich skin

ii) What problems do you encounter in marketing these ostrich products?
iii) Markets used (quantity) (per cent)
1. Zimbabwe
2. South Africa
3. Other countries (Africa)(specify)
4. North America
5. Asia
6. Others (specify)......................................

10. a) Live Ostrich Sales

	Quantity	Price	Where sold	Related Cost	Comments
Males					
Females					
Chicks					

b) Live Ostrich Sales

	Quantity	Price	Where sold	Related Cost	Comments
Eggs					
Skins					
Feathers					

11. What are the advantages and disadvantages of local and international markets.

Local Markets	International Markets
Advantages: 1. 2. 3. Disadvantages: 1. 2. 3.	Advantages: 1. 2. 3. Disadvantages: 1. 2. 3.

12. i) At what different levels of maturity do you sell your ostriches?
ii) What are the by-products in ostrich farming?
iii) What percentage of total farm income is income from ostrich farming?

13. Are you a member of any organisation?
1. TOPAZ
2. SHOC
5. Others (specify).....................................

What are the benefits from such affiliation?
....

14. i) Are there any conflicts in land-use between ostrich farming and other farming activities?
ii) How are you resolving these conflicts?

15. How difficult is the entry into the ostrich industry?
1. Purchasing of birds
2. Marketing of birds and ostrich products
3. Financing
4. Others (specify).....................................

16. Where do you get the information on ostrich farming?
1. TV/Newspapers/Radio
2. Representative organisations (specify)
3. Government
4. Other farmers
5. Trade fairs
6. Private Consultancy
7. Newsletter
8. Others (specify).....................................

17. What has been the government's response ;to your orientation towards ostrich production?
....

18. i) Are there any sub-contracting arrangements between communal and large commercial
farmers involved in ostrich farming?
ii) What are the benefits of such contractual arrangements?

19. What do you see as the impact of ESAP on the wildlife industry?

1. Fluctuation of prices
2. Retrenchment of farm labourers
3. Diversification too meet ESAP's challenges
4. Forex–Availability or non-availability

20. What do you see as the impacts of wildlife production on the environment?

<u>Positive Impacts</u>   <u>Negative Impacts</u>

....

21. How is the industry affected by drought and what mitigatory measures have you set in place?
....

22. Have your workers received specialised training in the raising of ostriches?

1. Duration
2. Where training was done

No. of ostriches	Total farm workers	Approx. vol.	Comments

23. What are the inputs for production that you are using on your farm?

i) Infrastructure: - Electricity
                                                      - Piped Water
                                                      - Roads

ii) Feeds: - Horticulture Produce
- Stock-feed (type, quantity, cost)..

iii) Veterinary Services: —Specialised Treatment
- Basic Hygiene..

Capital and Assets

No.	Description of item	Year acquired	Value	Forex duty

Codes:
1. Incubators   6. Buildings (dwellings, paddocks, chick pens)
2. Hatchers   7. Fencing
3. Solar Panel   8. Water supplies (dams, pumps, boreholes, pipeline)
4. Insulators   9. Birds
5. Land   10. ZESA power supply
11. Motor vehicle

Annex 6.4. Commercial Horticultural Farmer

(Supplementary questionnaire to general commercial farmer questionnaire)

A. Farm Ownership
A1. Full name of owner ....
A2. Sex of owner   Male   Female
A3. Race of owner ....
A4. Age of owner ....
A5. Type of horticultural enterprise
a) cut flowers
b) produce (vegetables)
c) fruit

B. History and Incentives
B1. When did you move into horticultural production? ....
B2. What crops or livestock enterprise were previously practised on the farm?
....
B3. What is the relationship between the horticulture enterprises and other enterprises?
a) complementary
b) supplementary
c) substitutes
Describe this relationship in more detail ....
B4. What promoted the shift to horticultural production?
a) ....

b) ....
c) ....
d) ....
B5. Why did farmer decide to grow this particular horticultural crop?
....

C. Land Issues
C1. Size of farm   Arable ....
                                     Grazing/non-arable ....
                                     Total ....
C2. How much is currently under use? ....
How much was under use before venturing into horticulture?..
C3. How much land is under irrigation? ....
C4. How much land is under greenhouses? ....

Land, Allocation, Production, Marketing

Crop	Area (ha)			Yield (kg/ha)	Use of product (kg)		
	Irrigated	Dryland	Greenhouse		Retained	Sold	
						Local Market	Export Market
Horticulture 1.							
2							
3							
4							
5							
6							
Other 1.							
2							
3							
4							
5							
6							

D. Marketing and Transport for Horticulture Crops
D1. What kind of transport is used to carry produce to the market?
a) refrigerated   open truck
                              closed van
b) non-refrigerated
D2. a) Does the farmer own the transport facility? ....
b) If not, who does? ....
D3a. Where are products sold (location)? ....
D3b. What is the distance of the farm from the market? ....
D4. What determines how much is sold locally and how much is exported?
....

Give advantages and disadvantages of local and export markets.

Advantages	Disadvantages
Local Market	
1.	1.
2.	2.
3.	3.
4.	4.
5.	5.
Export Market	
1.	1.
2.	2.
3.	3.
4.	4.
5.	5.

E. Labour
E1. Labour employed on the farm

		Permanent	Hired/Casual
1. Horticulture a) Produce	Male		
	Female		
	Total		
b) Cut flowers	Male		
	Female		
	Total		
c) fruits	Male		
	Female		
	Total		
Sub-Total Horticulture			
2. Other Enterprises a) Crops	Male		
	Female		
	Total		
b) Livestock	Male		
	Female		
	Total		
Sub-total other enterprises			
Grand total			

E2. Changes in labour due to horticulture
When you moved into horticulture did you dismiss or hire any workers? Give details.

Type	Sex	No. dismissed	No. hired
Professional	Male		
	Female		
	Total		
Semi skilled	Male		
	Female		
	Total		
Skilled	Male		
	Female		
	Total		
Unskilled	Male		
	Female		
	Total		
Grand total			

F. Access to Resources
F1. Extension
i) Where does farmer get knowledge on growing of horticultural crops
        a) farmer has received specialised training in horticulture
        b) farmer employs skilled workers who are trained in horticulture
        c) farmer get extension services from Agritex
        d) farmer gets extension services from CFU
        e) farmer gets extension services from private companies e.g input supplier and
        through workshops
        f) other (specify)

Give details on the above (areas covered, frequency, location) ....

ii) Does farmer receive adequate extension services?
Yes   No
If No please indicate what areas are not adequately covered
– planting
– growing
– harvesting
– marketing
– other (specify) ....

F2. Credit
i) Where does farmer get money to finance horticultural enterprises?

a) enterprise is self supporting
b) from other agricultural enterprise
c) from other non-agricultural enterprises
d) from AFC loans
e) from commercial banks
f) other (specify)

ii)   Does farmer have adequate financial resources from the above source/s?
     Yes   No

iii)   If No please suggest ways that could improve access to credit.

F3. Market Intelligence
i) Where does farmer get information on market trends?
        a) other farmers
        b) phone
        c) radio services (electronic media)
        d) farmer magazines (press media)
        e) does not get any

iia)   Does farmer get enough market intelligence
      Yes   No

iib)   If No please indicate how this can be improved?

iic)   If No how has this affected viability of the horticultural enterprises?

G. Constraints

G1. What are the main constraints hindering further expansion of the horticulture enterprise?

a)   Credit/capital/inputs
      – not enough money to acquire the necessary things to expand business

b)   Technology
      – the enterprise requires the use of specialised equipment which is not readily available

c)   Transport
      – shortage of transport facilities to deliver finished goods to the markets or to bring inputs to the farm

d)   Access to market facilities
      – difficulty of getting necessary materials to the business

e)   Irregular supply of inputs
      – required inputs are not always available and may not be available for some periods

f)   Government policy constraints
      – legal requirements and local authority by-laws which may not allow operating at higher levels

g)   Not interested in expansion of enterprise

h)   Time constraint
      – farmer would not have enough time to manage enterprise if it grew any larger than it already is.

i)   Land shortage
      – farmer does not have any more land on which horticultural enterprise can be expanded

j)   Bad debts
      – people do not pay up their debts when business extends credit to customers

k)   Water shortage

l)   Any other

Give details on the above ....

G2. Suggest possible solutions to the above constraints ....

Publications of the research programme "Political and Social Context of Structural Adjustment in Africa" published by the Nordic Africa Institute

Gibbon P., Bangura and A. Ofstad (eds.), 1992, *Authoritarianism, Democracy and Adjustment. The Politics of Economic Reform in Africa*. Seminar proceedings no. 26.

Gibbon, P. (ed.), 1993, *Social Change and Economic Reform in Africa*.

Chachage, C.S.L., M. Ericsson and P. Gibbon, 1993, *Mining and Structural Adjustment. Studies on Zimbabwe and Tanzania*. Research report no. 92.

Neocosmos, M., 1993, *The Agrarian Question in Africa and the Concept of "Accumulation from Below". Economics and Politics in the Struggle for Democracy*. Research report no. 93.

Kanyinga. K., A.S.Z. Kiondo and P. Tidemand, 1994, *The New Local Level Politics in East Africa. Studies on Uganda, Tanzania and Kenya*. Edited and introduced by Peter Gibbon. Research report no. 95.

Osaghae, E.E., 1995, *Structural Adjustment and Ethnicity in Nigeria*. Research report no. 98.

Gibbon, P. (ed.), 1995, *Markets, Civil Society and Democracy in Kenya*.

Gibbon P. (ed.), 1995, *Structural Adjustment and the Working Poor in Zimbabwe*.

Gibbon, P., 1995, *Liberalised Development in Tanzania*.

Bijlmakers. L.A., M.T. Bassett and D.M. Sanders; 1996, *Health and Structural Adjustment in Rural and Urban Zimbabwe*. Research report no. 101.

Gibbon, P. and A.O. Olukoshi, 1996, *Structural Adjustment and Socio-Economic Change in Sub-Saharan Africa. Some Conceptual, Methodological and Research Issues*. Research report no. 102.

Olukoshi. A.O. and L. Laakso (eds.), 1996, *Challenges to the Nation-State in Africa*.

Olukoshi, A.O. (ed.), 1998, *The Politics of Opposition in Contemporary Africa*.

Egwu, S.G., 1998, *Structural Adjustment, Agrarian Change and Rural Ethnicity in Nigeria*. Research report no. 103.

Olukoshi, A.O., 1998, *The Elusive Prince of Denmark. Structural Adjustment and the Crisis of Governance in Africa*. Research report no. 104.

Bijlmakers. L.A., M.T. Bassett and D.M. Sanders, 1998, *Socioeconomic Stress, Health and Child Nutritional Status in Zimbabwe at a Time of Economic Structural Adjustment. A Three Year Longitudinal Study*. Research report no. 105.

Mupedziswa, R. and P. Gumbo, 1998, *Structural Adjustment and Women Informal Sector Traders in Harare, Zimbabwe*. Research report no. 106.

Chiwele, D.K., P. Muyatwa-Sipula and H. Kalinda, 1998, *Private Sector Response to Agricultural Marketing Liberalisation in Zambia. A Case Study of Eastern Province Maize Markets*. Research report no. 107.

Amanor, K.S., 1999, *Global Restructuring and Land Rights in Ghana. Forest Food Chains, Timber and Rural Livelihoods*. Research report no. 108.

Ongile, G.A., 1999, *Gender and Agricultural Supply Responses to Structural Adjustment Programmes. A Case Study of Smallholder Tea Producers in Kericho, Kenya*. Research report no. 109.

Sachikonye, Lloyd M., 1999, *Restructuring or De-Industrializing? Zimbabwe's Textile and Metal Industries under Adjustment*. Resarch report no. 110.

Gaidzanwa, Rudo, 1999, *Voting with their Feet. Zimbabwean Nurses and Doctors in the Era of Structural Adjustment*. Resarch report no. 111.

Hashim, Yahaya and Kate Meagher, 1999, *Cross-Border Trade and the Parallel Currency Market—Trade and Finance in the Context of Structural Adjustment. A Case Study from Kano, Nigeria*. Research report no. 113.

Moyo, Sam, 2000, *Land Reform under Structural Adjustment in Zimbabwe. Land Use Change in the Mashonaland Provinces*.